An Archive of Hope

The publisher gratefully acknowledges the generous support of the General Endowment Fund of the University of California Press Foundation.

An Archive of Hope

Harvey Milk's Speeches and Writings

Harvey Milk

Edited by Jason Edward Black and
Charles E. Morris III

UNIVERSITY OF CALIFORNIA PRESS

Berkeley · *Los Angeles* · *London*

University of California Press, one of the most distinguished university presses in the United States, enriches lives around the world by advancing scholarship in the humanities, social sciences, and natural sciences. Its activities are supported by the UC Press Foundation and by philanthropic contributions from individuals and institutions. For more information, visit www.ucpress.edu.

University of California Press
Berkeley and Los Angeles, California

University of California Press, Ltd.
London, England

Library of Congress Cataloging-in-Publication Data

Milk, Harvey.
    An archive of hope : Harvey Milk's speeches and writings / Harvey Milk; edited by Jason Edward Black and Charles E. Morris III.
        pages cm
    Includes bibliographical references.
    ISBN 978-0-520-27548-5 (cloth : alk. paper)
    ISBN 978-0-520-27549-2 (pbk. : alk. paper)
    1. San Francisco (Calif.)—Politics and government—20th century—Sources.   2. San Francisco (Calif.). Board of Supervisors—History—20th century—Sources.   3. Gay liberation movement—California—San Francisco—History—20th century—Sources.
4. Gay men—Political activity—California—San Francisco—History—20th century—Sources.   5. Milk, Harvey—Archives.   6. Politicians—California—San Francisco—Archives.   7. Gay men—California—San Francisco—Archives.
    I. Black, Jason Edward.   II. Morris, Charles E., 1969-
III. Title.
    F869.S357M55   2013
    979.4'61053092-dc23   2012039811

22   21   20   19   18   17   16   15   14   13
10   9   8   7   6   5   4   3   2   1

Contents

Preface

An Archive of Hope is about Harvey Milk and gay, lesbian, bisexual, transgender, and queer (GLBTQ) memory and history. We believe that GLBTQ pasts, such as the multifaceted configurations of Milk, are invaluable and underutilized as the inventional resources for GLBTQ well-being, relationships, communities, culture, politics, and movement in the present and future.

This is easier espoused than enacted. Historically and presently, numerous constraints and disincentives have made inhabiting and mobilizing GLBTQ pasts very difficult, and in some instances, impossible. One ongoing challenge concerns the *where* of GLBTQ history and memory, where it can be found and how it is marked or unmarked; the term *archive* in this context should signify anything but ample, obvious, accessible, sanctioned. And we say this as people in awe of the gains made by GLBTQ collectors, archivists, librarians, historical societies, and museums in the United States. In an important sense, the more vexing challenge is what we might call the *please* of GLBTQ history and memory, that is, the will and desire for the past. The challenges come from a systemic problem (rarely if ever are GLBTQ history and memory encountered in schools), a communal problem (indifference to GLBTQ history and memory is acculturated), and a rhetorical problem (inducements to GLBTQ history and memory require much more attention to appeal and audience).

We don't remember when we first encountered Harvey Milk. Paradoxically, he seems to have been long a presence and also in short supply. Chuck had been screening Rob Epstein's powerful, Academy Award–winning documentary, *The Times of Harvey Milk* (1984), in his social protest seminars since the late 1990s; Jason for years had been teaching the "Hope Speech" and had worked with the Harvey Milk City Hall Memorial Committee to select quotations to appear on the Milk bust unveiled in San Francisco in 2008. Yet when we began talking about this project in 2006, we both had a strong sense that despite our belief in Milk's significant place in GLBTQ history and memory, he did not seem substantially recollected anymore, except perhaps in San Francisco itself (and that was a hunch). Only a handful of Milk's speeches and writings circulated publicly at the time, as now: four in an appendix in Shilts's *Mayor of Castro Street* and a token representative, "You Gotta Give 'Em Hope," in a small number of anthologies. How could this be? Harvey Milk matters—our mantra—so we decided to figure out what else there might be.

Having successfully persuaded The University of Alabama and Boston College to provide us grant monies for a project on Harvey Milk (rhetorical challenges to GLBTQ memory and history are multiple and varied), we first flew to San Francisco in 2007 to explore the Milk collection at the San Francisco Public Library (SFPL), which we knew had recently opened to the public in 2003. We were not sure what we would find, even though the Harvey Milk Archives—Scott Smith Collection index (GLC 35), available online, had us wide-eyed with imagined possibilities. To our amazement, we discovered at the SFPL a remarkable trove of Milk's words in various forms: speeches, editorials, columns, press releases, event fliers, campaign materials, correspondences, and interviews. Astonishingly, it became apparent from our conversations with the SFPL archivists and librarians that few others were availing themselves of the Milk archive, despite the rare opportunity here of a well-organized and available, institutionally supported and authorized collection of a GLBTQ historical figure better known and appreciated than most. (Interest seems to have increased significantly as our project has come to its completion, owing perhaps to the visibility generated by the film *Milk;* see "Condensed Milk: A [Somewhat] Shortlist of Harvey Milk Resources," http://sfhcbasc.blogspot .com/2012/05/condensed-milk-somewhat-short-list-of.html.)

Walking past Harvey Milk Plaza into the historic neighborhood of many GLBTQ dreams on that day in 2007, we toasted with a celebratory beer at Harvey's, the gay bar at Castro and 18th named in his memory and adorned with his images, all smiles over Milk's legacy being alive and well and available to be mobilized. A block away, at 575 Castro Street, marveling like pilgrims in front of what had been Milk's camera shop and political headquarters, beneath the second-story mural of Harvey wearing a t-shirt with his mantra, "You Gotta Give 'Em Hope," we committed ourselves as archival queers to doing what we could to help circulate and promulgate this invaluable archive. We went back to the SFPL in 2009, and the five years of this project have been consumed with the challenges of disposition, which is to say the culling, organizing, contextualizing, and rhetorically configuring this selected volume of Milk's speeches and writings. *An Archive of Hope* represents our best effort to do so (any shortcomings are squarely our own), an assemblage of artifacts from Milk's rhetorical and political corpus, most not seen publicly since they were originally published or delivered in the 1970s. Our hope is that Milk's voice, and ours, will in this book help to constitute one archival queer exhibition that contributes to the *where* and *please* of GLBTQ pasts.

Our fortune in this project has been an embarrassment of riches, and these brief lines of gratitude won't suffice but will have to do, at least in print. We simply can't believe that the fabulous Danny Nicoletta—so well-known and admired, so busy with his many significant projects—gave so much to our project, generously, copiously, whenever we asked. Danny is a GLBTQ treasure in his own right, and his proximity to Harvey Milk and Milk's memory, to GLBTQ San Francisco's past and present, for us made him our muse, our mentor, our Sherpa—electric and talismanic. We knew that *An Archive of Hope* had promise during our first meeting with Danny over dinner at Catch on Market Street, the very site where the Names Project transformed the world stitch by stitch into the AIDS Quilt. His encouragement has made all the difference.

The other guiding light of this project is Frank Robinson. Frank, too, is a great gift to GLBTQ history, and someone, we hope, will write his biography. Brilliant, gruff, witty, big-hearted, and a real "character," Frank both challenged and fostered our work. He made plain in no uncertain terms that he would not talk about Harvey Milk in a restaurant over lunch. So instead he welcomed us into his home, opened to us his files in the upstairs den, let us spread out materials in his kitchen, and sat for a long interview in his living room. Memory, of course, is both pleasure and pain, and we know Frank's conjuring of Harvey Milk was not always easy, more evidence of Frank's generosity of spirit. And what a storyteller Frank is: how lucky we were to be the beneficiaries. Then, when the day's research was done, Frank looked at us, smiled, and said, "*Now* you may take me to dinner." And dine we did, once at the historic Hotel Whitcomb's Market Street Café, one of his favorite spots.

Numerous others, in plentiful ways, materially and affectively, made our research and writing of this book possible, easier, pleasurable, better. The University of Alabama and Boston College offered financial support of our San Francisco trips through multiple grants.

At the James C. Hormel Gay and Lesbian Center in the San Francisco Public Library, Tim Wilson and Susan Goldstein warmly and enthusiastically endorsed and supported us and this project, and provided all the resources and expertise we needed and could have hoped for. Our many wonderful encounters with Tim in the reading room of the San Francisco History Center of the SFPL made us feel at home among friends, and when we returned in 2009, two years after our initial trip, the three of us fell right back into step.

For research and copyright assistance, we offer our thanks to Heather Cassell and Karen Sundheim at Hormel, Rebekah Kim and Daniel Bao at the GLBT Historical Society, Cynthia Laird at the *Bay Area Reporter,* Walter Caplan, David Lamble, Tom Spitz at KPIX/KBCW, Alex Cherian at the San Francisco Bay Area TV Archive, Ken Liss at O'Neill Library at Boston College, and Patrick Shannon at the Bancroft Library of UC Berkeley. Our research assistants, Benjamin Kimmerle and Gyromas Newman, handled many of our transcription assignments with good humor and good work.

San Francisco visits came with the warmest of welcomes and hospitality from friends and colleagues Gust Yep, John Elia, Ralph Smith and Russel Windes, Dan Saffer, Rink Foto, Jeff Sens, Jack Keatings and Tom Booth at Hotel Frank/Maxwell, and the staff at Harvey's.

At University of California Press, Kim Robinson's patience, counsel, and encouragement guided us through project vision and revision en route to a remarkably better book than the manuscript we submitted, for which we are so thankful. And we thank, too, Stacy Eisenstark for all her help during the production process.

Jason: This project, one borne from a mutual admiration of Harvey's story, has resulted in much more than the glorious fruits of an archival journey. For me, *An Archive of Hope* has also fostered a lifelong friendship—a story unto itself. Throughout the past seven years—from

San Francisco visits and Castro meanderings to writing sessions on a Boston rooftop and planning sessions on a Tuscaloosa riverboat—I have found a brother in Chuck Morris. I want to wholeheartedly thank Chuck for enlivening our work, for teaching me the nuances of queer worldmaking, and for supporting me when I needed it the most. *An Archive of Hope* would never have been realized and completed without his care and determination. I am genuinely honored and fortunate to consider Chuck a part of my family.

I would also like to express appreciation to my friends at The University of Alabama for all of their encouragement on this project. I am particularly indebted to Adam Sharples and Meredith Bagley for sharing their knowledge about LGBTQ memory and their mutual love for Harvey; to Beth S. Bennett, my good friend and mentor, for supporting *An Archive of Hope* every step of the way; to students in my undergraduate and graduate seminars for the many productive conversations about Harvey and the "hope trope"; and to my colleagues in the College of Communication & Information Sciences for their willingness to entertain my musings about and ardor for Harvey's story.

Finally, I am grateful to have a moment to thank my partner Jennifer Black and daughters Anabelle and Amelia for all of their love. I am blessed (and awed) by their understanding and patience—both related to this project and always. This anthology has been a part of our lives for the better part of a decade. My wish is that Harvey's name and *words* will remain constantly with us as a reminder of the possibilities of love and the resonance of hope.

Chuck: I beamed late one evening in 2006 when I read an email from Jason Black inviting me to consider collaborating with him on a Harvey Milk project. The idea excited me at that moment, but it would be our unfolding friendship that most enriched and sustained me as that idea transformed into this book. I now feel as if I've known Jason my whole life, and he's become indigenous to my world, for which I am enormously grateful and deeply happy.

During this project I lost two of my sweetest inspirations, Alex and Augustine, whose love and curiosity meant so much to me, and whose spirits still fill me.

Among the living, my friends make daily work and life richly rewarding, and for their laughter and comfort and wisdom I thank Dale, Dan, Rob, Tom, Andrew, David, Mary Kate, Chuck and Ginny, Jackie, Shea, Katie, Andrew, Austin, Vanessa, Karma and Sara, Jeff and

Isaac, Kendall, Erin, Lance, Bob, Pam, Bonnie, John, Keith and Bob, the Boston Rhetoric Reading Group, and all my field and Facebook pals.

Finally, I dedicate my effort here to my partner Scott Rose, my Gatto, for giving the deepest meaning and feeling to living and loving and intervening in the GLBTQ world, and to our boys, Jackson and Cooper, with all my heart.

Harvey

FRANK M. ROBINSON

Harvey Milk was one of the most significant of the American political figures of the twentieth century. He started as a Goldwater Republican and ended his life as the last of the store-front politicians—those who ran for public office with no money, their stores their campaign headquarters, and their following largely those who stopped in to buy something and stayed to talk politics with the owner.

An "openly gay man," as the newspapers of the time referred to Harvey, his constituency was the largely closeted gay population of San Francisco. Harvey was anything but—he was openly gay not only in the gay enclave of the Castro, but to the world at large.

He was to become the first gay man to win a major political office in the United States—despite the fact that gays were the last important group in the country who were subject to nationally approved prejudice. Tolerance was the most that a gay man could expect—acceptance was seldom granted.

In the city of San Francisco, the gay community was represented by politicians who were the "friends of gays" but never gay themselves.

It was Harvey's unique idea that gays should be represented by one of their own. The black community was represented by black politicians—they could hardly change the color of their skin. But gays had the option of hiding, and that was the course that most of them took. You could vote anonymously at the ballot box, but to acknowledge your homosexuality to the world at large could be extremely risky when it came to family, friends, or employment. It might be okay for Harvey to be openly gay, but it wasn't okay for most gays, and sometimes it could be physically dangerous.

Harvey was out to change all that. He turned his shop into a place for voter registration and urged all gays to "come out"—saying that people would never change their viewpoint on homosexuality unless they had actually met some homosexuals. Families might view their "single" aunts and uncles with suspicion, but as long as gay people "hid," they were tolerated.

By the time Harvey was elected to office as a San Francisco supervisor, those who suffered from the "love that dare not speak its name" had learned to shout.

Harvey was martyred after less than a year in office. His funeral procession led from 17th and Castro to City Hall and numbered 40,000. He was honored with a play produced locally; a biography, *The Mayor of Castro Street* by Randy Shilts, who wrote it for an advance of ten grand, peanuts in the publishing business; a successful television documentary, *The Times of Harvey Milk* (currently available on DVD); an opera that played in Houston, New York, and San Francisco; and a movie starring Sean Penn (he won an Oscar for it) with a screenplay by Dustin Lance Black (who also won an Oscar and gave an acceptance speech that earned him a standing ovation). After that, the small plaza at the corner of Castro and 17th, the staging area for so many of the rallies and marches Harvey led, was named after him.

And oh yes, you could buy a coffee mug with Harvey's picture on it from one of the souvenir shops on Castro.

But ask most young gay men about Harvey Milk and you'll get a blank stare and "Harvey who?"

A simple answer would be, "He's the man who changed your world." But memories are usually passed from one generation to another—from the third (grandfathers) to the second to the current one. For the gay community, except for a few, there is no second generation. It was largely wiped out by the AIDS epidemic.

This collection of speeches and writings is aimed not only at professors and researchers but also at a younger generation who might be assigned by their teachers to read it or who pick it up on their own.

Harvey.

In print.

A collection of his speeches and writings that resonated through the gay community and made it into a major political force in the country today.

Harvey was a tall, thin man in his early forties, with the improbable name of "Harvey Milk," who ran a camera shop on Castro Street. I lived in "Pneumonia Heights," a hill above the Castro, and used to walk down every morning for breakfast. One day he was out in front of his shop playing with Kid, the store's dog, and we started to talk. I told him I wrote books for a living, and he said he ran the store and once he'd run for supervisor.

He said he got 15,000 votes his first time out, and I was properly impressed. In Chicago the biggest political event we'd ever held was a "kiss-in" in front of City Hall—all one hundred of us.

He told me he was going to run for Supervisor again and asked whether I wanted to write speeches for him. "It'll be a hoot," he said. "We'll stir some shit."

Despite Harvey's 15,000 votes, I never for a moment thought he would win anything.

As a speechwriter, I soon discovered that I was just another cog in Harvey's embryo political machine. Scott Smith, his lover, ran the day-to-day management of the store as well as Harvey's campaigns (he and Harvey split after the first two. John Ryckman ran the third, and Anne Kronenberg, the fourth, as well as moved to City Hall with him when he won).

Jim Rivaldo and Dick Pabich wrote most of his campaign flyers. Some of the speeches Harvey gave nobody wrote for him. There were no teleprompters back then, and one of his speeches (Keynote Address, Gay Conference 5, Dallas, Texas) ran to seventeen typewritten pages. I'm pretty sure he spoke from a handful of notes, filling in as he went along. Mayor Feinstein—who had no love for Harvey because he frequently disagreed with her and wouldn't follow the party line—complained that Harvey talked too long and too often.

I wrote a number of Harvey's shorter speeches, as well as an occasional article for the *Bay Area Reporter's* "Forum." Harvey was far from illiterate—he could have written most of his speeches himself. But he couldn't do both and campaign as well. To a large extent, I was the pencil in Harvey's hand. We were both populists and agreed on practically all of his political positions. He was for the neighborhoods against downtown, and he championed the elderly, the unions, and the ethnic groups that made up the patchwork quilt of the city's population. He was insistent that those who drew a salary from the city should also live in the city. He never forgot the policeman who lived out of town and told him, "You couldn't pay me to live there"—meaning San Francisco.

He was tight with the unions, who were among his first supporters, and said a kind word about them whenever he could.

He was insistent about three things: The gay community should be represented by a gay man. The "friends of gays" who usually represented the community until Harvey came to town could change their positions depending on which way the political winds were blowing. An African American couldn't change the color of his skin and voted for one of his own. And an "openly gay man" would never be able to disavow his sexual orientation.

The latter was put to the test when gays had been granted civil rights in a few states, which upset Anita Bryant, a spokeswoman for the Florida orange juice growers. She started a campaign against gays that rolled across the country, gathering support as it went. In California, State Senator John Briggs picked up on it and introduced a bill to ban all homosexual teachers in the public school system. The bill was winning in the polls, and suddenly the "friends of gays" faded into the background.

It was Harvey who debated Briggs up and down the state (including the conservative stronghold of Orange County). Nobody wrote for him when he was on the road—he shot from the hip. ("How do you teach homosexuality? Like you'd teach French.")

The proposition lost.

High on Harvey's list of things to talk about was voting. He was well aware that power came from the ballot box, but many gays didn't bother to vote. He urged everybody in his audiences to "come out" and publicly acknowledge that they were gay. "How can people change their minds about us if they don't know who we are?"

Voting was easy. "Coming out" was another story. You could lose your family, your friends, and your job. Harvey was admired for being openly gay, but it wasn't a decision that many others were willing to make. It was easy to be "out" in the Castro—you could live there for weeks without meeting a straight man.

But being "out" in the world at large was a vastly different cup of tea.

Most of Harvey's positions were easy to write about—I'd been active in gay politics in Chicago and Harvey and I were two peas from the same pod.

The speech he gave most often was a barnburner, but I couldn't tell you who wrote it. It was Harvey's "hope" speech, and like Topsy it just grew. Harvey was fond of talking about "hope" in many guises and how it was important that younger gays, confused about their orientation, should be given "hope."

"You gotta give 'em hope."

The punch ending was that this kid in Altoona, Pennsylvania, had heard one of his speeches and called him. His parents would never understand him. Harvey was flattered by the call and told the boy that when he was of age, he should grab a bus and come out to California. There was silence for a moment and then the boy said quietly, "I can't. I'm crippled." (This was a highly emotional scene in the movie.)

Harvey polished the speech and used it often, though the rest of us kidded him because some days the boy lived in Altoona, other times in San Antonio or Buffalo. The boy really got around, we thought.

Harvey didn't have a battery of professional speechwriters who could make him sound like a latter-day John F. Kennedy. The strength of his speeches lay in his visceral connection with his audience.

It would take time for "gay power" to emerge, and it would bring hardships, but it would also bring freedom. Anybody who belonged to a minority group in the audience would nod and agree with that.

We expect our leaders to be exactly like us, and then we're disappointed when they turn out to be mere mortals—exactly like us. The attempt to impeach President Clinton failed because his audience instinctively understood that.

The police in Nazi Germany were brutal when it came to the Jews, because the Jews were undesirable anyway. Police brutality against homosexuals in the United States was tolerated because homosexuals were also undesirable. Right? That attitude spread like a cancer, and soon most of the country accepted it.

When it comes to taxes, you pay your fair share—but the insurance companies, the banks, the big corporations "pay little or nothing." You pay yours, but you're also paying theirs. Harvey wrote that thirty-five years ago, but it sounds very familiar today.

When it comes to our leaders, most of us instinctively recognize that "no person is born to greatness, but many people rise to it." Who knows what that scruffy kid down the block playing touch football will become? Harvey's audience recognized that and gave the kid the benefit of the doubt. Someday they might be voting for him.

"Nixon's appointments to the Supreme Court will affect our lives to a greater degree than anything he can do as president."

That's true of any president, and Harvey's audience knew it. The struggle for one political group or another to control the court is still going on today—the country swings left or right depending on the decisions of that court.

Harvey was prescient. His audience realized that the problems he pointed out in his lifetime would also be the problems of the future. Two steps forward, one step back: the history of our country.

Harvey was more than just a politician, more than a man running for political office.

He was an oracle and his audience identified with it. He spoke not only for today but also for tomorrow.

Speeches are important not only for the information they convey but for the insight they give into the people who delivered them. Hitler was brutal and sadistic, and it showed in his speeches. John F. Kennedy was altruistic; it came out in the man like sweat. Theodore Roosevelt—the first Roosevelt—was probably responsible for the expression "the bully pulpit." America had a manifest destiny—let's go get it!

The second Roosevelt, Franklin, was a healer. The country was bleeding when he took it, bound up its wounds, and bit by bit taught it to believe in itself again.

And Harvey?

Read his speeches and writings. He taught the gay community to respect itself; he taught it to believe in the power that it had and how to use it. A few of Harvey's campaigns and the local politicians knew that no anti-gay ordinance would ever be accepted by the city. The gays held veto power and they voted as a bloc.

Harvey wore a coat of many colors. He laughed a lot; he could be very funny; he could deliver a speech like an African American preacher, using the repetition of words and phrases until the crowd was roaring.

He started the first Castro Street Fair and showed the rest of the town how to throw a party. When the Ringling Brothers Barnum and Bailey circus came to town, he dressed as a clown and rode the cable cars to the delight of the tourists.

He never forgot those who had been less fortunate in life, and most of all, he showed his constituents how much he loved them. Some of us thought he loved campaigning more then he liked legislating.

He campaigned as a businessman, but in reality he was a terrible one. He wore hand-me-down suits, ground the beans for his coffee, and was an ace at a good spaghetti sauce. He was a man of the people— especially poor people (being a supervisor paid $9,000 a year; he had a very vivid idea of what being poor was like).

Why did he do it? Is there a lesson to be learned from reading what Harvey had to say? Can you see the man behind the curtain? You should; he never made any attempt to hide himself.

Harvey Milk was born into a world that didn't want him and left behind a world that discovered it would be difficult to do without him. Through his speeches and his courage he changed the lives of millions.

As teenagers, most gays used to haunt the library searching for mention of a gay man they could be proud of who in turn would make them proud of themselves. We desperately wanted to find a gay hero.

I never realized I had found mine until the day that Harvey died.

Harvey Milk's Political Archive and Archival Politics

CHARLES E. MORRIS III AND JASON EDWARD BLACK

In the Images of America memory book *San Francisco's Castro,* there appears a photograph depicting three volunteers anchoring the Harvey Milk Archives (HMA) booth at the 1982 Castro Street Fair.[1] Fittingly, the photograph was taken by Danny Nicoletta, Harvey Milk's protégé and photographer, who, for four decades now, has provided invaluable views of GLBTQ (gay, lesbian, bisexual, transgender, queer)[2] life in San Francisco. For those who personally remember, or for those who, against the odds, have somehow learned some GLBTQ history, the photograph may be haunting, temporally and tragically poised as it is between the immediate past of Milk's 1978 assassination and the unfolding present and future of HIV/AIDS in Ronald Reagan's New Right America. Even so, Milk's signature *hope* appears richly embodied in the photo's details—his huge smile beaming from a displayed portrait; the "Supervisor Harvey Milk" posters; the stack of Randy Shilts's newly published biography, *The Mayor of Castro Street;* and volunteer Tommy Buxton's laugh, implying a joyous carnivalesque occasion, communion, reprieve—suggesting that public memory powerfully affords comfort, community, and politics.

Like those HMA volunteers on Castro Street, we hope in this book to deepen and circulate the public memory of Harvey Milk. During the 1970s, Milk passionately lived as an activist and visionary, community builder, and stalwart and savvy campaigner, one of the first openly gay political officials in the United States. And Harvey Milk died with his boots on, a martyr—if not at the moment of his death, as some will quibble, then surely at the pronouncement of the unjust, undoubtedly homophobic verdict in his assassin's trial. Public memory is fraught, mutable, forceful, and consequential, and we believe it can be trans- formative in the lives of GLBTQ people—and everyone. What Harvey Milk bequeaths in the pages that follow is *An Archive of Hope*.

REMEMBERING HARVEY MILK

If you knew and loved Harvey, as so many in San Francisco still did, es- pecially in those first years after his death, you likely took heart and pride in those enthusiastic efforts to kindle his legacy. Perhaps you donated money to the HMA that day in 1982 on Castro Street. Or perhaps you participated in one of the many Milk memorial events that occurred in San Francisco and elsewhere in recent years: traveling aboard the "Gay Freedom Train" en route to "Avenge Harvey Milk!" at the first National March on Washington for Lesbian and Gay Rights in October 1979[3]; attending exhibits at the Gay Community Center and Castro Street Fair in 1979; watching photographer Crawford Barton's slide show at the Harvey Milk Gay Democratic Club (HMGDC) annual Milk dinner in May 1980; browsing archival materials that accompanied the newly rededicated Harvey Milk/Eureka Valley Library in May 1981; reminisc- ing at the HMGDC Milk slide show and cocktail party in City Hall that same month; joining devoted throngs in the annual Milk/Moscone Me- morial March; standing in line at Randy Shilts's book signings in 1982; or celebrating at Harvey's annual birthday party on Castro Street—a bounty of Milk memory!

So much commemoration in those early years of Milk's afterlives, in fact, that you might have thought Frank Robinson, Milk's speechwriter and campaign advisor (named as one of only four potential successors in Milk's political will), was unnecessarily concerned when he fretted in the inaugural 1983 issue of *The Harvey Milk Archives Newsletter*: "I do not know what Harvey's fate would have been if the Harvey Milk Archives had not been established. I am not sure what historians would have done, how they might have edited his speeches, how they might have subtly reshaped the past, how they might have interpreted the man who was the man who might have been."[4]

Robinson's insightful words should not be misunderstood as senti- mental hero worship or hagiography. Archival materials and their con- signation matter, always and profoundly, for histories and memories to survive and thrive, especially for those histories and memories that malignant individuals and institutions would readily consign to oblivion, and for those people who struggle for many reasons against manifold constraints to preserve and promulgate the past. Certainly this is true for GLBTQ histories and memories. Heather Love has written,

> The queer past has long served a crucial role in the making of queer community. . . . The desires that queers have invested in the past have transformed it. There are, as a result, many queer pasts: Some versions glitter with the collective fantasies of greatness; others have been rubbed smooth by constant handling; some are obscure, having been forgotten or put away; other versions of the past have been rendered ghostly through the weight of accreted longing; and some are covered by shadows, forgotten traces of ways of life that many would rather leave behind.[5]

There are, we believe, many queer pasts in Harvey Milk, as varied and valuable, as vulnerable, as those pasts Love describes and Robinson cherishes. The Milk archive, in whatever forms it exists and may eventually take, should never be taken for granted.

The extensive, largely behind-the-scenes efforts during the 1980s and 1990s to amass and preserve Harvey Milk's words, images, and ephemera deserve greater visibility. Scott Smith, heir and executor of Milk's estate, who, during their years as lovers, business partners, campaigners, and confidants, had done more than perhaps any other to influence Milk's transformation into the activist he became, devoted himself to cultivating and protecting Milk's legacy. He had help, too, from longtime friends and loyal supporters such as Frank Robinson, Danny Nicoletta, Anne Kronenberg, Jim Gordon, Linda Alband, Terry Henderling, Jim Rivaldo, Dick Pabich, Harry Britt, Denton Smith, Wayne Friday, Walter Caplan, John Wahl, John Ryckman, Alan Baird, Rich Nichols, Tom Randol, and Bob Ross, among others. After Scott Smith died in February 1995, some of those friends and associates contributed, culled, sorted, and inventoried materials in preparation for donation by Elva Smith, Scott's mother, to the San Francisco Public Library (SFPL). Correspondence suggests that negotiations among Elva Smith; co-executor Frank Robinson and the Ad Hoc Milk Archives Committee; and Jim Van Buskirk, Director of the James C. Hormel Gay and Lesbian Center at the SFPL, did not always proceed smoothly. Robinson's Letter to the Editor of the *San Francisco Bay Guardian* in July 1995 offers a sense of these archival politics: "Political regimes change, so do library personnel, and the intent of the ad hoc group is to make sure that the Archives will be protected for the use and benefit of future generations."[6] Nevertheless, The Harvey Milk Archives–Scott Smith Collection was officially donated to the SFPL in 1995 and transferred to the library in 1997.[7] It opened to the public in 2003.

Although for us this volume has been an enriching venture in GLBTQ memory work, which we hope readers will share, we should emphasize from the beginning that what we exhibit and narrate here—a substantial sample of transcribed documentary holdings representing Milk's typed, handwritten, recorded, and/or published words—constitutes but a fraction of Milk's public discourse. Many of Milk's speeches and writings have been lost because they were originally performed extemporaneously or published in outlets now remote; some of that corpus remains extant if as yet fully extracted in other archives and libraries, such as in microfilm series holdings of GLBTQ periodicals, objects, and documents housed at the GLBT Historical Society in San Francisco or the ONE Institute in Los Angeles, or materials in private collections. Despite Milk's presentiments of early death and his poignant foresight to tape-record a political will, he evidently was not much concerned with preserving or organizing his own archive for posterity; the state of his effects and affairs might fairly be described as chronically disheveled, a casualty of a devotedly engaged public life. We have decided to predominantly feature, with just a handful of exceptions, documentary texts of Milk's public political rhetoric derived from the Harvey Milk Archives–Scott Smith Collection at SFPL because of the concentration and diversity, history, and symbolism of this archival cache. However, we have been keenly aware from the start of this project, and cumulatively so throughout its production, that the Milk materials at the SFPL, invaluable for what they do contribute to Milk and GLBTQ history and memory, are nevertheless incomplete and should and undoubtedly will be beneficially complemented and supplemented in the future.[8]

It is also the case, as these selected documents evidence, that the traces of Harvey Milk's actual public discourse—scribbled or typed, scratched out, stump recycled, always in motion—bear the marks of having been lived rather than packaged. Milk's words are sometimes fragmentary, typically unpolished, and occasionally banal. At the same time, they always crackle with his energetic engagement. We might usefully think of these addresses, columns, statements, press releases, fliers, and open letters as quotidian translations from a single emergently public life; a locally situated if nationally aspirant gay street activist, consummate politician, and municipal official; a gay, white, Jewish, able-bodied, financially strapped but middle-class man. These words are embedded in complex, multitudinous, and intersectional contexts that enabled or thwarted Harvey Milk's presence, resonance, meaning, and influence in the 1970s, in the United States, in California, in San Francisco, in District 5, and in the Castro. We view such incomplete, tantalizing traces and echoes of distant times and larger stories, both inspirational and workaday texts, as rich enactments of Milk memory. As importantly, they constitute invitations to conversation, debate, reflection, teaching, learning, collaboration, community building, inter-generational relationships, and coalitional and oppositional politics—"how publics are formed in and through cultural archives"[9]—that inspire performative repertoires[10] of GLBTQ pasts that will be queerly reconfigured as the future unpredictably unfolds.

We also have usefully come to realize that some fairly will ask, "Why Harvey Milk?" Not everyone, then or now, considers Milk a pioneer, an icon, as he himself did, remarking to the Associated Press about his election in November, 1977: "I can really appreciate what Jackie Robinson was up against. . . . Every black youth in the country was looking up to him. . . . He was a symbol to all of them. In the same way, I am a symbol of hope to gays and all minorities."[11] Immodesty aside, Milk's claim on the GLBTQ pantheon might be rebuffed, or at least cause some bristling, despite his progressive populism and multi-issue advocacy, electoral success, visibility, assassination.[12] As some have argued, Milk was, after all, a local politician who served less than a year in municipal office, and we will never know what he might have accomplished politically had he lived.[13] Many in San Francisco thought him an arriviste. *Drummer* editor Jack Fritscher remembered that Milk was not well liked by many because he was "a political carpetbagger, because he was Manhattanizing laid-back San Francisco. He wasn't particularly cool. He was a New Yorker telling 'The City That Knows How' what to do in his 'Milk Forum' column in the *Bay Area Reporter*."[14] Many inside and outside of San Francisco, such as Minnesota activist Stephen Endean, who would go on to direct the Gay Rights National Lobby and founded the Human Rights Campaign Fund, despised "Milk's manner—his ego, his abrasiveness, his insistence on doing things his way—[which] ground on Endean's Midwestern sensibilities, and also probably on his insecurities."[15]

There are also perspectives that help us account for Milk's legacy in relation to broader cultural and political contexts. Fritscher offers gay immigration, single-issue voting, and assassination as crucial factors: "He was elected because he was gay, not because he was

'Harvey Milk.' . . . Beyond even Harvey's control, he was swept up in a symbolic role in ritual politics. The convergence of his times, not his life, propelled him. His latter-day sainthood came through a martyrdom that could have happened to anyone playing the role of gay supervisor. It was his bad fortune that 'Tonight the role of gay supervisor will be played by Harvey Milk.'"[16] Historian Jonathan Bell more generally links historical visibility with place and contingent circumstance, observing that San Francisco's attention is chiefly attributable to "the flamboyance and media-consciousness of its politicians and its importance as a microcosm of the social movements that have come to form the bedrock of the rights revolution of recent times."[17] From these vantages, Milk's posthumous renown should be understood as a complex production of his accomplishments, the where and when of his public life, the volume of his persona, and his dramatic demise.

These challenges and contextualizations are important and should shape any engagement with Milk's memory. We believe that they usefully complicate, but do not disqualify, a claim of Harvey Milk's significance, the value of his assembled words. Arguably, what materially matters most in GLBTQ worldmaking, then and now, occurs locally, whatever broader sweep and circulation a figure or place or event might foment or by happenstance occasion in the aftermath of activism. Most courageous GLBTQ activists since the first stirrings of political consciousness, during the arduous history of transformative acts and soundings, made a difference in particular spaces and sites, communities and forums, even as news of what they did—or they themselves—may have traveled. Milk remarked in 1978, "History is made by events . . . sometimes by large events with the world watching, but mostly by small events which plant the seeds of change. A reading of the Declaration of Independence on the steps of a building is widely covered. The events that started the American Revolution were the meetings in homes, pubs, on street corners."[18] Milk's successor on the Board of Supervisors, Harry Britt, came to a similar conclusion about *his* political fecundity:

> History will betray his own sense of who he was if we only remember him as a charismatic genius, a tragic figure wearing the face of a clown, a bigger-than-life model for gay pride. He was all that, of course, but the specialness of Harvey Milk was to be understood in terms of the specialness of San Francisco in the '70s and of the people whose hopes and dreams he was to take upon himself. . . . He could not have been what he was in an earlier period, or in another place. Most specifically, Harvey was a leader whose

destiny was the destiny of Castro's Street People, a motley gang of alienated refugees from the struggle to assimilate to the homophobic mainstream of American life.[19]

Thus a world of difference might be found in those local queer details called Milk, sine qua non inestimable.

Harvey Milk's words, too, teach us that successful activists *speak* locally, that the art of activist eloquence should be measured by the singularity of each ordinary persuasive opportunity, quotidian audience, or fleeting performance. Milk's purple passages and stump clichés teach us that hope's discourse, at close hearing by real people, is by turns and toil both sublime and hackneyed in situ. And with each of those hit-or-miss moments of rhetorical invention and embodiment, with each handshake, with each overbearing exchange, shameless self-promotion, flirtation, corny joke, and lump-in-the-throat moment when he was on a roll, Milk brought the GLBTQ folk of San Francisco that much closer to sexual justice and freedom, to gay rights. Milk campaign staffer Jim Rivaldo remembered, "I accompanied Harvey around the city and saw how readily people from all walks of life responded to an openly gay man with good ideas and an extraordinary gift for communicating them."[20]

Of course Britt's reminiscence—and he is not alone in this—elevates Milk onto a larger stage. Such hyperbole should not surprise or trouble us, as it is the currency and glue of public memory and social movements, both always replete with the propulsive lore of gods and devils.[21] Additionally, close associates of those inscribed into history and memory are often prone to flattering exaggeration. While wanting to avoid the distancing and distortion that comes with hagiography, we nevertheless believe Milk earned his inscription and our attention in GLBTQ history and memory by his contributions to gay rights writ large. Like GLBTQ activism itself during the 1970s, Milk was increasingly emerging on a national stage, with expanding influence. During the spectacular historic fluctuations of GLBTQ fortunes during 1977, Milk proved himself a movement leader and subject of national press coverage. Rodger Streitmatter, in spirit if not letter, conveys Milk's growing reputation and influence: "If San Francisco was the capital of Gay America, Harvey Milk was president."[22]

In a 1978 interview, Boze Hadleigh asked Milk, "As the most visible gay politician, aren't you going to be in demand as a national spokesperson?" His response: "That's starting already. A few groups have asked . . . but I'm so busy as it is, there's no time."[23] Nevertheless, during those few last months alive and working, Milk, along with tireless and talented activists Sally Miller Gearhart, Gwen Craig, Bill Kraus and so many others, led the successful statewide campaign to defeat Prop 6, called the "Briggs Amendment" after its sponsor, state assemblyman John Briggs, which would ban gay teachers from the California school system. Clendinen and Nagourney explain, "The decisive defeat of the Briggs initiative on November 7 [1978] was the greatest electoral victory the gay rights movement in the United States had known. It conferred a particular aura of historical celebrity on Harvey Milk, and at the victory party in San Francisco that night, he called for a gay march on Washington in 1979."[24] Assassinated 20 days later, Milk's place in the 1979 March for Lesbian and Gay Rights would be memorial, and thereafter sorting out and celebrating the historical contributions of the sanctified leader would be inevitably enhanced and muddled by the tropes of remembered martyrdom. The *Chicago Tribune* reported on November 30, 1978: "Milk, the leading avowed homosexual politician in California and perhaps the nation, will be especially missed. . . . 'Harvey Milk's assassination is a terrible blow to the gay-rights movement in this country,' said Robert McQueen, editor of *The Advocate,* San Francisco's leading gay newspaper. . . . [S]aid Harry Britt, one of Milk's closest friends and aides, 'Harvey Milk was the Martin Luther King of this nation's gay-liberation movement.'"[25]

Perhaps Ed Jackson was most insightful in capturing Milk's hold on the historical imagination when, in his 1984 review of Rob Epstein's documentary, he wrote, "*The Times of Harvey Milk* works powerfully on the viewer because of the Camelot-like resonances it sets off. On one level the story of one man's political career, it is also a morality tale about the dream of justice and the American faith in electoral politics. It traces the evolution of a populist hero who came to embody the hopes of an entire community, a hero tragically cut down in the prime of his political life."[26] Whatever the measure, on the street or on the pedestal, we believe Harvey Milk is historically significant, worthy of archiving and anthologizing, deserving of memory, and most importantly, accessible and relevant for cultural and political purposes in which he can prove invigorating and troubling still, and perhaps lifesaving.

HARVEY MILK: A BRIEF POLITICAL GENEALOGY

Given that Harvey Milk's public life did not begin until he was in his forties, and once begun lasted less than a decade—only ten months, eighteen days in office—it is a wonder that we should be bequeathed this archive. Indeed, it is a wonder such a public life began at all. Milk was not what most would consider destined for activism and politics. For most of his adult life Milk lived a quietly privileged domestic existence, passionately and monogamously devoted to his "marriages," his home, the opera, and other arts in New York. Though in retrospect some might consider him closeted, which is not quite the case, it is fair to say that Milk's private life was compartmentalized. His professional choices—in the Navy, as a schoolteacher, and for years in the financial world— reflected and no doubt solidified this conservatism. To the extent that he was political at all, as chroniclers like to recall, Milk had proven himself to be a Goldwater Republican. One can imagine those who knew Milk during most of life, those unaware of his sexuality but also his former lover Joe Campbell, doing a double take as he began making headlines in, of all places, San Francisco.[27]

Milk had made one other dramatic transformation prior to emerging as the "Mayor of Castro Street," and this may make it difficult to fathom Milk as the formidable politician he would become. Owing to the times, a young lover named Jack McKinley, and an experimental theater visionary named Tom O'Horgan (*Hair, Jesus Christ Superstar,* and *Lenny*), Milk had become a hippie. As Randy Shilts described it, "Milk found himself surrounded by some of the most outrageous flower children on the continent. Harvey started assimilating the new countercultural values, which spurned materialism, eschewed conformity, and mocked orthodoxy. With each month, Milk's hair became a little longer. With each political argument, his views became more flexible. With each new apartment, he discarded more of the tasteful furniture, stylish décor, and middle-class comforts he had cherished."[28] While briefly living in San Francisco in 1970, this Wall Street suit memorably burned his BankAmericard in response to the U.S. invasion of Cambodia. Two years later, with a new boyfriend named Scott Smith, Milk returned to California, flowers in his hair, roaming the state until finally settling for good in 1973 into a transitional neighborhood known by locals as Most Holy Redeemer Parish—what would become known as Castro Village and then, as now, the Castro.

Something queer was happening in San Francisco; indeed, it had been going on for quite some time. Always a haven for outsiders, San Francisco since World War II had become home to a sizeable population of GLBTQ people. Though more familiar for its 1970s blossoming, and overshadowed by mythic Stonewall, San Francisco *should* be remembered well for its much longer history of GLBTQ lives, cultures, and politics. In the 1950s Hal Call formed a chapter of the Mattachine Society, and Del Martin and Phyllis Lyon founded the Daughters of Bilitis, making the city a stronghold of homophile outreach. Jose Sarria, a drag institution at The Black Cat, who had tirelessly and resiliently stood up for his harassed, arrested, and beaten brothers, ran for Board of Supervisors in 1961, amassing 7,000 votes more than a decade before Milk's audacious first political campaign. Sarria's voice sounded the clarion call of a developing movement comprised of the organizations formed during that decade, including the League for Civil Education, Tavern Guild, Society for Individual Rights, and the Council on Religion and the Homosexual (CRH). The protest press conference held by the CRH in response to shameful police disruption of the New Year's Day Ball in 1965, as well as the trans people and other queers who resisted police brutality at Compton's Cafeteria in August 1966, stand alongside Stonewall as transformative events in the burgeoning national movement for GLBTQ liberation, rights, and pride. California establishment politicians were already responding to these grassroots activists in the nascent politics for sexual justice before the New York "birth" of liberation on Christopher Street in 1969.[29]

What GLBTQ San Francisco had been through the 1960s, though significant, would not have necessarily led one to predict the massive influx of immigrants and the expansion of cultures and politics in the subsequent decade.[30] John D'Emilio observes, "By the mid-1970s San Francisco had become, compared to the rest of the country, a liberated zone for lesbians and gay men."[31] Such growth was enabled by changing economic and demographic landscape of the city. San Francisco's transformation from a manufacturing center into a metropolis of corporate headquarters, tourism, and conventions, depleted the population's blue-collar, straight families in the many ethnic neighborhoods; consequently, it also enticed young professionals who found inexpensive housing in places like the Castro. Development politics were fraught, and tensions flared throughout the 1970s and beyond, inside and outside GLBTQ communities.[32] With San Francisco's development, however, accompanied by a growing reputation for sexual freedom, a GLBTQ homeland blossomed. D'Emilio explains that communities rapidly grew in a number of neighborhoods—Castro, Polk Street, Tenderloin, South of Market, Folsom Street, Upper Mission and Bernal Heights—constituting a "new social phenomenon, residential areas that were visibly gay in composition."[33]

With such visibility came more immigrants, social and sexual networks and spaces, communications, businesses, civic groups, political organizations, movement mobilization and action, public festivals, and celebrations. Reporting on the "economic boom" and "political clout" of GLBTQ San Francisco during the 1970s, the *Washington Post* concluded that it was the "most open of any [homosexual community] in the nation." Frances FitzGerald described the Castro as the "imminent realization" of gay liberation, "the first gay settlement, the first true gay 'community,' and as such it was a laboratory for the movement. It served as a refuge for gay men, and a place where they could remake their lives; now it was to become a model for the new society—'a gay Israel,' as someone once put it." Danny Nicoletta's recollection is equally effusive: "Into the Seventies, people arrived in San Francisco from all over the world with hopes of creating a life characterized by the consciousness attributed to the Sixties communal, holistic, non-violent, mystical, theatrical, and avant-garde. A facet of this idealism for myself and many others was that we were people who were gay searching for a place to be open and honest about this part of our lives—a place without fear of the hatred and persecution which had kept us in closets for so long."34

With such concentration, circulation, capital, and confidence, GLBTQ people also developed politically. The *San Francisco Chronicle* reported on its front page in 1971, "San Francisco's populous homosexual community, historically nonpolitical and inward looking, is in the midst of assembling a potentially powerful political machine."35 With the first gay rights marches, creation of the Alice B. Toklas Memorial Democratic Club, Jim Foster's path-breaking speech at the Democratic National Convention in 1972, and thriving lesbian-feminist communities, one might readily have believed the *Chronicle's* hyperbole, which became all the more manifest as the decade unfolded. Jonathan Bell's incisive analysis demonstrates that a broader confluence of contextual elements in California politics dating back more than a decade enabled such queer auspiciousness. From Bell's perspective, left liberalism guided a generation of influential and ascending politicians who fused economic and civil rights in a progressive vision of inclusion; politicians who were influenced by and collaborated with grassroots activists and who helped create the conditions under which such disenfranchised groups could make gains through electoral politics. This is not to say that Willie Brown, George Moscone, Phil Burton, Dianne Feinstein, Richard Hongisto, and other key political players of the era were unfettered champions of or exclusively responsible for gay rights, as Harvey Milk's critiques of superficial campaign courtship and battles with "the Machine" would later demonstrate. However, this analysis does help explain the conditions of possibility, "the distinctive contours of political life in San Francisco in the 1970s," within and through which Milk could emerge, mature, and ultimately succeed as a gay rights and community activist with a populist vision articulated through the discourses of economic justice, individual rights, political power, solidarity, and coalition.[36]

But of course it was not only because San Francisco existed as the "political base" and "spiritual home of California liberalism" that GLBTQ people flourished.[37] The intensifying, intensely satisfying, and interanimating dimensions of cultures and politics forged identification and identity, cultivated emotional bonds, deepened communities, fomented movement, and resulted in the sexual embodiment of freedom. Especially for gay men, such freedom was made all the more available and fluid by proliferating and booming bars, bathhouses, and clubs. With such growth came inevitable tensions, and there have been critiques, for example, of the gay male sexual culture.[38] However, sociologist Elizabeth Armstrong argues persuasively that those committed to gay rights (interest group politics and legal protections), gay pride (cultural identity and visibility), and sexual pleasure (its enactment and commercialization) created a synergistic movement of "unity through diversity."[39] Armstrong observes, "The political logic of identity made it possible to reconcile pride, rights, and sexual expression,"[40] despite differences among and the uniqueness of individuals, that solidified in economic power, political influence, and a sense of the collective instantiated through pleasure.

Significant, too, is the still broader context of national culture and politics, as well as the larger gay rights movement. Bruce Schulman writes in *The Seventies*, "[T]he emphasis on diversity, on cultural autonomy and difference, echoed throughout 1970s America. White ethnics picked it up, as did feminists and gay rights advocates and even the elderly. A new conception of the public arena emerged."[41] Contrary to narratives about cultural reversals and moribund activism, Dominic Sandbrook argues, "For all the efforts of the religious right and for all the talk of backlash against the legacy of the sixties, the fact remains that in moral and cultural terms, American society became steadily more permissive. More marriages broke up, more pregnancies were terminated, more children were born out of wedlock, and more gays and lesbians came out. In this respect at least, liberalism not only survived the 1970s but emerged triumphant."[42] Moreover, GLBTQ activism in particular should be understood as not only a legacy of the "long sixties" but as a distinctive influence on U.S. culture. Schulman goes so far as to conclude, "The gay rights movement transformed Americans' understanding of homosexuality, and of masculinity in general"; elsewhere he wrote, "Looking back . . . it is clear that the grassroots struggles for racial justice and sexual equality have exerted a more thoroughgoing impact than the liberal political economy of the Great Society."[43]

Such superlative assessments are warranted by hard-earned achievements of GLBTQ people and organizations, and the widening visibility that came with them. The often-cited *Time* cover story, "Gays on the March," from September 1975, remarked on the transformation:

> There are now more than 800 gay groups in the U.S., most of them pressing for state or local reforms. *The Advocate,* a largely political biweekly tabloid for gays, has a nationwide circulation of 60,000, and the National Gay Task Force has a membership of 2,200. . . . Since homosexuals began to organize for political action six years ago, they have achieved a substantial number of victories. Eleven state legislatures have followed Illinois in repealing their anti-sodomy laws. The American Psychiatric Association has stopped listing homosexuality as a psychiatric disorder, and AT&T, several other big corporations and the Civil Service Commission have announced their willingness to hire openly avowed gays.[44]

Little wonder, then, that even as the movement shifted from the brief revolution of gay liberation to the mainstay of gay rights reform (growing in numbers while contracting its agenda to single-issue politics), a heady mood of historic transformation pervaded. Like other GLBTQ people, John D'Emilio, himself both chronicler and activist, rode high on the collective effervescence: "The goals of activists had narrowed, yet activists in the mid-1970s almost uniformly displayed an élan that made them feel as if they were mounting the barricades. Activists increasingly engaged in routinized and mundane organizational tasks, yet they believed they were remaking the world."[45]

Harvey Milk emerged from within these layered political and cultural contexts, reflecting them but also, improbably, harnessing their energies and promises into a unique activist vision that would help define the rest of decade, locally and nationally, as an epoch in GLBTQ history. Of course, Milk did not commence his political career as the leader he would become. He began it quite sparsely and unremarkably in the spring of 1973 in his newly opened Castro Camera at 575 Castro Street.

The always threadbare business, which kept Milk in the financial straits to which he had not been accustomed during his earlier life, seems destined to the storied political front and headquarters it became. The real work of Castro Camera and its regulars focused not on rolls of film but on people, their freedoms, struggles, and neighborhoods in San Francisco.

Although Milk's deeper political inclinations may be attributable, by his own accounting, to the 1943 Jewish uprising in the Warsaw ghetto and his 1947 arrest as a teenager in Central Park for "indecent exposure," Milk often identified three moral shocks[46] in 1973 as effecting his awakening and sparking his first campaign for Board of Supervisors, the eleven-member body representing San Francisco's consolidated city-county government. First, shortly after Castro Camera opened, Milk had a heated altercation with a local bureaucrat who demanded a $100 deposit against sales tax in order for the business to operate, which seemed to him an outrageous violation of free enterprise and symptom of class inequity. Second, Milk blanched at the disparity between haves and have-nots in this "developing" city, disparity which appeared proximately in the form of a young teacher from a resource-strapped school asking if she could borrow a slide projector to teach her lessons. Finally, Milk had a visceral response to Attorney General John Mitchell's mendacious and evasive testimony during the Watergate Hearings, which he watched animatedly on a portable TV in the shop. Shortly thereafter, standing on a crate inscribed with the word "soap," Milk launched his first candidacy.[47]

A more auspicious political debut, short of winning, is hard to imagine. Perhaps especially so given the long odds Harvey Milk faced as an unknown newcomer, both to the city and to politics, with the wrong look and surprisingly fierce opposition. For starters, there was that ponytail few could ignore, the signature symbol of his troubling hippie persona. Milk was also openly and unabashedly gay, which, needless to say, for an at-large candidate in a citywide election battling five incumbents, made for a political liability.[48] We should recall and underscore how few GLBTQ candidates preceded Milk on any ballot in the United States, so few in fact, and with decidedly less candor and bravado, that it is not surprising (mythmaking notwithstanding) that he is often mistakenly celebrated as the first.

What may come as a surprise, however, is that Milk's gay problem mostly concerned GLBTQ people themselves, or as Brett Callis observes, "His candidacy was itself a major issue for gays in 1973."[49]

There was much passionate dispute in the GLBTQ press, social spaces, and political meetings, about how GLBTQ politics should proceed into or against the mainstream. Should the approach be accommodationist or radical? Should GLBTQ people enter politics to gain power or rely on the stewardship and largesse of straight allies? Should candidates make sexuality their defining marker, or should their ideology and platform take primacy over the fact that they happen to be gay? What might public engagement mean in relation to a politics of respectability? Should candidates be single-issue focused on gay rights or be committed to a broad set of issues?

From the beginning of his campaign, Milk was adversely targeted by the gay political establishment—the Society for Individual Rights (SIR) and the Toklas Club—whose key players and gatekeepers, by and large, had their own scars and believed in an accommodationist and gradualist approach to gay rights, gained through loyal support of elected straight liberal allies, what Milk derisively would later call the "gay groupie syndrome."[50] Michael Wong, a young, heterosexual, Chinese American who, in launching his own political career, courted counsel and support of prominent members of the Toklas Club, captured well in his diary this attempted fratricide by powerful members of the gay establishment:

> Gary Miller told me that Harvey Milk was "dangerous and uncontrollable." Duke Smith said that Harvey Milk was "high on something." Rick Stokes told me that Milk "had no support in [the] Gay Community . . . he's running all on his own." Jo Daly told me, "Maybe if we just ignore him, he'll go away." Jim Foster said that "it would be disastrous for the gay community if Harvey Milk ever received credibility." I couldn't have agreed with them more.[51]

Heeding such advice, Wong helped to block endorsements for Milk with San Francisco Young Democrats and San Francisco Tomorrow. Foster in particular, perhaps the most visible and influential gay establishment politician in San Francisco, openly opposed Milk until the bitter end, even after Milk had won over the *Bay Area Reporter,* SIR leader and *Vector* editor William Beardemphl, other publications, and a critical mass of GLBTQ voters.[52]

The intensity of the vitriol by Milk's political enemies within the GLBTQ community suggests that they saw in him something more than an upstart of questionable motives and dubious emotional stability. Wong wrote privately what insiders would not admit: "No candidate came close to his dynamic delivery. . . . He stole the show. . . . [E]verywhere he spoke, people were drawn to him. He was not slick and people related to him. He was causing the Toklas Club great concerns."[53] Moreover, Shilts astutely observed, "The disparity between Milk's image and his reality stemmed from the essential act with which he defined himself—rebellion. The campaign biography that emerged from his early media interviews reads like the blueprint for a maverick."[54]

And a queer, barnstorming, populist maverick he was. Milk's broad platform focused on a wide range of issues that prioritized San Francisco residents over the city's corporate and Chamber of Commerce interests. As the selected documents from 1973 reveal, Milk envisioned San Francisco as a city that would take its place among other great metropolises not for its bankbook or universities but for its populace, "a city that breathes, one that is alive and where the people are more important than the highways." Instead of downtown development and growth of the tourism industry, for Milk San Francisco's future depended on reducing wasteful and unfair governmental spending and taxation, promoting childcare centers and dental care for the elderly, eliminating poverty and addressing the unemployment rate by teaching skills and providing economic opportunities. Instead of fringe benefits for MUNI (San Francisco Municipal Railway) drivers, Milk advocated better service for MUNI riders, which would be achieved in part by mandating that city officials ride MUNI to work, and preventing congestion by reducing downtown parking garages. Instead of police harassment and arrests for marijuana possession, prostitution, and gay public sex, what he called "legislating morality" against "victimless crimes," Milk demanded improved police protection against rape, murder, and mugging, which would be achieved if policemen actually lived in the city they patrolled, and patrolled in greater numbers. As he argued in his September 1973 address to the Joint International Longshoremen & Warehousemen's Union and Lafayette Club, "It takes no compromising to give the people their rights . . . it takes no money to respect the individual. It takes no political deal to give people freedom. It takes no survey to remove repression." From promoting street arts and community art centers, to advocating for beer drivers' Local 888, to the district elections (Proposition K) he championed, Milk imagined the end of disenfranchisement and discrimination, better quality of life, and resurgence of democracy for all.

That Milk had indeed made a statement during the campaign is evidenced by the nearly 17,000 votes he garnered, finishing tenth in a field of thirty-two candidates. More heartening still, Milk realized that had there been district elections, voters in San Francisco's GLBTQ neighborhoods, despite the Toklas Club's opposition, would have delivered him to City Hall. SIR official and *Vector* editor William Beardemphl presciently observed in his *Bay Area Reporter* "Comments" column that, "Above and beyond his race for Supervisor, Harvey Milk IS opening the door to government a little wider so that all homosexuals of ability can enter politics without a destructive homosexual stigmata imposed on them."[55] Milk appears to have been emboldened by the experience and results, for he almost immediately cast his sights on the 1975 campaign and during the interim would become an even more dedicated and visible community and gay rights activist. During this period, Milk's political vision solidified and public voice amplified more prominently as he launched biweekly columns for the *Sentinel* ("Waves from the Left," February to September 1974) and *Bay Area Reporter* ("Milk Forum," May 1974 until the week of his death, November 1978) and regularly took to the streets in protest against homophobic discrimination, harassment, and violence, or in celebration of and communion with his GLBTQ neighbors, friends, and allies.

During 1974 and 1975, Milk continued his broad-based populism, but he also unmistakably sought to mobilize his own community toward seizing and consolidating its power through strength in numbers, solidarity, votes, and economic influence. In his effort at consciousness raising, Milk implored GLBTQ people that "the only important issue for homosexuals is Freedom. All else is meaningless. . . . Many people think that they are FREE because they have a lot of money and live in 'good' neighborhoods. But the homosexual is not free until there are NO laws on ANY books suppressing him and not until he, if he so wishes, can join the police force or any government agency as an open homosexual. It is as simple as that."[56] In his *Vector* editorial, among the selected documents, Milk invoked Martin Luther King, Jr., and memories of the Montgomery bus boycott to punctuate his call for "full citizenship" and struggle against homophobia: "the homosexual community is the last minority group that has received no civil rights. . . . In order for homosexuals to win our right to self-respect and equality, we must first assert our full existence and then its strength."

Once awakened, according to Milk's political calculus, GLBTQ people must act collectively to concentrate and strategically wield their power, which he theorized in economic, political, and communal terms. Milk's "Waves from the Left" column in the *Sentinel* on "Political Power," included in this volume, emphasized that change only comes through the exercise of material influence. That power begins with registering to vote, which is why Milk appropriated diverse occasions for that purpose and enlisted as many volunteers as he could muster (always recruiting) to help with drives (2,000 new voters for the 1974 gubernatorial election and many more for his own campaign in 1975). For those registered, Milk urged that political power works best in withholding votes until a sense of urgency among "friendly" candidates leverages sturdier pledges rather than automatically or prematurely offering votes for the price of a trivial campaign courting appearance.[57] Milk lashed out at his gay establishment nemeses for being what he called, in the selected editorial of the same name, "Aunt Marys," the equivalent of Uncle Toms, who sold out by toadying to straight liberal politicians who forgot their GLBTQ constituents once elected. Then GLBTQ voters should cast their ballots as a bloc, the sheer size of which would likely determine the outcomes of elections, making the community's presence unmistakable and influence palpable and in turn, quid pro quo, desirable capital. During 1974, Milk also began his practice of publishing endorsements, and disqualifications, with detailed political analysis specific to communal interests. Milk declared, "Every person in this state owes it not only to himself, but for all gay people who will follow us years from now[,] to vote for freedom."[58]

Second, Milk insisted, "Economic power is stronger than any other form of power. . . . There is tremendous amount of economic power and strength in the San Francisco gay community. It has never been effectively brought together. It looks as if it will now happen."[59] Milk's optimism stemmed from those existing and emerging associations— Gay Chamber of Commerce, Gay Community Guild, Tavern Guild, and Golden Gate Business Association—he supported, and the Castro Village Association he founded, which welcomed 5,000 for its first Castro Street Fair in August 1974 (25,000 in 1975, 100,000 in 1976).[60]

Third, Milk advocated the power of solidarity and coalition. He argued that GLBTQ people and politicians must eradicate endemic jealously and infighting; otherwise, such divisions amounted to complicity in their own oppression. In the *Bay Area Reporter,* Milk averred, "The day we can pick up a gay paper and not find any attacks on other gays, the movement will start to unite. It can never have full power as long as one person, for whatever reasons, attacks others in the movement . . . to go after another gay person for their doing their trip in the movement, is to attack the entire movement."[61] He convened a task force to explore paths to unification. Milk also urged the support of the Teamsters in the Coors Boycott as well as other unions, reasoning, "If we in the gay community want others to help us in our fight to end discrimination, we must help others in their fights."[62] About the neighborhood baseball challenge between the "gay all stars" and "champs of the local Twilight League," Milk effused, "Just the playing of the game did more to bring relations between the community than any other event, act, speech, law. . . . That game was a victory for better relationships between the straight youths and the gays."[63]

Beyond this communal power vision, Milk also became bolder in his confrontation with individuals and institutions harming GLBTQ people and other San Franciscans. Milk lambasted the city government for giving taxpaying members of the Gay Freedom Day Committee the "run-a-round" regarding permits and parade routes (but not other similar groups),[64] and in his Open Letter included in the volume, chided the *San Francisco Chronicle* for sensationalizing gay pride without sensitivity to the plight of GLBTQ people. He openly opposed political candidates like John Foran and Dianne Feinstein for their absent or phony solidarity, and ridiculed the Board of Supervisors for its failures, hypocrisy, and fawning compliance with downtown interests. "The time has come," he insisted, "Either the Board and the city agencies give to the gay community what any other group can get or don't come around courting our votes."[65] He unremittingly indicted police brutality and harassment, which he likened to Nazi oppression of the Jews, exemplified in his published and street protests of the Labor Day beatings at Toad Hall bar and subsequent jailing of the "Castro 14." In the face of such homophobic discrimination and violence, and bringing together all the elements of his platform, Milk called for economic and political mobilization.[66]

During the first campaign in 1973, Milk began telling reporters that some were calling him the "unofficial mayor of Castro Street," a clever moniker. His words and actions during 1974–1975 suggest that he may have perceived himself, and perhaps was beginning to be perceived by friends and enemies alike, as the unofficial, emergent leader of a (new) GLBTQ power movement.[67] Milk reflected in a *New York Times* interview, "I'm a left-winger, a street person. . . . Most gays are politically conservative, you know, banks, insurance, bureaucrats. So their checkbooks are out of the closet, but they're not. So you try to get something going, and all the gay money is still supporting Republicans except on this gayness thing, so I say, 'Gay for Gay.' That's my issue. That's it. That's the big one."[68] It is worth noting that Milk's candidacy operated within a state and local political culture that connected economic justice, rights discourse, and identity politics. Bell explains, "From the perspective of liberal politicians experimenting with a reconfiguration of the relationship between the individual and society it was inevitable that discussions of social marginalization in the 1950s and beyond would allow a widening of the left-of-center political lexicon that could be responsive to homophile activism. One of Harvey Milk's early successes as a leading gay activist in the Castro in 1973 was to help the Teamsters extend a boycott of Coors beer into the gay bars, linking gay rights to economic issues."[69]

However, Milk suggests in his *Sentinel* column "Where I Stand," among the selected documents, that any exclusive political categorization is a foolhardy venture, doomed to being inaccurate or incomplete. Note, for instance, pollster Mervin Field's analysis in *Time,* in which he commented on the two tides of the 1975 election: "One is the ebbing tide of traditional liberal, labor and cultural concepts—the idea that government can do it for you. Against this is the rising tide of the 'new conservatism'—which is related to fear about crime, the inability to get services from government, and fiscal responsibility."[70] The Harvey Milk of his second campaign, perhaps paradoxically, passionately espoused positions consonant with both tides Field identified.[71] The ponytail shorn, replaced by a second-hand, two-piece suit, Milk's hippie persona yielded to a clean-shaven one no less down to earth and outspoken but with broader visual and thus political appeal. Shilts reported that, "Milk's appearance and demeanor became so devastatingly average that he sometimes had to fend off allegations that he was actually heterosexual. 'If I were . . . there sure would be a lot of surprised men walking around San Francisco.'"[72]

Although Milk's second campaign has received comparatively scant attention, its significance should be understood in relation to the political traction he was gaining, the progressive muckraking he was advocating, and the gay rights agenda his visibility was advancing. The *Bay Area Reporter's* preview of Milk's campaign reveals the extent to which his vision had retained a balance and connectedness between GLBTQ concerns and those of all San Franciscans: "Milk's four-point program calls for a 'Fair Share' tax for those who work in The City but don't live here, for taxis and buses to be equipped so they can report crimes-in-progress directly to Police headquarters, for the Fire Department to be supplied with the most modern equipment available, and for 'the Board's present sense of priorities to be reoriented to the people and not to downtown interests.'"[73] Indeed, his "Milk Forum" columns throughout 1975 not only reiterated the GLBTQ power blueprint he had been articulating but addressed a broad range of local issues, including national and city economic conditions, MUNI deficiencies, Yerba Buena development, property tax assessments and housing, bail bondsmen, the Coors boycott (again), and the police strike.

Of course, his gay rights advocacy continued apace during the 1975 campaign. In his "Milk Forum" columns, he railed against City Hall for not providing funds for the Gay Freedom Day Committee while doing so for others, and decried the lack of media coverage of an event with more than 80,000 participants and spectators; he reminded his readers of the value of holding their vote pledges so as to get the most from their political "friends"; he urged a continuation of the GLBTQ Coors boycott even after the national Teamsters eliminated the local chapter's effort; he called for lobbying in support of AB489 and AB633, the consenting sex and fair employment legislation pending in the California Assembly.

Significant, too, about the 1975 election is that candidates, especially for the mayoralty, courted votes and endorsements from the GLBTQ community as never before. Perhaps because of Milk's trenchant critiques of the "gay groupie syndrome" and his passionate call for GLBTQ political power through decisive voting blocs, campaign hopefuls became increasingly attentive. How remarkable it must have been to read in the *Los Angeles Times* Supervisor John L. Molinari proclaiming, "The gay vote is a key element for any elected official in San Francisco."[74] Or to see mayoral candidate Dianne Feinstein chanting for the gay men's softball team against rival police department at their fourth annual game; or to hear that Feinstein had hosted and presided over the lesbian wedding of Human Rights Committee liaison Jo Daly and her partner. Or to finally witness the passage of the state law legalizing sex between consenting adults, thus defeating sodomy's long criminalization, thanks largely to State Senate Majority Leader and mayoral candidate George Moscone and his ally Willie Brown. Moscone's conservative opponent in the runoff that December learned the hard way that you ignored or maligned "you people," a term he used in a well-publicized meeting, at your political peril. Moscone publicly thanked Harvey Milk in his acceptance speech.[75]

Though Milk was not victorious, he finished seventh behind six incumbents out of a twenty-nine candidate field, despite renewed opposition from gay establishment politicos, with 52,649 votes, strongly supported from the Castro (where he garnered 60–70 percent) to Haight-Ashbury and Pacific Heights.[76] Jim Rivaldo, who along with Frank Robinson and Danny Nicoletta had joined Milk that year, proclaimed in light of the prescient color-coded map at Castro Camera, "We got the hippie, McGovern, and fruit voters."[77] Milk described the GLBTQ presence in this campaign season as having achieved "unprecedented political influence."[78] Despite the defeat, Milk had arrived. As Clendinen and Nagourney observe, "No one considered him a fluke anymore. He was part of a phenomenon, the sheer accumulation of gay influence in the city. . . . The boldest, most visible new element of that voting population was in the Castro, and by the end of 1975, Harvey Milk was clearly its voice—and the most public gay figure in the city."[79]

Were further proof needed of Milk's new political capital, it came in Mayor Moscone's appointment of him to the significant Board of Permit Appeals. (It had not hurt, of course, that Milk had publicly offered his unsolicited support to candidate Moscone in the run-off mayoral election against Supervisor John Barbagelata). Openly gay Commissioner Milk: a first in U.S. politics. As his friends and allies remembered, it certainly had a ring to it. Moscone called Milk "a pioneer." Even better, he said Milk wouldn't be a pioneer for long—the *Bay Area Reporter* headline read: "Moscone: Milk Appointment Is Just the Beginning."[80] The GLBTQ promise of the Moscone Administration was deepened by the appointment of Charles Gain as the first chief of police to publicly avow support for out cops on the force (for which Milk had been clamoring), as well as the election of District Attorney Joe Freitas, who pledged to end prosecutions for victimless crimes.[81] In "Milk Forum" he gushed, "[T]he gay community now has a mayor—for the first time ever!—who is not only understanding of our particular problems, but who wants to correct the inequalities."[82]

Ever the maverick, however, Milk served the shortest recorded term on the Permit Appeals Board; the Moscone dreams quickly soured. Milk had gotten wind of a purported deal among a number of state and national politicians, including Moscone, California Assembly Speaker Leo McCarthy, Congressmen Phil Burton and his brother John, and Assemblymen John Foran and Willie Brown. It was a multi-move, multilevel political orchestration that would mend rifts and solidify the new Democratic regime in California, with implications for the U.S. Congress. The last person in this political pact: Art Agnos, a McCarthy aide, who would be the heir apparent of the 16th Assembly District—Milk's District. Board of Supervisors President Quentin Kopp memorably called this political arrangement an "Unholy Alliance."[83]

That Mayor Moscone had dismissed Milk from the Board of Permit Appeals on the grounds that one could not hold such a position while campaigning—when he himself had done so a number of times—heightened the stench for some. In the *Bay Guardian* article entitled "Ganging Up on Harvey Milk," Bruce Brugmann and Jerry Roberts railed against what they described as "a naked, unabashed power play. . . . The hypocrisies abound."[84]

True to political character, Milk was outraged by the machinations. As he said in his declaration of candidacy, among the selected 1976 documents: "*I think representatives should be elected by the people—not appointed. I think a representative should earn his or her seat—I don't think the seat should be awarded on the basis of service to the machine.*" Given the math—what that impressive map indicated about voting patterns in Milk's campaigns, the 1974 vote total in the 16th District for John Foran, and the fact that Art Agnos was a political unknown— Milk's prospects for success appeared strong. "Milk vs. The Machine" became the slogan derived from media that fanned Milk's audacious challenge. This crusade seemed very much in keeping the vision Milk had championed since 1973. He wrote on his 1976 "Declaration of Candidacy" application: "My candidacy gives you a choice. Machine politics or an independent voice? . . . A Machine doesn't serve people, it rewards only people who slave it. I will fight to prevent San Francisco from becoming a Chicago politically."[85]

Perhaps it is too obvious to call Milk's Assembly campaign a transitional moment, given the requisite performance on the larger stage and greater complexities of California state politics. The transition we have in mind here, however, is toward a national political arena, one that made possible his deft leadership in engaging and exploiting the more familiar homophobic national spectacle of 1977. Although Milk had always commented on issues of national concern, in 1976 his commentaries on the impact of the Coors boycott, the Supreme Court's homophobia,[86] Nixon's legacy, the presidential primary election, California's Nuclear Initiative, Angola, the failed revolutionary legacy of 1776, Bob Dole, and of course on GLBTQ lives and the gay rights movement all seem to suggest an ever-expanding political vision. After his own race had ended in June, Milk focused much attention on the presidential race. A picture of Milk shaking hands with Jimmy Carter appeared in the *Bay Area Reporter,* and his endorsement of Carter, announced in the selected document, "'Uncertainty' of Carter or the 'Certainty' of Ford," was enthusiastic despite Carter's discomfort and ambivalence regarding the GLBTQ community. (Milk would later challenge President Carter to address the human rights of GLBTQ people and encouraged a writing campaign to lobby the White House.) Milk counseled his readers and supporters to learn lessons from the African American community by exercising their voting power in the election, by voting as a bloc for Carter and other candidates sympathetic to gay rights.[87]

At the same time, that broader vista only held meaning in relation to the communities in which one lived, the people for whom one strived and struggled politically. Milk's hero, as he wrote in the column included in this volume, "My Concept of a Legislator," was Harry Truman, who

> never developed contempt for the common man, perhaps because he had personally waited on so many of them in his Kansas City clothing store. Once in public office, he never patronized his constituents, perhaps because he never forgot the time when he had to file bankruptcy. The people who supported Truman were those who had to sweat for their daily bread, many who may not have been as articulate as others with their tongues, but were loving in their hearts, those who instinctively recognized that no person is born to greatness, but many people rise to it.

His political vision and platform clearly had not changed, and he approached the campaign against the Machine as he had the others, by tirelessly attending every meeting possible, shaking hands and conversing, and by building bridges among those who shared stakes in the Sixteenth District. Frank Robinson remembered, "Everything could be going against him, but he would come back to the headquarters jubilant because he has persuaded one old lady to vote for him. . . . It was as if every person he won over represented an important victory. . . . Those moments meant more to him than anything in the world."[88]

Throughout the campaign, and even into the first hours of the election returns, there was cause for hope. *Hope,* the theme and trope that would come to define Milk's legacy, had emerged during the 1976 campaign in part because Art Agnos told him, after one of their countless tandem events, that his stump speech was too dour. Perhaps this time Milk underestimated his opponent, who was backed by every prominent politician at the state and local level (including, at the eleventh hour, Gov. Jerry Brown, who had sworn neutrality) and endorsed by the very press (such as the *Bay Guardian*) that had encouraged Milk and castigated the Machine. The gay establishment, of course, actively supported Agnos; that low moment when they imported openly lesbian Massachusetts state representative Elaine Noble to endorse Agnos (to throw her weight against Milk, whom she had never met) must have stung deeply. Some openly accused Milk himself of being involved in a political deal with the Machine, which he bitterly denounced as a smear campaign. Moreover, Milk may have strategically overestimated his support among Castro voters, spending more time emphasizing non–gay rights issues while Art Agnos highlighted his solidarity with the GLBTQ community. The full-page Agnos campaign ad in the *Bay Area Reporter* a week before the election packed a punch, however inaccurate: "'Who is really upfront for Gay rights no matter who the audience is?' . . . If Harvey Milk won't speak out for gay rights at the Labor Council in S.F., what will he do in Sacramento?" It has been suggested that the 35 percent of the votes Agnos received in the high turn-out Castro (Milk garnered 62 percent), compared to the lower turn-out minority neighborhoods where Milk fared worse than he had planned and concentrated, arguably made the difference in the election. The toll was also personal, including the disintegration of his relationship with Scott Smith, and the death threats that resonated with his long-standing foreboding about an early demise.[89]

Against those long odds, Milk only lost by 3,630 votes of 32,000 cast, though the triumphalism of his enemies writing his political obituary must have only deepened the exhaustion of his third campaign—two in two years—and third defeat. Had he squandered his chance for election to the Board of Supervisors in 1977, as he had his appointment to the Board of Permit Appeals, because of his political willfulness? Were those pundits correct who suggested the margin of Milk's loss meant that the gay establishment could no longer deliver the vote, thus paving the way for a run in 1977? Was the most significant, and dramatic, act of Milk's operatic political career yet to come?

One can imagine Milk losing faith in Hope. In addition to the precariousness of his political future, Milk now sought change amid shifting, worsening political contexts in California and nationally, with obvious impact at home. Cultural anxieties in California were running high despite new Governor Jerry Brown's "big thinking": "Beneath the glamour of California life, the undercurrent of anxiety had rarely run harder and faster than in the mid-1970s. With the economy in recession, jobless rates stood at almost 10 percent, and the state was coming under growing pressure to raise taxes and slash services. Factories and employers were heading south, their tanks and theaters were closing, and people were increasingly moving out of the big cities."[90] Was there glumness in Milk's interview with the San Francisco State University student paper, *Zenger's?* "I'm deeply in debt, my store's deeply in debt. It's a struggle to get out. . . . I just took my stand and lost, unlike other politicians who get involved just to fill their egos and their pockets. But I knew the consequences of running, but it's vital that someone raises the questions. Such as, why is there crime? Not how to stop it by using more police. Why is there unemployment and why has industry been driven out of town?"[91]

More ominously, evangelical and social conservatives, alarmed by what they perceived as widespread moral deterioration in a climate of tolerance and permissiveness precipitating a crisis in the American family, began in earnest to mobilize a movement that would hit full stride after Ronald Reagan's election in 1980. Paul Boyer explained, "In this decade, the nation's evangelical subculture emerged from self-imposed isolation to become a powerful force in mainstream culture and politics. . . . When *Newsweek* magazine proclaimed 1976 as 'The Year of the Evangelical,' the editors underscored a phenomenon that was well under way."[92] As Bruce Schulman put it, "Thunder was gathering on the right." Worse yet, its lightening, prayers being answered, should smite GLBTQ people. "In the rhetoric of the New Right, feminists were second only to homosexuals in the list of villains threatening the American family," according to Dominic Sandbrook. "If there was one threat that particularly disturbed preachers, it was homosexuality."[93] Texas televangelist James Robison's battle cry of 1980 could be found forming in the throats of the devout half a decade earlier: "I'm sick and tired of hearing about all of the radicals, and the perverts, and the liberals, and the leftists, and the communists coming out of the closet. It's time for God's people to come out of the closet, out of our churches, and change America."[94] And so they did.

The year 1977 proved to be one of the most important in GLBTQ history to date, the best and worst of times, though its memory has been overshadowed by Stonewall and by the tragic events of 1978. The year began with such promise. The long-sought district elections had finally been won the previous November, changing the landscape of municipal politics and quite likely the political fortunes of Harvey Milk, as that color-coded map had long predicted. In his first "Milk Forum" column for the new year, he touted Carter's presidency and district elections as "changes of influence . . . changes in priorities" that meant good news for GLBTQ people.[95] A gay rights ordinance protecting against homophobic discrimination in employment, housing, and public accommodations had just passed in Dade County, Florida, a noteworthy civil rights victory in what would become a series of such advancements over the course of the year, in unlikely bastions such as St. Paul, Wichita, Iowa City, Champaign-Urbana, Aspen, and Eugene. A number of states were considering similar legislation. Wyoming became the 19th state to legalize sex between consenting adults of either gender. Shilts described the "year of the gay": "The year, it seemed, surely would show that the gay movement had reached the juggernaut status; nothing could stop this idea whose time had come."[96]

Ironically, the year would be consequential for the movement because an evangelical pop singer and sunny endorser of Florida orange juice named Anita Bryant thwarted the gay rights juggernaut in a Manichean showdown. Bryant's wholesome persona, Donna Reed looks, mellifluous voice, conservative values, and devout faith—embodiments of what we now know familiarly as family values rhetoric—made her a powerful spokesperson for a homophobic campaign to repeal the Dade County gay rights ordinance that in its own right threatened to become a national juggernaut and a harbinger of the New Right. Calling itself "Save Our Children," the repeal effort trafficked in the invidious and intoxicating fear appeals regarding homosexual "recruitment." As Bryant, in a characteristic harangue, charged, "What these people really want, hidden behind obscure legal phrases, is the legal right to propose to our children that there is an acceptable alternate way of life. . . . No one has a human right to corrupt our children. Prostitutes, pimps, and drug pushers, like homosexuals, have civil rights, too, but they do not have the right to influence our children to choose their way of life." Bigotry never sounded so sweet. It took no time at all to gather the required signatures (plus 50,000 more in addition) to secure a special election in June of 1977 that would become known as "Orange Tuesday." Gay rights operatives from both coasts took their stand on the battleground of Miami. But their rational arguments proved to be no match for commercials featuring provocative images from the San Francisco Gay Freedom Day parade, and the refrain of children in peril, accompanied occasionally by Bryant's rousing version of "Battle Hymn of the Republic" (and her labeling of gay people as "human garbage").[97]

Harvey Milk brilliantly rose to the challenges of this shameful episode in U.S history (though children are not taught this blight in today's classrooms). For months prior to the vote in Dade County, Milk used "Milk Forum" as a bully pulpit to mobilize against Anita Bryant, calling for a boycott of Florida orange juice, her firing, and an indictment against her for "inciting violence against Gay people." He chided those who did not take her seriously, who were apathetic about participating in the boycott, and he excoriated the National Gay Task Force (NGTF), which defended her right to free speech. In response, he exclaimed, "Well, what about the rights of all those people who are fire-bombed because they are Gay? What about the rights of all who are, and will be, discriminated against because they are Gay? What about the rights of all who become victims of Anita Bryant's preaching? What about the rights of Ovidio Ramos? Where is our great NGTF when it comes to Gay people who are beaten and lose their jobs?"[98] Milk linked Bryant's hate speech to recent public discourse by Supervisor Feinstein and Assistant District Attorney Douglas Munson in San Francisco that homophobically associated the "crime wave" with public sex spaces in their effort to relocate such businesses to a dilapidated section of the city.[99]

On June 7, the repeal passed with nearly 70 percent of the vote. Milk had not been enlisted by the gay establishment for the fight on the ground in Florida, but unlike more "respectable" representatives he became the de facto leader of the throngs of GLBTQ and allied people in the Bay Area who reacted to the repeal. Arguably, Milk was now a national leader of the gay rights movement. As in cities around the country, thousands took to the streets of San Francisco on Orange Tuesday and every night for the better part of a week thereafter, during which Milk's presence towered. That first night is best remembered because Milk transformed the massive demonstration that threatened to turn violent ("Out of the Bars and into the Streets!") into a five-mile peaceable march throughout the city, culminating in a rally of 5,000 at the steps of City Hall; the front-page *Chronicle* photograph of Milk with his familiar bullhorn captured well the spirit and achievement of the massive demonstration and its leadership. Clendinen and Nagourney observed:

> [T]he midnight march was wholly a product of the city's new gay population, one angry and aroused, with its own neighborhood, its own distinct cultural values, its own community organizations and leaders, and its own way of reacting to events. Anita Bryant's victory had helped bring them into focus. As a large red banner emblazoned with the words "Gay Revolution" was run up the flagpole on Union Square that night, there was a new reality in San Francisco, and it was emerging in the middle of a crucial political campaign.[100]

Milk quelled violence even as he wasted no time in escalating his bellicose rhetoric so as to frame Dade's outrage as a catalyst for intensified activism. "Without the President and the national leaders taking a stand, this will be a struggle like the black civil rights or the anti-Vietnam movements. . . . There will be violence and bitterness and the nation will be seared, but if we have to do battle in the streets we are ready to."[101]

As the selected 1977 documents vividly convey, Milk believed Orange Tuesday to be a watershed event, "a victory deeper than the actual vote," a swiftly rising tide of visibility, consciousness, and mobilization. "This was our Watts, our Selma, Alabama." In a powerful turn of affect and logic, Milk thanked Anita Bryant, for "she herself pushed the Gay Movement ahead and the subject can never be pushed back into the darkness. . . . [S]he has, in fact, started what so many of us have talked about—a true national Gay Movement."[102] And Milk did shape his public discourse on Orange Tuesday with an eye toward the coming election. In his candidacy announcement later that month, during the Gay Freedom Day celebrations, Milk asked where the city's elected officials had been during those days of protest, where had been the "appointed gay officials," such as his replacement on the Board of Permit Appeals and soon-to-be campaign rival, Rick Stokes. "Like every other group," Milk averred, "we should be judged by our leaders."

And GLBTQ leadership was needed more than ever. Anita Bryant's homophobic discourse surely had something central to do with the rise of anti-GLBTQ violence in San Francisco as elsewhere. Although city gardener Robert Hillsborough was murdered by a young man deeply conflicted about his own sexuality, John Cordova's chanting of "faggot" while repeatedly stabbing his victim marked it as a crime constituted if not directly caused by the same hate speech that Milk found politically galvanizing. Hillsborough's mother said of Anita Bryant, "My son's blood is on her hands."[103] This very same fund of hate speech provided gubernatorial hopeful and California state senator John Briggs with an expedient platform, announcing just days after Orange Tuesday his campaign to remove from the public schools "gay teachers" or anyone affirming homosexuality in the classroom. Local politicians took the opportunity to attempt repeal of the recently won district elections and to recall GLBTQ-friendly officials such as Moscone, Hongisto, and Freitas, a nail biter not resolved favorably until the mid-summer special election. Across the nation, concerted efforts began to roll back gay rights, repeal campaigns that by 1978 would prove successful in St. Paul, Wichita, and Eugene.[104] Assemblyman Art Agnos decided not to pursue promised gay rights legislation within the current climate created by Bryant and the Dade repeal.[105]

Within this broad combustible and propulsive political context, Milk stayed true to the vision he had forged through three previous campaigns. He never wavered from his position that GLBTQ people needed an "avowed gay leader" in office, one who was not beholden to those straight liberal "allies" who retreated from their pledged support whenever the political temperature on homosexuality rose precipitously. During this campaign, Milk first called for a statewide "gay caucus" and convention that would mobilize community across political, social, and other lines to create a unified front and influential bloc designed to test the commitment of any aspirant politician—local, state, or national—on gay rights issues. In the 1977 selected documents and elsewhere, Milk again was writing about what he called "gay economic power" and the representational power of a visible "lifestyle."[106] In his speech to the San Francisco Gay Democratic Club, he claimed that his motivation for running (running and running and running) was that "I remember what it was like to be 14 and gay." Inspiring that kid from Altoona, or Des Moines, or wherever the closet needed to be opened in the now familiar refrain of the evolving Hope speech, was Milk's sine qua non.[107]

Yet, even with a heightened emphasis on gay rights, Milk's campaign vision and platform still embodied the populist, neighborhood activist fighting for all people in District 5 and across San Francisco, voicing issues that mattered to African Americans, Latinos, women, the elderly, and heterosexuals. In "Milk Forum," he openly called for a coalition with other minorities.[108] As he declared in his 1973 Address to the San Francisco Joint International Longshoremen & Warehousemen's Union and Lafayette Club, "People are more important than buildings and neighborhoods, more important than freeways." This was still Milk's mantra, one that made his call to GLBTQ people that "we must learn from history that the time for riding in the back of the bus is over" broadly resonant, even in this virulently homophobic period.

Milk's campaign, despite more favorable circumstances than in any of his previous attempts, nevertheless required a fight.[109] He was once again openly opposed by prominent members of the gay establishment, including his accommodationist challenger, wealthy attorney and bathhouse entrepreneur Rick Stokes, who outspent him nearly three to one. Moreover, the threat loomed that a split gay vote in District 5 could lead to a victory for the formidable straight liberal candidate, Terence Hallinan. However, Milk had momentum in this electoral season that nearly perfectly reversed his showing in 1976. He won the endorsements of the GLBTQ press, including longtime antagonist *Sentinel,* as well as most of the GLBTQ Democratic clubs, and unexpectedly gained the straight press support of the liberal *Bay Guardian* and relatively conservative *San Francisco Chronicle*. With such visible and influential backing, and the help of campaign manager Anne Kronenberg as well as Dick Pabich, Jim Rivaldo, Cleve Jones, Frank Robinson, and Danny Nicoletta, Milk finally won, taking 30 percent of the vote in a field of seventeen, finishing first in sixty out of ninety-eight precincts and second in another thirty-three. Harry Britt, who would succeed Milk as city supervisor in little more than a year, remembered:

> Election night, 1977, was a night when we looked at each other in the clutter of Harvey's camera store headquarters in a new way. I don't think many of us had looked beyond that night—now we allowed ourselves to envision new possibilities, to sense that the magic Harvey had seen in us and built power around could spread and create a different future in which power and acceptance of diversity might come together. The people of District 5—GLBTQ and straight—had understood Harvey's call to that future. Seemingly, he would now be able to lead us to his Promised Land.[110]

Milk's triumphal message consummated the vision he had forged since 1973. "This is not my victory, it's yours and yours and yours. . . . If a gay can win, it means that there is hope that the system can work for all minorities if we fight. We've given them hope."[111]

Harvey Milk's forty-two and a half weeks as the first openly gay elected city official in the United States is captured metaphorically by the iconic photograph depicting his walk from the Castro to City Hall on Inauguration Day, January 9, 1978. The joyous occasion appears in the smiles on the faces of Milk and his constituents, including his troubled and troublesome boyfriend Jack Lira, around whose shoulder Harvey's arm is intimately draped (openly sharing the day with his lover meant so much, personally and symbolically). In glancing at the photograph, it could be a depiction from a Gay Freedom Day parade; indeed, in an important sense, it was. But it might also have been a demonstration, not unlike those that followed the same path after Robert Hillsborough's murder and Orange Tuesday, marching again for GLBTQ justice and equality. Although Milk now operated officially as a gay rights leader on the inside—as he had always insisted was necessary—rather than struggling against discriminatory power from Castro Street, he never stopped the street theater, the marching, the neighborhood activism, the campaigning. As he had stated in his 1977 Victory Statement, "I understand the significance of electing the first Gay person to public office and what his responsibility is not only to the people of San Francisco but to Gay people all over. It's a responsibility that I do not take lightly. Whoever shoulders that responsibility must be willing to fight. It won't be an easy task."[112] Where Milk was concerned, and as the photograph speaks, all political work, even the bureaucratic sort, constituted a mode of activism.

Electing to be sworn in on the steps of City Hall, where more might see and the spectacle might flash more brilliantly despite the falling rain, Milk's inaugural words foretold the spirit of his leadership to come: "Anita Bryant said gay people brought drought to California. Looks to me like it's finally started raining. . . . This is not my swearing-in, this is your swearing-in. You can stand around and throw bricks at Silly Hall or you can take it over. Well, here we are."[113] Milk's first official act as supervisor introduced an anti-discrimination ordinance assuring gay rights in all employment, housing, and public accommodations in San Francisco. In his first major address, included among the 1978 selected documents, Milk told his audience, "I understand that my election was not alone a question of my gayness but a question of what I represent. In a very real sense, Harvey Milk represents the spirit of the neighborhoods of San Francisco. For the past few years, my fight to make the voice of the neighborhoods of this city be heard was not unlike the fight to make the voice of the cities themselves be heard. The American Dream starts with the neighborhoods." A month later, Milk emphasized that his domestic policy chiefly concerned an "emotional commitment" or "patriotism" regarding the city and its "new demographics": "The city is no longer primarily white, established, middle class, or even primarily married with children. It's yellow, brown, black, with a steady influx into the middle economic class of people who were formerly lower economic class. It's also increasingly young marrieds with no children, or young couples who aren't married, or extended families, or gays, or singles, and most certainly seniors." Ever the populist, progressive bridge builder, Milk would pave the way for a city he believed one day in the near future would be most heavily populated and influenced by Chinese and GLBTQ Americans.[114]

Milk quickly discovered that laboring in City Hall on behalf of San Francisco and its neighborhoods differed substantially from the grassroots efforts that championed it. Anne Kronenberg, now one of Milk's administrative aides, explained:

> Any glamorous illusions I had about coming to City Hall were quickly dispersed. I learned that the job was difficult, often thankless and always frustrating. Everybody thought we could solve their problems whether it was cars parked on sidewalks, dog poop in the park or street signs that needed repair. We were district representatives and Harvey was elected to handle these problems, to be the voice of District 5 in City Hall. Each morning

Harvey would empty his pockets stuffed with scribbled napkins filled with names, numbers and constituent problems. . . . Life in City Hall was not as Harvey envisioned it either. It was one thing running a campaign, it was quite another working within a bureaucracy to accomplish your goals.[115]

Milk was often on the losing end of 6–5 votes on the Board. He often clashed with his fellow supervisors, perhaps especially, as the months passed, with District 8 supervisor Dan White.[116] Although White's campaign discourse in his conservative, Irish Catholic district had been unmistakably homophobic, Milk told his skeptical friends and colleagues that White was "educable" and promising. White's early solidarity corroborated Milk's intuition: persuading Board president Dianne Feinstein to appoint Milk chairman of the coveted Streets and Transportation Committee, voting with Milk to save the Pride Center and to honor the twenty-fifth anniversary of a lesbian couple, and endorsement in committee of Milk's gay rights ordinance. Milk aide Dick Pabich observed, "He's supported us on every position, and he goes out of his way to find out what gay people think about things."[117] Their relationship soured, however, after Milk reversed his position on the psychiatric treatment facility White sought to keep out of his neighborhood, casting the deciding vote. White's thin-skinned and grudging character forged Milk's perceived betrayal into an abiding animus and internecine rivalry. White would cast the only negative vote against the ultimately successful gay rights ordinance. As we know, White's vindictiveness could and would go beyond the pale—tragically so.

Yet despite the bureaucratic drudgery required to solve the practical problems of his constituents, evidenced by quotidian correspondence found in his archives, and the frictions and frustrations of routine political wrangling on a Board with an opposition majority, Milk thrived. After memorably informing Mayor Moscone that Milk was "number one queen now,"[118] the two, once politically at odds, became allies. Moreover, as Mike Wong observed,

Harvey was probably the most popular elected official in San Francisco today. . . . The women . . . who once labeled Harvey as anti-woman were now his supporters. Gay people found a committed defender of gay rights. The Toklas members had come to respect their once enemy. Liberals who once shunned him found him to be most receptive and enjoyable to work with. Neighborhood groups knew that they had a powerful ally on the Board. Harvey's re-election list [by supervisorial lottery as part of the Board restructuring post-district elections, Milk was among those supervisors who would have to run for reelection in 2 rather than 4 years] now included endorsements from most of his former opponents and people who never gave him the time of day.[119]

Milk's leadership also began to become more visible and influential on the state and national political scenes. He successfully helped organize the California Gay Caucus, creating a politically united front that would achieve coalitional solidarity and thus create pressure on political candidates of every stripe to support gay rights. The caucus enacted Milk's vision long sought in his voter registration efforts and calls for GLBTQ power and indigenous leadership, embodying his belief that "Gay political clout must move forward in the face of the recent defeats in St. Paul and Wichita."

Dominating Milk's attention during most of what remained of that first year in office, and solidifying his reputation as a local activist stalwart with an expanding national reputation, was state senator John Briggs's crassly opportunistic and virulently homophobic campaign to rid the California schools of GLBTQ teachers—what became certified as Proposition 6 in May and otherwise known as the Briggs Initiative.[120] Given Briggs's disrepute, even within his own party, he undoubtedly surprised most by taking the mantle of Anita Bryant and making the entire state of California the battleground staked elsewhere that year only in municipalities like Wichita and Eugene. Few would have expected this fight to culminate in Milk's crowning achievement—and swan song.

Within that broader post-Dade County context, there was little reason to be optimistic about stemming the national wave of homophobia that Briggs had managed to ride into temporary political prominence and menace. Much as in the case of Bryant's campaign, the Briggs Initiative inflamed the electorate because it concerned children, discourse rife with bogeys of sodomy, molestation and murder of innocents, and the classroom as a breeding ground of homosexual indoctrination. As Briggs argued in an apocalyptic editorial entitled, "Deviants Threaten the American Family": "Children in this country spend more than 1,200 hours a year in classrooms. A teacher who is a known homosexual will automatically represent that way of life to young, impressionable students at a time when they are constantly exposed to such homosexual role models, they may well be inclined to experiment with a life-style that could lead to disaster for themselves and ultimately, for society as a whole."[121] Elsewhere Briggs warned, "If you let one homosexual teacher stay, soon there'll be two, then four, then 8, then 25— and before long, the entire school will be taught by homosexuals."[122]

For potential victims of Prop 6, the scope and implications of its broad language—"advocating, soliciting, imposing, encouraging, or promoting private or public sexual acts . . . between persons of the same sex in a manner likely to come to the attention of other employees or students"—struck deeply rooted personal and communal fears of (state-sponsored) exposure and ruination, and the greater ease and likelihood of being ensnared. Sol Madfes, executive director of the United Administrators of the San Francisco school district, explained, "The Briggs Initiative would leave teachers in the position of being accused—and then having to prove their innocence. . . . The board or superintendant will listen when a parent starts yelling. The attitude is—where there's smoke, there's fire. Under Briggs, the opportunity would be there to crucify somebody by accusation."[123] The first poll in September indicated 61 percent to 31 percent in favor of Prop 6.[124] GLBTQ press and activists urged calm and solidarity in the face of certain defeat.

Milk's response, as we might expect, was to fight. According to his battle plan, articulated and reiterated throughout the documents in this section, one must ceaselessly talk, speaking out to explode the homophobic myths and hysteria that the Religious Right and opportunists such as John Briggs exploited to their ideological and political advantage. Milk implored:

> I believe that we can win in November . . . but only if we mount a full-fledged campaign. One that covers all bases, both positive and defensive. Yes, defensive, too. For not to answer the false charges is, to some, an admission that the charges are not false. Otherwise, we would repudiate them. There is no time like the present to start to repudiate them. For the sooner we start, the sooner we can lay them to rest. So, we need to have every gay person talk to as many non-gay people as possible about the issues—both real and false. It will be a monumental effort and, because many gays will remain in their closet, it makes it that much more important for those of us who are out.

And talk he did, refuting the lies and distortions that asserted that homosexuality is a choice, that homosexuals are the primary perpetrators of child molestation and abuse, that homosexuals recruit by becoming "role models" for the "lifestyle," and simultaneously promoting the idea that homosexuality is natural, given, omnipresent, good, and undeserving of discrimination, harassment, and violence. In mobilizing GLBTQ people to rise up against Briggs, Milk employed patriotic collective memory, quoting Patrick Henry, the Declaration of Independence, the Statue of Liberty's credo, and "The Star-Spangled Banner." In characterizing the viciousness of the Briggs Initiative, and as a means of rousing resistance by shattering apathy, Milk favored the Holocaust trope, likening Briggs to Hitler and GLBTQ people to Jews oppressed by the genocidal Nazi regime: "We are not going to allow our rights to be taken away and then march with bowed heads to the gas chambers. On this anniversary of Stonewall, I ask my Gay sisters and brothers to make their commitment to fight. For themselves, for their freedom, for their country."[125] What had become his signature opening line, full of humor and bite, said it all: "I'm Harvey Milk and I'm here to recruit you."

Randy Shilts characterized the public debates Milk and Briggs staged across the state through the fall of 1978 as "fast food politics," owing to the by now boilerplate responses to questions repeated over and over again, and perhaps in part because these political gladiators fighting for the lives of their constituents had become friendly on the road and in the wings of their public verbal battles.[126] But even if the message had become prepackaged and efficient, such mantra-like repetition and simplicity, and the familiarity of the performance, offered Milk's best hope of eroding the bulwark of Briggs's homophobic invective. We believe it made the difference in defeating Prop 6. Others have offered different and compelling reasons for the shift away from Briggs: heterosexuals' eventual realization that Prop 6 would create a slippery slope endangering their free speech and privacy; high-powered bipartisan appeals against the initiative by Ronald Reagan, Jerry Brown, Jimmy Carter, and nearly every other state politician (even if some, namely, the good straight liberal allies Milk had long said could not be trusted, were quieter in their solidarity than the rest); concerted effort by sophisticated GLBTQ politicos and their allies in Los Angeles and elsewhere; and Briggs himself, with his support eroding as election day neared, becoming even more hyperbolic. Nevertheless, these other influences absent Milk's tireless voice would have been necessary but insufficient to defeat Briggs. Harvey Milk held sway. On November 7, Prop 6 was defeated by more than a million votes, 3.9 million to 2.8 million, 58 percent to 42 percent.[127]

In his victory speech, Milk cast his gaze on the future: "This is only the first step. The next step, the more important step, is for all those gays who did not come out, for whatever reasons, to do so now. To come out to all your family, to come out to all your relatives, to come out to all your friends—the coming out of a nation will smash the myths once and for all."[128] Milk, who often invoked the civil rights movement and especially Martin Luther King, Jr., as analogy, had delivered his mountaintop speech—quite literally, given the events that unfolded in the immediate wake of Briggs's defeat.

Much has been said by others about those final weeks between the euphoria of Prop 6's demise and the assassinations of Harvey Milk and George Moscone on November 27, 1978: the emotional unraveling of Dan White; his resignation from the Board of Supervisors; his strong-armed rescinding of that resignation and appeal for reinstatement; the political jockeying and lobbying that ensued during the interim; his learning from a reporter that Moscone would not reappoint him; his armed entry of City Hall through a basement window; his execution of George Moscone; his execution of Harvey Milk; Dianne Feinstein's devastating revelation to City Hall employees and reporters, "Mayor Moscone and Supervisor Harvey Milk have been shot . . . and killed. Police have a suspect. Supervisor Dan White." Much too has been said about Milk's eerie fatalism, his longstanding prediction that he would die early, and his preoccupation with the possibility of assassination—existential trembling no doubt exacerbated by proliferating death threats, the deep exhaustion of the anti-Briggs campaign, the Jonestown massacre in Guyana, and the suicide of boyfriend Jack Lira. Because he recorded it a year before his death, we include in this volume a portion of his political will. Milk's myth is burnished by such hauntings, our retrospective understanding that he knew somehow that he would never get to the promised land with his gay brothers and sisters. But we leave that myth and thirty years' worth of Milk memory—the candlelight march on the night of the assassination, White's sham trial, his Twinkie defense and reduced sentence, the White Night riots, the annual commemorations, the archive, *The Mayor of Castro Street, The Times of Harvey Milk, Harvey Milk: An Opera in Three Acts,* Harvey Milk Plaza, Harvey Milk High School, his bust in City Hall, *Milk,* Harvey Milk Day, and much more—for another volume.[129]

Rather, we think it fitting simply to note the profound silence on November 27, 1978. In response, we let Harvey, again and again in the pages that follow, speak for himself.

WHY MILK MEMORY MATTERS

In an important sense, the timing of this collection could not be better. Our project promises to be illuminated by the still lingering afterglow of the Focus Features film *Milk,* directed by Gus Van Sant, written by Dustin Lance Black (for which he received an Academy Award), and starring Sean Penn as Harvey Milk (he, too, earned the Oscar). This acclaimed biopic rediscovered and, for both GLBTQ and straight audiences, introduced the name and political life of Harvey Milk. We cannot emphasize this enough: We would venture to estimate that a large percentage of an entire GLBTQ generation, and most of multiple generations of straight people, would not have recognized the name Harvey Milk before 2008. *Milk* retrieved, if within the limits of Hollywood history, the Castro's first decade as a GLBTQ homeland, Mecca, or Oz, the time before HIV/AIDS when sex, sociality, solidarity, and struggle created affective bonds and visibility never before experienced to such an extent by GLBTQ peoples in the United States. Christopher Castiglia and Christopher Reed view *Milk*—and *Milk's* appropriation of Rob Epstein's 1984 documentary *The Times of Harvey Milk*—as part of the reparative and transformational counter-memory that undoes "degenerational unremembering" and deploys the past for social and political GLBTQ benefits in the present.[130] Mathias Danbolt suggests that the film also productively juxtaposes heady memorialization with "archives of homophobic violence"—black and white images of state repression of gay men, the viscera of shame, and Milk's brutal end—so that we "remember that the fight for a society livable for all continues in the present"—that is, as a mode of activist mobilization.[131]

The stakes of the film deepened and widened because of the timing of its release in late fall of 2008, on the eve of the historic Obama election and amid the clamor of battle over Proposition 8 ("California Marriage Protection Act"), the ballot initiative and constitutional amendment that would by definition exclude same-sex marriage in California. Numerous articles marked parallels between the Prop 8 fight and Harvey Milk's successful campaign against Proposition 6. Proposition 6 failed, perhaps Milk's greatest political achievement; Proposition 8 passed, for many a devastating reversal of short-lived marriage equality. Despite the wrenching disappointment, many believed that *Milk* re-politicized GLBTQ peoples, reignited the movement. "We need Harvey Milk now," someone told *USA Today,* "This movie reminds us what it's like to fight for our rights, something I think many of us have forgotten how to do." Echoing the *Advocate,* which dramatically announced "the Resurrection of Harvey Milk," people wondered aloud, "What would Harvey do?" and "What if Milk had lived?" Such questions and the discourses that inspired them revealed a robust public memory of Milk.[132]

In the few years since the film, Milk's legacy has remained amplified, as an inspiration for the 2009 Equality March on Washington; in panels sponsored by the San Francisco GLBT Historical Society and featured in its new museum space; in the public performances of Cleve Jones and Dustin Lance Black; in Danny Nicoletta's photographic exhibitions; in the philanthropic efforts of nephew Stuart Milk and his Harvey Milk Foundation; in the 2009 posthumous awarding of the Presidential Medal of Freedom; in California's 2010 passage and subsequent annual celebrations of Harvey Milk Day; in public debate about how the space at 575 Castro should be embodied and utilized; in the National Gay and Lesbian Task Force petition to the United States Postal Service to create a Harvey Milk postage stamp; in Congressman Bob Filner's 2012 proposal that a naval ship be named the USS *Harvey Milk* in recognition of Milk's service and the end of "Don't Ask, Don't Tell." Our hope with this volume and beyond it is that Harvey Milk will resonate for generations of GLBTQ people fighting for their rights and protections and an end to homophobia and heterosupremacy, and for those engaged in queer world making.

At the same time that we believe *An Archive of Hope* reflects and extends this resurgence of Milk memory, we also feel strongly that it would be wise to consider this moment fleeting, to fret over the prospects of losing Milk once more. We note that Milk memory faded in the decades between his assassination and *Milk,* despite the critical acclaim for *The Times of Harvey Milk* (the *Advocate* review in February 1985: "*Harvey Milk*' Dilemma: Critical Raves, But Apathetic Audiences"), despite his being named one of the 100 most influential figures of the twentieth century by *Time* in 1999, despite the opening in New York City of the Harvey Milk School in 2003.[133] Writing on the 20th anniversary of Milk's assassination in 1998, John Cloud's lament accounts for memory's faltering:

[M]any gays don't know who he is. "The memory in this community doesn't last more than a few years," [gay historian John] D'Emilio says. Elaine Herscher, a *San Francisco Chronicle* reporter who has covered gay politics off and on for two decades, agrees: "The people under 45, even in the Castro, really don't know him." San Francisco officials have done their best to change this; every few years they rename a building or two for Milk (including, most recently, an elementary school that became the Harvey Milk Civil Rights Academy). When two men trying to build a Milk memorial in Washington, D.C., held a ceremony there to honor him last year, fewer than a dozen people turned out. It's too bad Harvey Milk is being forgotten.[134]

We have been haunted throughout our research by an editorial Milk protégé and AIDS Quilt founder Cleve Jones published in the *Bay Area Reporter* in November 2005 in support of the Harvey Milk Memorial Committee. Jones recounted that he and a friend, while having a drink at Edge in the Castro, struck up a conversation with a young gay man who responded to their reminiscing with the question, "Who was

Harvey Milk?" More alarming, once having been told Milk's story, a story that had helped make possible three gay men having such a conversation in a gay neighborhood in the United States, this twenty-something could not grasp the legacy, comparing without irony Milk's impact to that of pop singing star Avril Lavigne.[135] Twenty years earlier, Frances FitzGerald, surveying a decade's worth of Milk commemoration, concluded:

> The Castro mourned Harvey Milk, and yet it could not seem to make him into a living legend—that is, into a legend that would nourish and sustain it. The Castro saw him as a martyr but understood his martyrdom as an end rather than a beginning. He had died, and with him a great deal of the Castro's optimism, idealism, and ambition seemed to die as well. The Castro could find no one to take his place in its affections, and possibly it wanted no one.[136]

Jones would likely take issue with FitzGerald, as he did with his new acquaintance in the Castro. His point, which we emphasize, is that GLBTQ history and memory are fragile, rarely taught, and subject to trivialization even by those within GLBTQ communities. We believe the antidote to such presentism and erasure is to engage in an ongoing effort to circulate queer pasts and conjure their presence wherever possible, in classrooms and community meetings, at pride celebrations and fundraising events, and, yes, even in those gay social spaces where "history lessons" might be, well, out of the ordinary. What George Chauncey observed in the context of gay male subculture in the early twentieth century remains vital and necessary for diverse GLBTQ communities today: "[W]e need to invent—and constantly reinvent—a tradition on the basis of innumerable individual and idiosyncratic readings of [queer] texts. . . . embed its transmission in the day-to-day social organization of [our] world. . . . passed on in bars and at cocktail parties, from friend to friend, from lover to lover, from older . . . serving as mentors to younger . . . just beginning to identify themselves as gay."[137] The stories we tell about GLBTQ pasts provide resources, inspiration, and challenge in present struggles—from historic battles over gay marriage and preventing suicides by bullied queer youth, to endemic racism, sexism, classism, ableism, and ageism—and shape the queer futures we imagine and chart.

Toward that end, in December 2010, California state senator Mark Leno introduced SB48, the Fair, Accurate, Inclusive, and Respectful (FAIR) Education Act, legislation that would revise the existing Education Code so as to include GLBTQ people among those other racially and culturally diverse groups already protected against "adverse portrayals" in the state curriculum; moreover, it would require adoption of educational materials that would accurately portray the role and contribution of GLBTQ people in society.[138] On April 4, 2011, more than seventy GLBTQ and ally high school students rallied on the Capitol steps in Sacramento and lobbied on behalf of FAIR as part of the annual Queer Youth Advocacy Day; a day later, on April 5, the Senate Judiciary Committee passed SB48 by a 3–2 vote. On April 14, it passed the State Senate, 23–14; and it passed the Assembly, 49–25 on July 5. Governor Brown signed FAIR into law on July 14, 2011; tellingly, the jubilant announcement of FAIR becoming law on the popular GLBTQ blog towleroad.com was accompanied by the well-known photograph of Harvey Milk in the Gay Freedom Day parade, 1978.[139] With this legislation signed into law, California's position as the largest purchaser of textbooks in the United States could greatly influence what the nation's students are taught, a potentially powerful counter to the social science curriculum as it will be shaped by the second largest textbook purchaser, namely Texas.[140] However, as of this writing, multiple anti-gay grassroots efforts have been underway to seek repeal of FAIR. Further hindering the enactment of FAIR, although the law went into effect in January 2012, most school districts may find a loophole created by state budget cuts. Textbook revisions have been deferred until at least 2015.[141]

Leno justified the bill in part by arguing that a GLBTQ affirmative curriculum may function to reduce homophobic vernacular, bullying, and bashing. Arguably, this vision has been legitimated by the case of Stoke Newington School in north London, which claimed in 2010 to have all but eradicated bullying by introducing in its classrooms Alan Turing, Oscar Wilde, James Baldwin, Andy Warhol, and other prominent GLBTQ figures.[142] Put differently, had California Governor Schwarzenegger not vetoed legislation in 2006 prohibiting negative characterizations of homosexuality in textbooks, he would have had less cause to sign legislation in 2007 seeking to protect vulnerable GLBTQ youth from homophobic violence, such as fifteen-year-old Lawrence King, who was shot in the back of the head in early 2008, by a classmate, for being gay and gender nonconforming.[143] Dustin Lance Black captured this promise in his 2009 Academy Award acceptance speech:

> When I was 13 years old . . . I heard the story of Harvey Milk. And it gave me hope. It gave me the hope to live my life, it gave me the hope to one day live my life openly as who I am and that maybe even I could fall in love and

one day get married. . . . If Harvey had not been taken from us 30 years ago, I think he'd want me to say to all of the gay and lesbian kids out there tonight who have been told that they are less than by their churches or by the government or by their families that you are beautiful, wonderful creatures of value and that no matter what anyone tells you, God does love you and that very soon, I promise you, you will have equal rights, federally, across this great nation of ours.[144]

As a heartening case in Milk memory's imagined application writ large, the private all-boys Town School in San Francisco took its second grade seven- and eight-year-old students on a field trip to the Castro in the spring of 2011 as part of its annual Day of Service, designed "to give our boys perspective on how they can make a small yet meaningful impact on their community." This "neighborhood study," as it was called, "focused on history, social and civil rights, the importance of diversity, and Harvey Milk," including a tour and lessons by a local historical guide at sites such as Pink Triangle Memorial Park, the Hope for the World Cure Mural, the Human Rights Campaign Action Center, Harvey Milk's camera shop, and "the Harvey Milk Elementary School, which is adorned with wonderful murals depicting Harvey Milk's commitment to diversity. While at the school, the guide shared Harvey Milk's analogy, likening a better world to a sandbox where all children play together harmoniously."[145] In response to a surprisingly few protests by parents and others, headmaster Brewster Ely, who called the endeavor "a wonderful success," wrote in a public letter:

At Town we have long taught that it is important to be open minded about difference, and we are pleased that we have boys at school who have gay parents. A few families who felt uncomfortable with the Castro trip chose to keep their sons home, and we recognize their decision to do so. One anonymous parent felt compelled to contact the local CBS News desk and register her unhappiness about the trip through the media. On Friday, CBS ran a story in which I was quoted as saying, "The school and the administration see the Castro as a respected community in San Francisco, and we want our students to develop an appreciation for whoever lives in our community." In an unexpected way, this coverage provided the school and its leadership with a public forum to share the value we see in diversity and in fostering in our boys a respect for and understanding of difference.[146]

The embodied and mediated engagements of this field trip and its subsequent public discourse—experience, provocation, education, critique, activism, at an early age and cross-generationally—comprise the promises of Milk or any other GLBTQ memories.

The benefits of Milk and other memory work taught, exhibited, and performed in U.S. classrooms, in the immediate present and near future, come from enacting Stuart Biegel's advice: "Even just mentioning LGBTs and acknowledging their existence, currently and throughout history, is an important step. Even if nothing else is done, such an act will be a significant contribution."[147] Such appears to be the case with *The Milk Effect* (2012), fifteen-year-old Max Geschwind's ten-minute film in which he interviewed West Hollywood's five City Council members, as well as the four candidates in the state's 50th Assembly District race, on the impact of Milk's legacy. *The Milk Effect* concludes by having "his fellow Fairfax High students recite one of Milk's most famous speeches, creating a poignant reminder of how future generations are affected by the past." Prior to seeing *Milk,* Geschwind had never heard of Harvey Milk, but inspired by the film and his work on West Hollywood's planning committee for Harvey Milk Day, he decided to make his own commemoration. In turn, Geschwind inspired his own classmates, who did not know what Milk had achieved.[148]

Longer term, as Kevin Kumashiro has theorized it, such "disruptive knowledge" functions more broadly as a queer world-making initiative called "antioppressive education."[149] Perhaps in the span of time it takes these Town School boys and their generation to grow into adulthood, more systemic transformation can be imagined, as expressed in the headmaster's closing words: "It is my hope that these events ultimately engender an even greater appreciation for diversity and a respect for all people. I close with a statement from our Town School philosophy: Town values being a diverse community that nurtures integrity, sensitivity and respect in its boys, and prepares them to become productive and contributing members of an ever-changing world."[150]

For all of these reasons, we emphasize that when Harvey talked, he was hard to forget, and his memory matters more now than ever. As ongoing instigation and inspiration, we recall sociologist Stephen O. Murray's refutation of the theory he had read in the influential volume *Habits of the Heart,* which argued that GLBTQ people, collectively speaking, should not be understood as a community. A "real community," according to Bellah and his colleagues, "does not forget its past." Rather it circulates "stories of collective history and exemplary individuals," as well as "painful stories of shared suffering." They concluded, "Where history and hope are forgotten and community means only the gathering of the similar, community degenerates into lifestyle enclaves." Murray admirably invoked history courses and bookstores, the AIDS

Quilt, oral history projects, and the San Francisco Gay and Lesbian Historical Society (Milk, too, appears in his apologia) to demonstrate GLBTQ "community-generated public remembrance."[151] In this age of neoliberalism, in which the private rewards of marriage and adoption may take us as GLBTQ people deeper into our homonormative domiciles rather than more expansively into community and coalition building, we believe the gains of public remembrance must be constantly fostered and reestablished, and that we might usefully allow Bellah and his colleagues' ungenerous characterization to haunt us. *An Archive of Hope,* like Harvey Milk, must always be restless, reaching, establishing grounds of presently unknown possibilities of queerness yet to be.[152]

By way of closing, we are also reminded of what Horacio Ramírez described, in recounting legendary San Francisco performer Teresita la Campesina and queer Latino communal memory, as the vexing but vital work of "talking history" or developing the "talking archive": "the process of narrating the lives of those who passed on and the meanings the archives communicate back to those committed to listening."[153] For the sake of the future of GLBTQ pasts, which is to say the future of us all, we aim to keep Harvey talking, and we hope generations will earnestly engage in the work of queer listening.

NOTES

1. Strange de Jim, *San Francisco's Castro* (San Francisco: Arcadia Books, 2003), 73.

2. Although the terms *gay* and *lesbian* would be historically more accurate in keeping with the vernacular of Milk's era, we risk the anachronism "GLBTQ" throughout this essay because, although it, too, has many limitations (gender and sexually non-normative people have always exceeded the language that describes, constitutes, enables, and constrains them), we believe it meaningfully gestures toward the great diversity among individuals, enclaves, and communities existing at that time in San Francisco. That said, in certain instances we use the word *gay* specifically, such as in the case of "gay establishment," because of its historical accuracy in depicting gay male dominance in a particular social or political sphere or mode, or the phrase "gay rights," which functions as exclusionary synechdoche but also circulated as an nearly universal designation of the movement during the 1970s. Any slippage in nomenclature, which we have found vexingly easy to commit, is our own error, and we are comfortable with the frictions inherent in our effort to queerly cross time through available language. Coincidentally, a 1977 three-part series in the *Bay Area Reporter* explored the genealogy of the term *gay,* revealing its emergence as an idiom and its sexual politics. The articles did not discuss *gay* as an exclusive term representing a diverse population of gender and sexual non-normativity. Jack Warner,

"'Gay'—Our Word, Their Word? Why Call Them Gay?" Parts I, II, and III, *Bay Area Reporter*, March 3, 1977, 7; March 31, 1977, 30; and April 4, 1977, 12.

3. Dudley Clendinen and Adam Nagourney, *Out for Good: The Struggle to Build a Gay Rights Movement in America* (New York: Simon and Schuster, 1999), 407.

4. Frank M. Robinson, "Harvey's History—And Ours," *The Harvey Milk Archives Newsletter* 1 (January 1983), 4, Harvey Milk Archives—Scott Smith Collection (GLC 35), San Francisco Public Library.

5. Heather Love, "The Art of Losing," in *Lost and Found: Queerying the Archive*, eds. Mathias Danbolt, Jane Rowley, and Louise Wolthers (Copenhagen: Nikolaj, Copenhagen Contemporary Art Center, 2009), 69.

6. Frank M. Robinson, Letter to the Editor, *San Francisco Bay Guardian*, July 20, 1995, personal papers of Frank M. Robinson.

7. Some items from the estate, especially ephemera, were donated to the GLBT Historical Society and the ONE Institute. The GLBT Historical Society, for example, now houses Milk's famous barber chair from Castro Camera, in which we both have had the thrill of sitting.

8. Vince Emery's valuable volume *The Harvey Milk Interviews* is an excellent case in point. We had the happy coincidence of meeting Mr. Emery in the reading room at the San Francisco Public Library and have been bolstered by knowing during our project that he, too, was anthologizing Milk's archival materials. As we can all attest, there is much more to be done. Vince Emery, *The Harvey Milk Interviews* (San Francisco: Vince Emery Productions, 2012).

9. Ann Cvetkovich, *An Archive of Feelings: Trauma, Sexuality, and Lesbian Public Cultures* (Durham, NC: Duke University Press, 2003), 9.

10. In Diana Taylor's influential theory, the documentary (archive) and performative (repertoire) manifestations, preservations, and deployments of memory are distinct but interrelated and should be cultivated together. Taylor, *The Archive and the Repertoire: Performing Cultural Memory in the Americas* (Durham, NC: Duke University Press, 2003).

11. "Homosexual on Board Cites Role as Pioneer," *New York Times*, November 10, 1977, 24.

12. That is, for those who would welcome individuals functioning, synecdochally and otherwise, as the vehicles of history and memory; many are wary of such (identity) politics of historical representation.

13. This counternarrative to the "great man" hagiography is deftly crafted in Brett Callis's work, which has not been given the attention it deserves. Brett Cole Callis, *From Castro Street to City Hall: Harvey Milk and Gay Politics in San Francisco, 1973-1977* (Master's thesis, University of Hawaii, 1991; UMI 1346930).

14. Jack Fritscher, *Gay San Francisco: Eyewitness* Drummer (San Francisco: Palm Drive Publishing, 2008), 117. Fritscher's claim that "homomasculine" culture has been ignored and erased by those chronicling GLBTQ history is compelling, and his "eyewitness" to GLBTQ culture in San Francisco over the past 35 years has been insightful and invaluable. By way of contextualizing his observations about Milk, it is also worth noting a politics of remembrance perhaps shaped by long-standing intercommunity tensions. Castells and Murphy

observe, "[M]any gays . . . started another 'colonization' in the much harsher area South of Market. . . . Their marginality from the gay community was not only spatial. Socially, they tended to reject the politicization and positive counterculture of the new liberation movement. They emphasized the sexual aspects of the gay condition. The more the gay community appeared in the process of legitimation, the more a strongly individualised minority, generally poorer and less educated [Fritscher has a Ph.D.], headed toward self-affirmation of a new sexual 'deviance,' many of them joining the sado-masochistic networks: South-of-Market became the quarters of 'leather culture.'" Manuel Castells and Karen Murphy, "Cultural Identity and Urban Culture: The Spatial Organization of San Francisco's Gay Culture," in *Urban Policy Under Capitalism,* eds. Nathan I. Fainstein and Susan S. Fainstein (Beverly Hills, CA: Sage, 1982), 254–255. For a more laudatory perspective on the gay community South of Market, see Gayle S. Rubin, "The Miracle Mile: South of Market and Gay Male Leather, 1962–1997)," in *Reclaiming San Francisco: History, Politics, Culture,* eds. James Brook, Chris Carlsson, and Nancy J. Peters (San Francisco: City Lights Books, 1998): 247–272.

15. Clendinen and Nagourney, *Out for Good,* 405.

16. Fritscher, *Gay San Francisco,* 117.

17. Jonathan Bell, *California Crucible: The Forging of Modern American Liberalism* (Philadelphia: University of Pennsylvania Press, 2012), 259.

18. Harvey Milk, "On the Milk Stool," *Coast to Coast* (Los Angeles), 1978, Harvey Milk Archives–Scott Smith Collection (GLC35), Box 26 (1973–1978), Clippings.

19. Harry Britt, "Harvey Milk as I Knew Him," in *Out in the Castro: Desire, Promise, Activism,* ed. Winston Leyland (San Francisco: Leyland Publications, 2002), 78.

20. Jim Rivaldo, "Remembering How Harvey Milk Helped Pave the Way," *Bay Area Reporter,* June 21, 2001, 40.

21. James M. Jasper, *The Art of Moral Protest: Culture, Biography, and Creativity in Social Movements* (Chicago: University of Chicago Press, 1997), 201.

22. Streitmatter argues that the significance of such activism in San Francisco, and Milk's role in it, was amplified because of an expanding gay press: "Seeing that the major events were being covered by the establishment media, lesbian and gay journalists adopted a new tack: they transformed local events into national ones. By the conventional definition of news, the vote on a city gay rights ordinance was of local interest only; by the revised gay press definition, such a vote was the fodder for the front page of gay newspapers everywhere. In short, the newspapers "nationalized" gay news. Streitmatter, *Unspeakable: The Rise of the Gay and Lesbian Press in America* (New York: Faber and Faber, 1995), 220.

23. Boze Hadleigh, "Harvey Milk: Ten Years After," *Christopher Street,* September 1988, 16.

24. Clendinen and Nagourney, *Out for Good,* 403.

25. Ronald Yates and Michael Coakley, "Milk's Murder Stuns San Francisco Gays," *Chicago Tribune,* November 30, 1978, 7.

26. Ed Jackson, "Gay Liberation 101—Plus," *The Body Politic,* November 1984, 30.

27. For biographical material regarding Harvey Milk's life before politics, see Harvey Milk Archives—Scott Smith Collection (GLC 35); Harvey Milk—Susan Alch Correspondence (GLC 19); Harvey Milk—Joseph Campbell Correspondence; Randy Shilts Papers, Mayor of Castro Street series, James C. Hormel Gay and Lesbian Center, San Francisco Public Library; and Randy Shilts, *The Mayor of Castro Street: The Life and Times of Harvey Milk* (New York: St. Martin's Press), 1982

28. Shilts, *The Mayor of Castro Street,* 38.

29. For pre-Castro GLBTQ San Francisco history, see John D'Emlio, "Gay Politics and Community in San Francisco since World War II," in *Hidden from History: Reclaiming the Gay and Lesbian Past,* eds. Martin Bauml Duberman, Martha Vicinus, and George Chauncey, Jr. (New York: New American Library): 456–476; Allan Bérubé, *Coming Out Under Fire: The History of Gay Men and Women in World War Two* (New York: Free Press, 1990); Susan Stryker and Jim Van Buskirk, *Gay by the Bay: A History of Queer Culture in the San Francisco Bay Area* (San Francisco: Chronicle Books, 1996); Nan Alamilla Boyd, *Wide Open Town: A History of Queer San Francisco to 1965* (Berkeley: University of California Press, 2003); Horacio N. Rocque Ramírez, "A Living Archive of Desire: Teresita la Campesina and the Embodiment of Queer Latino Community Histories," *Archive Stories: Facts, Fictions, and the Writing of History,* ed. Antoinette Burton (Durham: Duke University Press, 2005); Marcia M. Gallo, *Different Daughters: A History of the Daughters of Bilitis and the Rise of the Lesbian Rights Movement* (San Francisco: Seal Press, 2007); Susan Stryker, *Transgender History* (San Francisco: Seal Press, 2008); J. Todd Ormsbee, *The Meaning of Gay: Interaction, Publicity, and Community among Homosexual Men in 1960s San Francisco* (Lanham, MD: Lexington Books, 2010); Allan Bérubé, *My Desire for History: Essays in Gay, Community, and Labor History,* eds. John D'Emilio and Estelle B. Freedman (Chapel Hill, NC: University of North Carolina Press, 2011), Chapters 1–4; John D'Emilio, *Sexual Politics, Sexual Communities: The Making of a Homosexual Minority in the United States, 1940–1970,* 2nd ed. (Chicago: University of Chicago Press, 1998), Chapter 12; and Bell, *California Crucible,* Chapter 10.

30. For detailed explanations of the complex changes in San Francisco that made possible the significant growth of GLBTQ culture and politics, and the development of the Castro as we have come to know it, see Fritscher, *Gay San Francisco;* Timothy Stewart-Winter, "The Castro: Origins to the Age of Milk," *The Gay and Lesbian Review Worldwide* 16 (January–February 2009), 12–15; Josh Sides, *Erotic City: Sexual Revolutions and the Making of Modern San Francisco* (New York: Oxford University Press, 2009); Martin Meeker, *Contacts Desired: Gay and Lesbian Communications and Community, 1940s–1970s* (Chicago: University of Chicago Press, 2006); *Screaming Queens: The Riot at Compton's Cafeteria,* dir. Victor Silverman and Susan Stryker (Los Angeles: Frameline, 2005); Joshua Gamson, *The Fabulous Sylvester: The Legend, the Music, the Seventies in San Francisco* (New York: Henry Holt and

Company, 2005); Winston Leyland, ed., *Out in the Castro: Desire, Promise, Activism* (San Francisco: Leyland Publications, 2002); *The Castro,* dir. Peter L. Stein (San Francisco: KQED, 1998); Clendinen and Nagourney, *Out for Good,* Chapter 10; Benjamin Heim Shepard, *White Nights and Ascending Shadows: An Oral History of the San Francisco AIDS Epidemic* (London: Cassell, 1997); Streitmatter, *Unspeakable;* Richard Edward DeLeon, *Left Coast City: Progressive Politics in San Francisco, 1975–1991* (Lawrence, KS: University of Kansas Press, 1992), Chapter 3; John D'Emilio, "Gay Politics, Gay Community: San Francisco's Experience," in *Making Trouble: Essays on Gay History, Politics, and the University,* ed. John D'Emilio (New York: Routledge, 1992): 74–95; Frances Fitzgerald, *Cities on a Hill: A Journey through Contemporary American Cultures* (New York: Simon and Schuster, 1986); John D'Emilio, *Sexual Politics, Sexual Communities: The Making of a Homosexual Minority in the United States, 1940–1970* (Chicago: University of Chicago Press, 1983), Chapter 10; Manuel Castells, *The City and the Grass- roots: A Cross-Cultural Theory of Urban Social Movements* (Berkeley, CA: University of California Press, 1983), Chapter 14; Shilts, *The Mayor of Castro Street;* and Edmund White, *States of Desire: Travels in Gay America* (New York: E. P. Dutton, 1980): 30–69.

31. D'Emilio, "Gay Politics and Community in San Francisco since World War II," 468.

32. Chester Hartman, *The Transformation of San Francisco* (Totowa, New Jersey: Rowman and Allanheld, 1984; and Stewart-Winter, "The Castro."

33. D'Emilio, "Gay Politics and Community in San Francisco since World War II," 468.

34. Larry Kramer, "Gay Boom Seen in Bay Area," *Washington Post,* April 7, 1978, F2; Fitzgerald, *Cities on a Hill,* 48; and Daniel Nicoletta, "So Long at the Fair," *The Harvey Milk Archives Newsletter* 1 (July 1983), 1. See also Danny Nicoletta, "Harvey Milk and the Castro of the 70s," *East Village Boys* (January 21, 2009), http://www.eastvillageboys.com/2009/01/21/dan-nicoletta-harvey-milk-and-the-castro-of-the-70s/; and Daniel Curzon, "Why We Came to Sodom," *The North American Review* 268 (December 1983): 21–23.

35. Quoted in Stewart-Winter, "The Castro," 14. See Clendinen and Nagourney, *Out for Good,* Chapter 10.

36. Bell, *California Crucible,* Chapter 10, 261.

37. Bell, *California Crucible,* 263, 265.

38. D'Emilio observes, "The explosive growth of the gay community and its political activism also made internal differences visible. For some gay men liber- ation meant freedom from harassment; for radicalesbians it meant overthrowing the patriarchy. Bay Area Gay Liberation participated in anti-imperialist coali- tions while members of the Alice B. Toklas Democratic Club sought to climb within the Democratic Party. The interests of gay entrepreneurs clashed with those of their gay employees. Gay male real-estate speculators displayed little concern for 'brothers' who could not pay the skyrocketing rents. Gay men and women of color found themselves displaced by more privileged members of the community as gentrification spread to more and more neighborhoods. Sexual orientation created a kind of unity, but other aspects of identity brought to the

surface conflicting needs and interests." D'Emilio, "Gay Politics and Community in San Francisco since World War II," 468. On the critique of gay male sex culture, see Sides, *Erotic City*, Chapter 3.

39. Elizabeth Armstrong, *Forging Gay Identities: Organizing Sexuality in San Francisco, 1950–1994* (Chicago: University of Chicago Press, 2002), esp. Chapters 5 and 6.

40. Armstrong, *Forging Gay Identities*, 104.

41. Bruce J. Schulman, *The Seventies: The Great Shift in American Culture, Society, and Politics* (New York: The Free Press, 2001), 72.

42. Dominic Sandbrook, *Mad as Hell: The Crisis of the 1970s and the Rise of the Populist Right* (New York: Alfred A. Knopf, 2011), 364.

43. Schulman, *The Seventies*, 180; and Bruce J. Schulman, "Comment: The Empire Strikes Back—Conservative Responses to Progressive Social Movements in the 1970s," *Journal of Contemporary History* 43 (2008), 697. See also Simon Hall, "Protest Movements in the 1970s: The Long 1960s," *Journal of Contemporary History* 43 (2008): 655–672.

44. "Gays on the March," *Time*, September 8, 1975, 32.

45. John D'Emilio, "After Stonewall," in *Making Trouble: Essays on Gay History, Politics, and the University* (New York: Routledge, 1992), 248.

46. Moral shock, as conceptualized by sociologists James Jasper and later Deborah Gould, is constituted by a singular happening or multiple events, sudden or cumulative, which creates sufficient cognitive, affective, and ethical or moral disruption such that one is compelled toward political action; it might be understood as contextual inducements that awaken or propel, or motivate in a material sense, an activist (or collectively, movement) into being. In rhetorical studies, Bonnie Dow draws on Kenneth Burke to theorize how such "existential disruptions" can be—arguably, *must* be—rhetorically produced or framed to function effectively. See Jasper, *The Art of Moral Protest*, 106; Deborah Gould, *Moving Politics: Emotion and ACT UP's Fight Against AIDS* (Chicago: University of Chicago Press, 2009), 134–143; and Bonnie J. Dow, "AIDS, Perspective by Incongruity, and Gay Identity in Larry Kramer's '1,112 and Counting,'" in *Readings on the Rhetoric of Social Protest*, 2nd ed., eds. Charles E. Morris III and Stephen Howard Browne (State College, PA: Strata, 2006): 320–334.

47. Shilts, *The Mayor of Castro Street*, 10, 71–72.

48. In his thesis, Callis argues, as did some of Milk's critics, that during his political ascendancy, and specifically in his first three campaigns, Milk downplayed his sexuality, such as omitting his sexuality or gay rights issues from his official candidate statement, in his alliance with unions, or in his appeals to non-GLBTQ voters, a politically opportunistic calculus intended to strengthen the viability of his candidacies. His opponent in the 1976 Assembly campaign, Art Agnos, declared, "Milk is running a closet campaign in front of straight audiences and an upfront one in the gay community." This perspective deepens our engagement with the closet politics inevitably imbricated in a gay candidacy at the time—or in our own time, as the documentary *Outrage* demonstrates. That said, we are not convinced that Milk's tactics at any time during his political career constituted a variation of what Kenji Yoshino has conceptualized as "covering." Regardless of tactical foregrounding and de-emphasis, the broader

context of Milk's public persona and framing, and his bedrock personal and political commitment to gay rights, even granting sometimes lamentable variations among outlets and audiences, rendered him functionally and unmistakably "out." Callis is correct in observing that Milk was never a single-issue, that is exclusively gay rights, candidate. Callis, *From Castro Street to City Hall,* 31, 51, 70, 97–98. See also *Outrage: Do Ask, Do Tell,* dir. Kirby Dick (New York: Magnolia Pictures, 2009); and Kenji Yoshino, *Covering: The Hidden Assault on Our Civil Rights* (New York: Random House, 2006).

49. Callis, *From Castro Street to City Hall,* 24, Chapter 2.

50. Deeper understanding of the gay political establishment in San Francisco can be found in the pages of the two leading gay papers, *Bay Area Reporter* and the *Sentinel,* as well as in SIR's newsletter, *Vector.*

51. Michael Wong, "Harvey," Harvey Milk Archives—Scott Smith Collection, Series 4, Box 13, 2; and Harvey Milk, "Milk Forum: Gay Groupie Syndrome," *Bay Area Reporter,* February 20, 1975, 10–11.

52. Callis, *From Castro Street to City Hall,* 29–30, 37–38.

53. Wong, "Harvey," 1–2. Note, too, Daniel Curzon's memory of first encountering Milk: "Harvey wasn't St. Harvey then; in fact, he hadn't even been elected to the Board of Supervisors in San Francisco, but he was extremely articulate and charismatic as he spoke from his seat at the conference. I was turned on by him, to be honest." Daniel Curzon, *Dropping Names: The Delicious Memoirs of Daniel Curzon* (San Francisco: IGNA Books, 2004), 30.

54. Randy Shilts, "The Life and Death of Harvey Milk," *Christopher Street* (March 1979), 30.

55. William E. Beardemphl, "Comments," *Bay Area Reporter,* October 3, 1973, 6.

56. Harvey Milk, "Waves from the Left," *Sentinel,* February 14, 1974, 5.

57. Harvey Milk, "Waves from the Left," *Sentinel,* June 20, 1974; and Harvey Milk, "Gay Groupie Syndrome," *Bay Area Reporter,* February 20, 1975, 10–11. See also Callis, *From Castro Street to City Hall,* Chapter 3.

58. Harvey Milk, "Waves from the Left," *Sentinel,* May 9, 1974, 3, 5; Harvey Milk, "Clear Choice for Voters," *Bay Area Reporter,* May 15, 1974, 1–2; and Harvey Milk, "Waves from the Left," *Sentinel,* June 20, 1974, 3.

59. Harvey Milk, "Waves from the Left," *Sentinel,* February 28, 1974.

60. Harvey Milk, "Waves from the Left," *Sentinel,* July 3, 1974, 5; and Harvey Milk, "Castro Street Fair," *Bay Area Reporter,* 8.

61. Harvey Milk, "Milk Forum: Gay Unity: Fact or Fiction," *Bay Area Reporter,* December 23, 1974, 8.

62. Harvey Milk, "Milk Forum: Teamsters Seek Gay Help," *Bay Area Reporter,* November 27, 1974, 2.

63. Harvey Milk, "Waves from the Left," *Sentinel,* July 18, 1974, 5.

64. Harvey Milk, "Waves from the Left," *Sentinel,* April 11, 1974, 5.

65. Harvey Milk, "Waves from the Left," *Sentinel,* April 11, 1974, 5; and Harvey Milk, "Waves from the Left," *Sentinel,* August 29, 1974, 5.

66. Harvey Milk, "Milk Forum: Castro Busts," *Bay Area Reporter,* September 4, 1974; and Harvey Milk, "Waves from the Left," *Sentinel,* September 12, 1974, 5.

67. Historically, indeed by definition, movement leaders do not seek elective office. Milk, however, defied categorization. He was a pastiche, philosophically, politically, and rhetorically, one moment speaking in the tones and absolutes of gay liberation (though he claimed not to be a revolutionary and rebuked the extremes of left and right), then sounding like a gay rights reformist (though he rejected gradualism and assimilationism); little wonder he clashed with both the radicals of Bay Area Gay Liberation (BAGL) and the moderates of the Alice B. Toklas Memorial Democratic Club. As part of this explanation, note that Milk emerged during the period of transition between the movements known as Gay Liberation and Gay Rights/Gay Identity. For discussions of changes in the GLBTQ movement in the 1970s, see Barry D. Adam, *The Rise of the Gay and Lesbian Movement*, rev. ed. (Boston: Twayne, 1995); Clendinen and Nagourney, *Out for Good*; Craig A. Rimmerman, *From Identity to Politics: The Lesbian and Gay Movements in the United States* (Philadelphia: Temple University Press, 2001); Armstrong, *Forging Gay Identities*; and David Eisenbach, *Gay Power: An American Revolution* (New York: Carroll and Graf, 2006).

68. In Herbert Gold, "A Walk on San Francisco's Gay Side," *New York Times*, November 6, 1977, SM17.

69. Bell, *California Crucible*, 265.

70. "Elections: San Francisco Squeaker," *Time*, December 22, 1975, http://www.time.com/time/magazine/article/0,9171,879568,00.html#ixzz1AHre4cvD.

71. GLBT Studies scholar Wayne Dynes observed, "Later mythology has portrayed Harvey Milk as a radical leftist, but more careful scrutiny shows that he retained elements of his conservative background to the very end. At bottom, he held an almost Jeffersonian concept of the autonomy of small neighborhoods, prospering through small businesses and local attention to community problems. . . . Milk anticipated the later strategy of the 'rainbow coalition,' but because of his personal gifts, and the time and place in which he lived, he was able to make it work more effectively for gay and lesbian politics than any other single individual has done before or since." Quoted in Paul Russell, *The Gay 100: A Ranking of the Most Influential Gay Men and Lesbians, Past and Present* (New York: Kensington Publishing, 1995), 97.

72. Shilts, "The Life and Death of Harvey Milk," 31.

73. "Harvey Milk to Run for Supervisor," *Bay Area Reporter*, March 20, 1975, 3.

74. Quoted in Clendinen and Nagourney, *Out for Good*, 344; see also Philip Hagar, "Gay Power Emerging at Ballot Box," *Los Angeles Times*, September 30, 1975, A1.

75. Clendinen and Nagourney, *Out for Good*, 343–345; and Shilts, *The Mayor of Castro Street*, 105–106.

76. Clendinen and Nagourney, *Out for Good*, 343–344; Callis, *From Castro Street to City Hall*, 79-80; and Shilts, *The Mayor of Castro Street*, Chapter 7.

77. Shilts, "The Life and Death of Harvey Milk," 32.

78. Harvey Milk, "Milk Forum: Untitled," *Bay Area Reporter*, December 11, 1975, 8.

79. Clendinen and Nagourney, *Out for Good*, 340.

80. George Mendehall, "Finding the Answers: Moscone: Milk Appointment Is Just the Beginning," *Bay Area Reporter*, February 5, 1976, 7.

81. Wong, "Harvey," 6; Shilts, *The Mayor of Castro Street*, 107, 120–121. It should be noted that pioneer lesbian activist Phyllis Lyon was appointed by Moscone to the Human Rights Commission the same year. Del Martin, "Phyllis Lyon," in *Before Stonewall: Activists for Gay and Lesbian Rights in Historical Context,* ed. Vern L. Bullough (Binghamton, NY: Harrington Park Press, 2002): 169–178.

82. Harvey Milk, "Milk Forum: Musical Chairs," *Bay Area Reporter,* January 8, 1976, 4.

83. Jerry Burns, "Kopp Accuses Phil Burton and McCarthy of 'Unholy Alliance,'" *San Francisco Chronicle,* February 10, 1976, 4.

84. Callis, *From Castro Street to City Hall,* Chapter 4, 93, 89; Bruce Brugmann and Jerry Roberts, "Ganging Up on Harvey Milk," *San Francisco Bay Guardian,* February 13, 1976; and "Milk Will Run—Loses Permit Board Seat," *San Francisco Chronicle,* March 10, 1976, 6.

85. Harvey Milk, "Declaration of Candidacy," n.d., Harvey Milk Archives–Scott Smith Collection (GLC35), Box 3, Series 2a, Harvey Milk Candidacy for Assembly 1976, Official Forms; George Mendenhall, "Finding the Answers: Harvey Milk vs. The Machine," *Bay Area Reporter,* February 19, 1976; George Mendenhall, "Finding the Answers: Of Harvey's Running," *Bay Area Reporter,* March 18, 1976; and Shilts, *The Mayor of Castro Street,* Chapter 9.

86. Milk's editorial concerned the 1976 Supreme Court affirmation by a 6–3 vote, without oral argument or written opinion, of the lower court ruling upholding the Virginia sodomy statute in *Doe v. Commonwealth's Attorney for the City of Richmond* (E.D.Va., 403 F.Supp. 1199, affirmed, --- U.S. ----, 96 S.Ct. 1489, 47 L.Ed.2d 751 [1976]). See Robert D. McFadden, "Homosexuals and A.C.L.U. Dismayed by Court's Ruling," *New York Times,* March 30, 1976, 17. Milk's animus toward what he called the Nixon Court was well founded. GLBTQ legal scholar William Eskridge observes, "The Burger Court not only denied rights in almost every decided case involving gay litigants or materials but narrowed Warren Court decisions that potentially empowered gay people against homophobes. . . . By treating sex as dirty conduct rather than expression and 'homosexuals' as presumptive sodomites rather than citizens, the Burger Court did what it could to preserve the remnants of the closet. Don't ask, don't tell sums up the Burger Court philosophy, itself derived from the approach still in rural and small-town America: gay people should be unseen but not heard." William N. Eskridge, *Gaylaw: Challenging the Apartheid of the Closet* (Cambridge, MA: Harvard University Press, 1999), 146.

87. Harvey Milk, "Milk Forum: A Lesson from the Convention," *Bay Area Reporter,* July 22, 1978.

88. Quoted in Shilts, *The Mayor of Castro Street,* 138.

89. Harvey Milk, "Milk Forum: Our Uncle Toms Learn from Nixon," *Bay Area Reporter,* May 13, 1976, 17; *Bay Area Reporter,* May 27, 1976, 19; Wong, "Harvey," 6–16; Shilts, *The Mayor of Castro Street,* Chapter 9; Shilts, "The Life and Death of Harvey Milk," 33–34; Callis, *From Castro Street to*

City Hall, 95–103; and Ron Moscowitz, "Harvey Milk Blames 2 Factors for Defeat," *San Francisco Chronicle,* June 10, 1976, 7.

90. Sandbrook, *Mad as Hell,* 276.

91. Mark Vaz, "Zenger's Interview: Harvey Milk: The Candid Political Activist of San Francisco's Gay Community Speaks, *Zenger's,* November 3, 1976, found in James C. Hormel Gay & Lesbian Center of the San Francisco Public Library, GLC35, Milk–Smith Collection, Box 26, 73–78.

92. Paul Boyer, "The Evangelical Resurgence in 1970s American Protestantism, in *Rightward Bound: Making America Conservative in the 1970s,* eds. Bruce J. Schulman and Julian E. Zelizer (Cambridge, MA: Harvard University Press, 2008), 29. See also Perry Deane Young, *God's Bullies: Native Reflections on Preachers and Politics* (New York: Holt, Rinehart, and Winston, 1982).

93. Sandbrook, *Mad as Hell,* 267, 348.

94. Matthew D. Lassiter, "Inventing Family Values," in *Rightward Bound,* 14.

95. Harvey Milk, "Milk Forum: Changes of Influence in '77," *Bay Area Reporter,* January 6, 1977, 8–9.

96. Shilts, *The Mayor of Castro Street,* 155. See also Gold, "A Walk on San Francisco's Gay Side."

97. For details of the Dade County repeal fight and its aftermath in 1977, see Tom Mathews, "Battle over Gay Rights," *Newsweek* (June 6, 1977), 16–26; Clendinen and Nagourney, *Out for Good,* Chapters 22–26, Bryant quoted 292; Young, *God's Bullies,* Chapter 3; Cleve Jones, *Stitching a Revolution: The Making of an Activist* (San Francisco: HarperSanFrancisco, 2000), Chapter 5; Eisenbach, *Gay Power,* Chapter 10; and Fred Fejes, *Gay Rights and Moral Panic: The Origins of America's Debate on Homosexuality* (New York: Palgrave Macmillan, 2008), Chapters 3–5.

98. Harvey Milk, "Milk Forum: Where Does the Political Left Stand on Anita Bryant?" *Bay Area Reporter,* April 14, 1977, 9. See also Harvey Milk, "Milk Forum: Leave Anita Alone?" *Bay Area Reporter,* March 17, 1977, 4; and Harvey Milk, "Milk Forum: Pools within Pools," *Bay Area Reporter,* March 31, 1977, 8. Cuban gay activist Ovidio "Herb" Rámos was a spokesperson for the Latin Committee for the Human Rights of Gays, working in Miami, where Bryant's hate speech in the Catholic Cuban community had been fanned by Catholic and Protestant leaders. He participated in a debate on March 14 with representatives of Save Our Children on a Spanish-language radio station. The vitriol of the comments spewed by those listeners who called in—advocating deportation, concentration camps, and execution—was so devastating that two days later Rámos committed suicide. Fejes, *Gay Rights and Moral Panic,* 128–129; and Young, *God's Bullies,* 53–54.

99. Harvey Milk, "Milk Forum: Porno Bill to Close Polk/Castro Bookstores and Flicks?" *Bay Area Reporter,* January 20, 1977, 4; Harvey Milk, "Milk Forum: The Damage Has Been Done—Again," *Bay Area Reporter,* February 3, 1977, 10; Milk, "Leave Anita Alone?"; and Harvey Milk, "Milk Forum: Finding a Home for Porno Houses," *Bay Area Reporter,* June 9, 1977, 10.

100. Clendinen and Nagourney, *Out for Good,* 336–337.

101. Grant Winthrop, "Florida Vote Upsets San Francisco Homosexuals," *Boston Globe,* June 20, 1977.

102. See Tina Fetner, "Working Anita Bryant: The Impact of Christian Anti-Gay Activism on Lesbian and Gay Movement Claims," *Social Problems* 48 (August 2001): 411–428.

103. Shilts, *The Mayor of Castro Street,* 164. In a January 1979 editorial, Eric Rofes drew explicit linkages among Bryant's crusade, Hillsborough's murder, and Dan White's assassination of Harvey Milk within a broader context of escalating homophobic attacks. "To deny there is a connection [among these events] . . . is to deny there is a connection between the rational hatred of homosexuality and the irrational violence directed against gay people." Eric Rofes, "Milk Death, Homophobia Link Hard to Deny," *Boston Globe,* January 8, 1979, 11.

104. See Fejes, *Gay Rights and Moral Panic,* Chapters 6 and 7.

105. Shilts, *The Mayor of Castro Street,* 160.

106. Harvey Milk, "Milk Forum: 40,000 Throng Castro St. Fair," *Bay Area Reporter,* August 18, 1977, 11; and Harvey Milk, "Milk Forum: A Lifestyle Emerges," *Bay Area Reporter,* September 1, 1977, 11.

107. For analysis of the Hope Speech, and Milk's discourse generally, see Karen A. Foss, "Harvey Milk: 'You Have to Give Them Hope,'" *Journal of the West* 27 (April 1988): 75–81; Karen A. Foss, "The Logic of Folly in the Political Campaigns of Harvey Milk," in *Queer Words/Queer Images: Communication and the Construction of Homosexuality,* ed. R. Jeffrey Ringer (New York: NYU Press, 1994): 7–29; Karen A. Foss, "Harvey Milk and the Queer Rhetorical Situation," in *Queering Public Address: Sexualities and American Historical Discourse,* ed. Charles E. Morris III (Columbia, SC: University of South Carolina Press, 2007): 74–92; and Jason Edward Black & Charles E. Morris III, "Harvey Milk, 'You've Got to Have Hope' (24 June 1977)," *Voices of Democracy Journal* (National Endowment for the Humanities) 6 (2011): 63–82.

108. Harvey Milk, "Milk Forum: You Draw the Conclusion," *Bay Area Reporter,* August 4, 1977, 8.

109. For discussion of the 1977 campaign, see George Mendenhall, "Finding the Answers: Milk vs. Stokes in the Castro," *Bay Area Reporter,* December 9, 1976, 13–14; Harvey Milk, "Milk Forum: Haight Street: A New Direction or Back Behind the Iron Gates?" *Bay Area Reporter,* October 13, 1977, 14; Wayne Friday, "Milk for Supervisor District 5, *Bay Area Reporter,* October 27, 1977, 16–17; Harvey Milk, "Milk Forum: Running against a Moralist," *Bay Area Reporter,* October 27, 1977, 20; Shilts, *The Mayor of Castro Street,* Chapter 11; Callis, *From Castro Street to City Hall,* Chapter 5; Clendinen and Nagourney, *Out for Good,* Chapter 24; Anne Kronenberg, "Everybody Needed Milk," in *Out in the Castro: Desire, Promise, Activism,* ed. Winston Leyland (San Francisco: Leyland Publications, 2002): 37–43; Shilts, "The Life and Death of Harvey Milk," 36–39; Wong, "Harvey," 19–25; Bill Sievert, "Divided They Stand—The Milk-Stokes Split," *The Advocate,* July 13, 1977, 13; and Jerry Burns, "17 Wage Wide-Open Battle for District 5 Supervisor," *San Francisco Chronicle,* November 4, 1977, 4.

110. Harry Britt, "Harvey Milk as I Knew Him," 80.

111. Quoted in Shilts, *The Mayor of Castro Street,* 183.

112. Harvey Milk, "Milk Forum: Victory Statement," *Bay Area Reporter,* November 10, 1977, 77.

113. Quoted in Shilts, *The Mayor of Castro Street,* 190. For discussion of Milk's inauguration and opening acts and speeches as supervisor, see Shilts, *The Mayor of Castro Street,* Chapter 12; and Randy Alfred, "Milk Sworn In: SF Gay Goes to City Hall," *GAYVOTE* (San Francisco Gay Democratic Club newsletter) 1 (January 1978): 1, 4, found in James C. Hormel Gay & Lesbian Center of the San Francisco Public Library, GLC35, Milk–Smith Collection, Box 4, Series 2a. G.

114. In his "Milk Forum," he declared, "The coalition of minorities—including the feminist and Gay movements—are starting to join on all issues that affect anyone in the coalition." Harvey Milk, "Milk Forum: The Jarvis-Gann Initiative," *Bay Area Reporter,* March 30, 1978, 14.

115. Kronenberg, "Everybody Needed Milk," 41. For an account of Milk's work in City Hall during 1978, see Emery, "Appendix: Milk's Supervisorial Activities," *The Harvey Milk Interviews,* 317–339; Bruce Pettit, "Anne Kronenberg & Dick Pabich: Harvey Milk's Dynamic Aides Speak Out," *Bay Area Reporter,* March 2, 1978, 8–9; and Bruce Pettit, "Milk's Last Three Months," *Bay Area Reporter,* July 20, 1978, 7.

116. See Shilts, *The Mayor of Castro Street,* Chapter 12.

117. Pettit, "Anne Kronenberg and Dick Pabich"; and John Geluardi, "Dan White's Motive More about Betrayal than Homophobia," *San Francisco Weekly* (January 30, 2008), http://www.sfweekly.com/2008-01-30/news/white-in-milk. See also Mike Weiss, *Double Play: The Hidden Passions Behind the Double Assassination of George Moscone and Harvey Milk* (1984; San Francisco: Vince Emery Productions, 2010).

118. Shilts, *The Mayor of Castro Street,* 193.

119. Wong, "Harvey," 29, 30.

120. Briggs' campaign against gay teachers was particularly appalling because ideology, such as Bryant's evangelicalism, did not motivate him. Reporter Robert Shrum wrote, "Briggs recalled that, 'Reagan was going down the tubes in 1976 until he came up with Panama as an issue.' So Briggs came up with his own issue, 'the homosexual issue,' rating it 'the hottest social issue since Reconstruction.'" Although Briggs claimed "it was when he flew to Miami to volunteer for Bryant's crusade that the Lord inspired him with the Briggs Initiative," his inspiration, as Shilts argued, likely came rather from his will to power: "it seemed highly doubtful from the start that John Briggs ever really had anything personal against gays. He was just running for governor. 'It's just politics . . . just politics.'" After the gubernatorial prospects faded, Briggs pressed on with Prop 6 because it likely represented his last best hope for the political limelight. Shrum, "Gay-Baiting in California: Sexual Politics in the Classroom," *New Times,* September 4, 1978, 23–24; and Shilts, *The Mayor of Castro Street,* 157–58, 241.

121. Quoted in Clendinen and Nagourney, *Out for Good,* 381.

122. Shilts, *The Mayor of Castro Street,* 239.

123. Quoted in Shrum, "Gay-Baiting in the Classroom," 22.

124. Shilts, *The Mayor of Castro Street,* 242.

125. For a discussion of Holocaust rhetoric in the history of the struggle for gay rights, see Arlene Stein, "Whose Memories? Whose Victimhood? Contests

for the Holocaust Frame in Recent Social Movement Discourse," *Sociological Perspectives* 41 (1998): 519–540. Throughout his career, Milk used Hitler, the Nazis, and Jewish traitors as analogies and rhetorical frames in denouncing his political enemies. In addition to Document 10 on police brutality, note these examples: "As [Anita Bryant] gains support (and she is) she takes stronger and stronger anti-gay stands. Reminds me of how Hitler rose to power by using the Jews as bait. I don't see Bryant becoming another Hitler, but the tactic is similar. Hitler even had many Jews on his side at first, defending his 'rights'"; "Letting [Anita Bryant] get away with her bigotry and hatred is not too far from letting the Nixons and the Hitlers get away with their sicknesses"; "Hitler lives on in Briggs." Milk, "Leave Anita Alone?"; Milk, "Pools within Pools"; and Harvey Milk, "Milk Forum: Jarvis-Gann," *Bay Area Reporter,* June 22, 1978, 12.

126. Shilts, *The Mayor of Castro Street,* 229. For description of a typical debate, see for example Jean Dickinson, "Briggs-Milk Debate: Scoring Points in WC [Walnut Creek]," *Contra Costa Times,* September 17, 1978, 1, found in James C. Hormel Gay & Lesbian Center of the San Francisco Public Library, GLC35, Milk–Smith Collection, Box 26, 73–78 Clippings. For discussion of the October 11, 1978, televised debate hosted by KQED in San Francisco, in which Milk was partnered with San Francisco State University Speech Professor and lesbian-feminist activist Sally Miller Gearhart, see Raul Ramirez, "Verbal, Physical Scuffling Mark Debate on Prop. 6," *San Francisco Examiner,* October 12, 1978, 10; and Jones, *Stitching a Revolution,* 49–51.

127. Clendinen and Nagourney, *Out for Good,* 381–390; and Shrum, "Gay-Baiting in the Classroom," 24–27.

128. Quoted in Shilts, *The Mayor of Castro Street,* 250.

129. Warren Hinckle, "Dan White's Final Solution," *Inquiry Magazine,* October 29, 1979: 8–20; See Shilts, *The Mayor of Castro Street,* Chapters 15–18; Weiss, *Double Play; The Times of Harvey Milk,* dir. Rob Epstein (New York: New York Films, 1984); Warren Hinckle, *Gayslayer! The Story of How Dan White Killed Harvey Milk and George Moscone and Got Away with Murder* (San Francisco: Silver Dollar Books, 1985); Stryker and Van Buskirk, *Gay by the Bay;* Jones, *Stitching a Revolution;* Leyland, *Out in the Castro;* de Jim, *San Francisco's Castro;* William Lipsky, *Gay and Lesbian San Francisco* (San Francisco: Arcadia Publishing, 2006); and *Milk: A Pictorial History of Harvey Milk* (New York: Newmarket Press, 2009).

130. As a friendly amendment to Castiglia and Reed's insightful reading of the "metamemory" in *Milk,* by which they mean intertextual layers of the past operative in the film, including Epstein's *The Times of Harvey Milk,* we would emphasize that the invaluable countermemory initiatives they prescribe entail multiple and complex rhetorical challenges, including the inventional work of creating inducements to memory in the first place (gay film qua gay film cannot be presumed sufficient, however sexy the trailer) and providing the requisite contextual scaffolding (too often disparagingly understood as "history lessons") that would enable cross-generational engagement through memory literacies. We are not convinced, for instance, that the intertextual materials Castiglia and Reed rightly identify would be legible as such for many audience

members. We continue to puzzle over the vexing question of how scholar activists, what we term *archival queers,* without seeming patronizing or pedantic while being collaborative, would enhance interest in a memory text and offer enough backstory or "annotation" to make the text meaningful beyond basic narrative conventions or facile hero/martyr tales—not that *Milk* is guilty of either. Christopher Castiglia and Christopher Reed, *If Memory Serves: Gay Men, AIDS, and the Promise of the Queer Past* (Minneapolis: University of Minnesota Press, 2012), Introduction and Chapter 1, 66–69. See also Charles E. Morris III, "Archival Queer," *Rhetoric and Public Affairs* 9.1 (2006): 145–151; and K. J. Rawson and Charles E. Morris III, "Queer Archives/Archival Queers," in *Re/Theorizing Writing Histories of Rhetoric,* ed. Michelle Baliff (Carbondale: Southern Illinois University Press, forthcoming 2013).

131. Mathias Danbolt, "Touching History: Archival Relations in Queer Art and Theory," in *Lost and Found: Queerying the Archive,* eds. Mathias Danbolt, Jane Rowley, and Louise Wolthers (Copenhagen: Nikolaj, Copenhagen Contemporary Art Center, 2009), 27, 28.

132. Marco R. della Cava, "Timing Is Finally Right for 'Milk' Amid Uproar over Gay Marriage," *USA Today,* November 24, 2008, 2D. See also Jesse McKinley, "Back to the Ramparts in California," *New York Times,* November 2, 2008, 5; Michael Cieply, "Activists Seek to Tie 'Milk' to a Campaign for Gay Rights," *New York Times,* November 22, 2008, C1; Matt Budd, "'Milk': We Need Him Now More Than Ever," *The Huffington Post,* November 26, 2008, http://www.alternet.org/story/108847/; and Michael Martin, "The Resurrection of Harvey Milk," *The Advocate,* November 18, 2008, 33–44.

133. Edward Guthmann, "*Harvey Milk*' Dilemma: Critical Raves, But Apathetic Audiences," *Advocate,* February 5, 1985, 34; and John Cloud, "Harvey Milk: The Pioneer," *Time,* June 14, 1999, 183.

134. John Cloud, "Why Milk Is Still Fresh," *Advocate,* November 10, 1998, 33.

135. Cleve Jones, "Support Milk Memorial Project," *Bay Area Reporter,* November 24, 2005. For an interesting corollary, see Josh Getlin's lament about the dimming memory of George Moscone on the 30th anniversary of the assassinations, and on the eve of *Milk's* premiere. "Remembering George Moscone," *Los Angeles Times,* November 23, 2008, http://www.latimes.com/news/opinion/la-oe-getlin23-2008nov23,0,1670616.story.

136. FitzGerald, "The Castro," 80.

137. George Chauncey, *Gay New York: Gender, Urban Culture, and the Making of the Gay Male World, 1890-1940* (New York: Basic Books, 1994), 283. See also Greg Vogel, "Gay Historians: Remembrance of Rich Heritage," *Advocate West,* July 23, 1986, 8.

138. Mark Leno, "Senate Bill No. 48," December 13, 2010, http://info.sen.ca.gov/pub/11-12/bill/sen/sb_0001-0050/sb_48_bill_20101213_introduced.pdf; Gerry Shih, "Clashes Pit Parents vs. Gay-Friendly Curriculums in Schools," *New York Times* March 4, 2011; and Susan Ferriss, "New Bill Requires Gay History in Textbooks to Fight Bullying, *The Sacramento Bee,* December 13, 2010, http://blogs.sacbee.com/capitolalertlatest/2010/12/sen-leno-hopes-gay-history-bil.html.

139. Karen O'Camb, "FAIR Education Act and Gender Nondiscrimination Act Pass Key California Legislative Committees," *LGBT/POV,*

April 6, 2011, http://lgbtpov.frontiersla.com/2011/04/06/fair-education-act-and-gender-nondiscrimination-act-pass-key-california-legislative-committees/; Jennifer Medina, "California May Require Teaching of Gay History," *New York Times*, April 15, 2011, http://www.nytimes.com/2011/04/16/us/16schools.html?_r=2&scp=3&sq=gay&st=cse; MatthewS. Bajko, "California Schools Already Teaching Gay History," *Bay Area Reporter*, April 21, 2011, http://www.ebar.com/news/article.php?sec=news&article=5645; Stacy Teicher Khadaroo, "Could California Lead Nation in Teaching of Gay History in Schools?" *Christian Science Monitor*, July 7, 2011, http://www.csmonitor.com/USA/Education/2011/0707/Could-California-lead-nation-in-teaching-of-gay-history-in-schools; and "California Governor Signs Fair Education Act, Requiring Schools to Add LGBT History to Curriculum," towleroad.com, July 14, 2011, http://www.towleroad.com/2011/07/breaking-california-governor-signs-fair-education-act-requiring-schools-to-add-lgbt-history-to-curri.html.

140. Huma Kahn, "Politics of Education: New Texas Social Sciences Curriculum Standards Fraught with Ideology, Critics Say," *ABC News*, May 21, 2010, http://abcnews.go.com/Politics/Media/education-texas-social-sciences-curriculum-standards-stirs-nationwide/story?id=10700720.

141. Lyanne Melendez, "Opponents Working to Repeal 'Fair Education Act,'" KGO-TV San Francisco, March 7, 2012, http://abclocal.go.com/kgo/story?section=news/education&id=8572972; and Seth Hemmelgarn, "Repeal Effort of California's FAIR Education Act Cleared for Signatures," *Bay Area Reporter*, February 24, 2012, http://www.lgbtqnation.com/2012/02/repeal-effort-of-californias-fair-education-act-cleared-for-signatures/.

142. Miranda Bryant, "Anti-Gay Bullies Are Taught a Lesson or Two," *The Evening Standard* (London), October 26, 2010, http://www.thisislondon.co.uk/standard/article-23891416-anti-gay-bullies-are-taught-a-lesson-or-two.do. On bullying, see C. J. Pascoe, *Dude You're a Fag: Masculinity and Sexuality in High School* (Berkeley, CA: University of California Press, 2007); Robin Kowalski, Susan Limber, and Patricia Agatston, *Cyber Bullying: Bullying in the Digital Age* (Oxford: Blackwell Publishing, 2008); Michelle Birkett, Dorothy Espelage, and Brian Koenig, "LGB and Questioning Students in Schools: The Moderating Effects of Homophobic Bullying and School Climate on Negative Outcomes," *Journal of Youth and Adolescence* 38 (2009): 989–1000; Stuart Biegel, *The Right to Be Out: Sexual Orientation and Gender Identity in America's Public Schools* (Minneapolis: University of Minnesota Press, 2010), Chapter 5; Rebecca Haskell and Brian Burtch, *Get That Freak: Homophobia and Transphobia in High Schools* (Black Point, Nova Scotia: Fernwod Publishing, 2010); *Bullied*, dir. Bill Brummel, 2010; *Bully*, dir. Lee Hirsch, 2012; and The Queering Education Research Institute, accessed June 1, 2012, http://www.queeringeducation.org/.

143. Rebecca Cathcart, "Boy's Killing, Labeled a Hate Crime, Stuns a Town," *New York Times*, February 23, 2008,http://www.nytimes.com/2008/02/23/us/23oxnard.html.

144. Dustin Lance Black, "Academy Award Acceptance Speech," February 22, 2009, http://www.glaad.org/2009/02/22/dustin-lance-blacks-moving-acceptance-speech/.

145. Amy Graff, "The Mommy Files: Is San Francisco's Castro Neighborhood Appropriate for Young Kids?" *SFGATE* (*San Francisco Chronicle*), June 5, 2011, http://www.sfgate.com/cgi-bin/blogs/sfmoms/detail?entry_id=86303; For similar efforts, see Bajko, "California Schools Already Teaching Gay History."

146. Brewster Ely, "Dear Town School Parents and Community," April 5, 2011, in Graff, "The Mommy Files" *SFGATE* (*San Francisco Chronicle*), http://www.sfgate.com/cgi-bin/blogs/sfmoms/detail?entry_id=86303.

147. Biegel, *The Right to Be Out,* 146. See also Stuart Biegel, "Teachable Moments," *The Advocate* (April 2011): 20–21; Therese Quinn and Erica R. Meiners, *Flaunt It! Queers Organizing for Public Education and Justice* (New York: Peter Lang, 2009); Nelson M. Rodriguez and William F. Pinar, eds., *Queering Straight Teachers: Discourse and Identity in Education* (New York: Peter Lang, 2007); Eric Rofes, *A Radical Rethinking of Sexuality and Schooling: Status Quo or Status Queer* (Lanham, MD: Rowman & Littlefield, 2005); and William F. Pinar, ed., *Queer Theory in Education* (Mahwah, NJ: Lawrence Erlbaum, 1998). For the lesson plans in GLBTQ history provided by GLSEN (Gay, Lesbian, and Straight Education Network), see http://www.glsen.org/cgi-bin/iowa/all/library/record/2461.html?state=tools&type=educator (accessed June 1, 2012).

148. James F. Mills, "Got Milk? Filmmaker Creates a Harvey Milk Documentary," *West Hollywood Patch,* June 13, 2012, http://westhollywood.patch.com/articles/got-milk-young-filmmaker-creates-a-harvey-milk-documentary.

149. Kevin K. Kumashiro, *Troubling Education: Queer Activism and Antioppressive Pedagogy* (New York: RoutledgeFalmer, 2002); and Kevin K. Kumashiro, *Against Common Sense: Teaching and Learning Toward Social Justice* (New York: RoutledgeFalmer, 2004).

150. Ely, "Dear Town School Parents and Community."

151. Stephen O. Murray, "Components of Gay Community in San Francisco," in *Gay Culture in America: Essays from the Field,* ed. Gilbert Herdt (Boston: Beacon Press, 1992), 115–116. See also Robert N. Bellah, Richard Madsen, William M. Sullivan, Ann Swidler, and Steven T. Tipton, *Habits of the Heart* (Berkeley: University of California Press, 1985), 153–154.

152. See José Esteban Muñoz, *Cruising Utopia: The Then and There of Queer Futurity* (New York: New York University Press, 2009).

153. Ramirez, "A Living Archive of Desire," 130.

PART ONE

Milk and the Culture of Populism

I

"Interview with Harvey Milk"

Kalendar, August 17, 1973

Harvey Milk's political career began in the summer of 1973 in a campaign for San Francisco Board of Supervisors, launched in a principled yet soon-to-become signature emotional outburst against systemic class bias and its material harms, increasing corporate power at the expense of hard-working ordinary people, and the abuses of Watergate. Milk was an unknown, unlikely candidate, a hippie Castro Street merchant without political connections or experience, whose passion and populist vision had to overcome knee-jerk negative reactions to his ponytail, his being openly gay, and his candor and outspokenness. But as everyone—friends and foes alike—would soon discover, Milk was a "natural" political performer and activist.

This interview fittingly was published in the San Francisco free gay paper, Kalendar, *given shortly after declaring on Castro Street his candidacy for Board of Supervisors, while standing upon that wooden box inscribed "soap." Milk's motives and mission as a "gay candidate" seeking a diverse constituency and wide-reaching transformative vision are here first articulated, a political platform that remained remarkably cohesive throughout his career. Milk's preoccupations included homophobic discrimination; gay rights and the means to achieve them; bureaucratic privilege, abuse, and obligation; the economy; victimless crime; answering the needs of ordinary citizens; and nurturing neighborhoods. We also get a glimpse of what would become Milk's unmistakable political demeanor. Here we experience Milk's strong and long-lasting first impression.*

. . .

"Freedom of speech and action is only tokenism in this country. Where there is repression there is violence that makes a mess of the world. It's force and repression," he said.

It was Saturday morning. I sat in a hill-top Castro apartment looking past a lavender-leaved Wandering Jew at the lazy skyline of San Francisco.

Assignment: Harvey Milk, outspoken gay candidate for Board of Supervisors. The Place: His apartment. I had met him a few minutes earlier in the camera shop he runs with his lover Scott. The shop was large with the air of an art studio in the beginning days. (The shop is, in fact only three months old).

Harvey was at the front desk grinning broadly at me as I came through the door.

First impression? A rush of invigorating air. Gemini. It figured.

He showed me photography displays on the walls, telling me he encouraged people to hang their best prints there as a kind of unofficial show of the week. The project obviously excited him.

I made quick physical appraisal of him as we talked and looked at the photographs. Long brown hair pulled back in a pony tail that hung half way down his back. Hazel eyes. Trim body . . . moving with a virile forcefulness.

After a few minutes, we left Scott in charge and walked up to the apartment.

He put some coffee to grind and we sat at the kitchen table talking.

"I'm forty-three," he said, "and I can do one of two things. I can concentrate on a lot of money while I enjoy perhaps another ten years of active gay life. Then after fifty-three I can just coast. Call the whole thing good. Afterall, I've had a lot of fun, fantastic experiences."

"Or I can get involved and do something about all the things I think are wrong in our society."

"I remember that not too long ago in New York in Central Park, gay people couldn't bathe out in the sun on the weekend with their shirts off without being busted by police."

"I'm forty-three, so I'm past that but Scott, my lover, is twenty-three and there's another generation coming up and somewhere someday somebody's got to say 'I'm going to fight, not only for myself, but to make it easier for the next group.'"

"I've got to fight. Not just for me but for my lover and his lover eventually, whoever it is. I've got to fight for them too."

"Homosexuals are still criminals; until that changes, we are not free. When Herb Caen in his famous comment about my running said, 'What do these people want?' it reminded me of a southern colonel in the war who asked a similar question concerning blacks."

"I want freedom for gay people. I don't want . . . laws or citations instead of jail terms. I don't want more bars or baths or newspapers. I want legal freedom to be who I am."

"If we take the criminal element off of us, the next generation can't be told we are criminals. They can accept us."

"Right now the parent says to the child, "homosexuals are good and bad, nothing to be upset about.""

"The kid says, 'Then why do you call them criminals?'"

"The parent says, 'well . . .'"

"The kid is left unanswered and we're still against the law."

It was clear to me that Harvey Milk was not afraid to speak his mind. "For years, like everybody else, I've been bitching," he says. "But what really pisses me off, really got me moving, was Watergate."

"Every day I'd end up screaming at the TV set: 'You lying mother fuckers.'"

"Also everyone is out to get the gay vote. Politicians are concerned. They want us. They want our votes. But it's just lip service so long as we remain criminals and nothing is done to change it."

"The Board of Supervisors says they can't do anything about it because it's state law, but they can cut the balls off the police department by cutting the budget. But they pass the police budget like Washington passes the Pentagon's. Without questioning."

"So I'm running. It's going to be a campaign. If other gay people think I'm wrong, let them run, too."

"I'm not representative politically of the whole gay community. There's no such thing as being representative of the gay community in that way. There's some gays who are John Birchers. Others are communist."

"But when the election's over, I'm not just another politician who promised to support gay freedom. I'm still gay and I have a lover I am sexual with."

"If there comes an oppression as there did in Germany for the Jews, it won't matter where we were different in our economic thinking."

"Hitler didn't care if the Jew was an ultra liberal or a conservative. He was Jewish and he went into a concentration camp."

"We're in bed together . . . by the fact that we're all homosexuals. If we don't understand that, we're in trouble."

"The ex-chief of police is running for the Board of Supervisors. If he gets elected, it's going to get more conservative. It's going to crack down more. They've already closed Broadway. Next month it may be the porno shops. After that . . ."

For the next hour we talked about a variety of controversial subjects including election of the Board of Supervisors by district, full time supervisors, lower taxes, the economy, religion, the theater and drugs.

His ideas came racing out at me as I sipped my coffee. I could feel the excitement in him, the intensity, the idealism he had to build a better world.

Supervisor, he feels, is something that should require a man's full time.

"If $9,000 a year is not enough for Ron Pelosi, I say, let him step down."

"All tax income should be invested," he declares, "so the interest coming in on it will lower our taxes."

The fact that the people who handled Watergate are building our economy is frightening to him. His experience as a security analyst in New York, Dallas and San Francisco he uses to evaluate the present situation.

"I know, for instance, oil companies can tell you to the gallon how many gallons of gasoline they are going to produce, refine and sell for the next three years. And all of the sudden the oil company says there is not enough oil. That's bullshit. It's because they wanted the Canadian/Alaskan pipeline built. They said if we don't have this built there's going to be a shortage of gasoline. So the legislation passed and now there's not going to be a shortage for the rest of the year. The public is spoon fed and the press doesn't do anything about it."

His religion is music, Mahler, Bruckner, Wagner and Strauss. He likes the Rolling Stones, too.

"I think Mahler and Bruckner are more religious than the pope," he says. During his early days on the stock market in New York City he became acquainted with Tom O'Horgan who was later famous as the director of HAIR on Broadway.

In those days O'Horgan was putting plays on in his loft. Harvey helped him produce an all male cast of MAZE there.

The friendship eventually resulted in Harvey leaving San Francisco and the stock market to help Tom O'Horgan in producing LENNY and JESUS CHRIST SUPER STAR.

But Harvey's heart was in San Francisco and he left the theater to return. He is appearing, however, in a bit part of a film version of Ionesco's RHINOCEROS to be released in January.

I dreaded my next question, being tired of it and all the answers I thought he might give, but feeling it was too important not to ask.

"What is your stance on drugs?" I asked.

He's never smoked marijuana, he says, even though he's lived with people off and on for over twenty years who have. He drinks a little wine now and then, but that's about it. And coffee.

What other people do, he feels, is their affair so long as they don't harm someone else with it.

"I'd like to know a little more about your past—who you've been," I said, relieved to change the subject.

He smiled and I knew he liked to talk about that, could see he felt good about what had happened to him.

"I was born on May 22, 1930," he said, "about 20 miles outside New York City on Long Island in a little fishing village."

"When I was twelve I found out that religion was phony or hypocritical. At fourteen I found out I was a homosexual."

"That almost brought me back into religion because I went to a rabbi and I told him."

"The rabbi said something to me that really stuck. He said you shouldn't be concerned about what people said to you about how you lived your life as long as you felt you were living it right. He said that people spend more time legislating about morality and telling people how to spend their lives than about how to make life more enjoyable. Most legislators want to be god. Since they can't be, they try to legislate other people. They only think they are god-like. That's wrong. But instead of being angry and upset about them, you should have rachmones for them—a Jewish word that means: 'Have sorrow and pity with love and compassion.'"

"That almost brought me back into religion, but I found out he was a rare bird."

"I left home at seventeen and never went back except for special occasions and therefore grew to love and respect my parents."

"Went to teacher's college upstate New York."

"Campaigned actively for Harry Truman even though I wasn't old enough to vote."

"The Korean War was going on at that time and it was then patriotic to fight for you country, so after college I joined the Navy."

"When I got out, I realized I couldn't be a teacher because if it was discovered that I was a homosexual it would be the end of that, even though I wanted to be a teacher."

"I knocked around the country four or five years—yo-yoed between California and Florida and New York. Worked in gay bars. Finally got to New York and settled down somewhat. Had a lover for five years."

"Got involved in the stock market. Spent eight years working as a research analyst for the stock market."

"During that time I had another love affair that lasted eight years."

"Then I met Tom O'Horgan . . ."

And the story goes on.

About the present situation and his campaign he said: "Maybe one day people will do it legally. Maybe they'll just accept us."

"Meanwhile I'm going out for the straight vote as well as the gay."

Harvey gave a wry smile.

"Some of my best friends are straight," he said.

The things that keep him going are the fact that he has a lover he loves, the music of Mahler and Bruckner, and the words of his rabbi to have rachmones for people, have sorrow and pity for them and love.

2

"Address to the San Francisco Chapter of the National Women's Political Caucus"

September 5, 1973

Harvey Milk's first campaign derived its energy and vision from a populism that embraced those effectively disenfranchised people without a representative voice in mainstream politics, those who suffered and struggled in a city of decaying neighborhoods and a system of inequity and injustice. Milk opposed the corporate, or "downtown," interests and their backers in the Chamber of Commerce and on the Board of Supervisors, challenging the very meanings and entailments of "development." In this city increasingly symbolized by high rises, Milk emerged as a grassroots Democratic politician mobilizing as his chief constituents the have-nots as electoral agents of change against this "mentality" of the privileged, what elsewhere he characterized as the "Marie Antoinette Syndrome," and advocating instead for a different configuration of urban infrastructure, dwelling, and community.

Milk's populist vision surely must have resonated with members of the San Francisco chapter of the National Women's Political Caucus who comprised his audience for this address. NWPC formed in 1971 with the purpose of recruiting and training feminist candidates for political office to achieve equal representation for women and to resist sexism, racism, poverty and their material consequences. Although many rightly have critiqued the gay rights movement of this era for its lack of inclusiveness of all GLBTQ people (for being gay-white-male-centric), and to a lesser degree Milk's own insensitivities to women generally and lesbians specifically during his career, this early document attests to the expansive reach of Milk's originary platform.

. . .

The reason that the economy is fouled up . . . The reason that there is so little meat in the supermarkets and that there is a gasoline shortage is that the same people . . . the same mentality, that handled all aspects of Watergate also handles all aspects of our economy. The reason that the City of San Francisco is becoming fouled-up is that the same people . . . the same mentality that is for spending money to tear down ugly freeways while there is a need for more child care centers; the same mentality that is for building convention halls instead of developing the poverty areas—this mentality is setting the priorities and tax rates for our City. This mentality votes against nudity; votes for the death penalty; votes to maintain a police budget, over 50 percent of which is wasted in attempting to contain victimless crimes while rape, burglary, and/or theft continue to increase. . . . This is the mentality that succumbed so readily to the political pressure applied by MUNI drivers and their union, in spite of warnings from top MUNI officials that service would decrease if the suggested fringe benefits were increased . . . Supervisors don't ride trolleys . . . so they went ahead and approved the fringe benefits.

A city . . . any city takes one of two basic approaches. It either looks at the immediate present and tries to get through (and through the next election); or it looks at the future and tries to set up a system that will take the city through that future. . . . The Founding Fathers did this with the Constitution. . . . There were things wrong with the original document . . . that is what the amendments have tried to correct. But (with a few great exceptions and I don't have to tell this particular audience what they are) it works. For it is long range in its thinking. A city can concern itself about the clogged sewers of today and worry about tomorrow when tomorrow and tomorrow's problems come; or it can prepare itself for tomorrow. . . . This city and its present leadership is too concerned with today, with too little thought of tomorrow . . . that mentality must stop. . . . We must not only do something about today's problems, but we must also put effort, energy, and money into tomorrow's city. For we all will die someday and there will be another generation to take our places, and we do not have the right to lay our mistakes at their feet.

3

"Address to the Joint International Longshoremen & Warehousemen's Union of San Francisco and to the Lafayette Club"

September 30, 1973

If the best-remembered Hope Speech, or more precisely its peroration, has become Harvey Milk's rhetorical signature, his mantra, then this address should be rightfully recalled as his manifesto. This passionate critique of the status quo and blueprint for economic justice, civil rights, public health—in a word, community—underwrote every argument, every position, every campaign that would comprise Milk's political career and corpus. The interdependency, mutuality, and equality of Milk's city on a hill—indeed, this speech constitutes a remarkable queering of that familiar trope, marking a predominantly conservative rhetorical legacy from John Winthrop through Ronald Reagan to the present day in the United States—provided the foundation on which hope for GLBTQ people, for women, for people of color, for seniors, for poverty-stricken children, for all, was built. Its fundamental premise, its most eloquent articulation—"It takes no compromising to give the people their rights. It takes no money to respect the individual. It takes no political deal to give people freedom. It takes no survey to remove repression"—should reside in the pantheon of oratorical landmark refrains in U.S. history.

In thinking about the audiences for this address, and its thrust, other aphorisms also come to mind, such as Oscar Wilde's quip "Morality is simply the attitude we adopt toward people whom we personally dislike." Milk believed such attitudes might be changed, perhaps especially if you could look a voter in the eye, shake hands, or address a crowd.

Although Milk's coalition politics with Teamsters in the Coors Boycott of 1974 and after has been emphasized by historians and filmmakers, he sought to forge solidarity with the working class and labor activists from the very beginning. Likewise he appealed to other constituencies perhaps thought politically unreachable, such as members of ethnic gentlemen's clubs. An openly gay candidate might reasonably bypass such seemingly incommensurate if not hostile audiences, especially when delivering a rally cry against legislating morality (and its underlying bigotry). However, Milk was as fearless as he was unabashed—and he was a true believer in the promise of that beacon called San Francisco.

. . .

A city, any city can take one of several approaches to the future; whichever approach it takes not only affects the citizens of today but also greatly affects the children of tomorrow—the citizens of tomorrow.

San Francisco, like any other major city, has that choice, and before we get too far down any route we must be sure that it is the route we really want to travel. The present leadership seems to have taken the money route: bigness and wealth. They would like to be remembered as making San Francisco a major money center: a big bank book. The trouble with this approach is that there is no way whatsoever that this city can ever gain anywhere near the wealth that the New Yorks, the Chicagos have. No matter how much we try we will always be somewhere down on the list. If someone ever wants to add up the bank accounts of our cities New York is always going to come out on top.

Or, our city could take the route of becoming the seat of learning. But, there is no way it will be able to surpass the Bostons . . . there are just too many great universities throughout the land. We can never become *the* seat of learning.

Then there is the route that for some reason or other no major city has ever tried. That is the route that has little room for political payoffs, deals . . . that is the route that leaves little in the way of power politics . . . that is the route of making a city and exciting place for *all* to live: not just an exciting place for a few to live! A place for the individual and individual rights. There is no political gain in this nonmoneyed route, and thus you do not find people with high political ambitions leading this way. There are no statistics to quote . . . no miles of highway built to brag about, no statistics of giant buildings built under your administration. What you have instead is a city that breathes, one that is alive and where the people are more important than highways.

How does this route stand with our present leadership? They are more impressed with statistics than with life. I want a city that is not trying to become a great bankbook.

San Francisco can start right now to become number one. We can set examples so that others will follow. We can start overnight. We don't have to wait for budgets to be passed, surveys to be made, political wheelings and dealings . . . for it takes no money . . . It takes no compromising to give the people their rights. It takes no money to respect the individual. It takes no political deal to give people freedom. It takes no survey to remove repression.

We can start immediately by rereading the Constitution of the United States. We can start immediately by no longer trying to legislate morality. The Constitution calls for the separation of church and the state . . . and, yet we find that our legislatures end up spending millions of dollars and years of their lives trying legislating morality . . . that money, that time, that energy should be spent in making the city a place for all people. When our Supervisors are more concerned about tearing down a freeway than dental care for the elderly or child care centers; when our Supervisors are more concerned about MUNI drivers' benefits and not the least bit concerned about improving service for the riders; when our Supervisors are more concerned about building a multi-million dollar tourist and convention center instead of putting that money into an "Operation Bootstrap" to teach the unemployed of San Francisco skills so that there will not be the need to rely on the tourist for jobs; when our Supervisors realize that the best way to attract visitors is not through convention centers but through giving the people of San Francisco real job opportunity so that we can beat poverty; when such a consciousness takes place, when such a human sense of priorities gains hold, it will indeed be number one.

We can start immediately by giving the people of San Francisco and not the people who live in Marin first priorities. . . . we can start immediately be giving the people who live here and not the tourists first priorities. When we hire someone from outside the city to work for the city that person takes our tax money and spends it in Marin . . . he cannot be loyal towards the city for he does not live here. The rent he pays, the food he buys, the products for his home . . . all that is purchased with San Francisco tax money from business outside the city. He does not understand the problems of the city . . . how could he? . . . he does not live here at nighttime. To make the city a better place . . . to lower the city's unemployment rate, all city employees must be residents of the city. The policeman who works in the city during the day is not involved in the city's nighttime problems. Right now San Francisco has seen an increase in police force, an increase in police budget, an increase in stolen cars, an increase in burglary and a decrease in our population! Why? Two reasons: 1. many police do not live in the city . . . I never want to hear what I heard last week . . . a police officer in the downtown sector made this comment to me: "I wouldn't live in this city if you paid me!" . . . We do pay him! The second reason is that half of the police budget and effort is wasted on trying to enforce victimless crime laws . . . *that is trying to bring back Prohibition! All prohibition did was to create the greatest crime waves and syndicates the country has ever had . . . and it created a lot of murder.* AND ALL IN THE NAME OF MORALITY!! Can't we learn? It was the moralist of the '20s that created Crime Inc., and now the same moralistic types are once again, in their blindness to force their morality on others, creating organized crime . . . can they not learn? Do they ever read history? Because of the failure of their family, of their church they are attempting to make the police force into ministers while crimes against victims increases . . . this false morality is against the Constitution. If they do not like the Constitution let them amend it. Let them scrap the Declaration of Independence and in the meantime let them go back to God with their morality and become ministers . . . true ministers. *Instead of spending time trying to get the death penalty passed let them reread the Ten Commandments.* Let them teach the Commandment: Thou Shall Not Kill. I know of no Commandment that says: Thou Shall Not Smoke Marijuana. I know of no Commandment that says: Thou Shall Not Read Dirty Books. I know of no Commandment that says: Thou Shall Not Walk Around Naked. Why are they such moralists when it comes to man-made Commandments and such anti-moralists when it comes to God's Commandments?

Let me have my tax money go for my protection and not for my prosecution. Let my tax money go for the protection of me. Protect my home, protect my streets, protect my car, protect my life, protect my property. Let my minister worry about me playing bar dice. Let my minister and not some policeman worry about my moral life. Worry about gun control and not marijuana control . . . worry about dental care for the elderly and not about hookers . . . worry about child care centers and not what books I want to read . . . worry about becoming a human being and not about how you can prevent others from enjoying their lives because of your own inabilities to adjust to life.

4

"An Open Letter to the Mayor of San Francisco"

Public letter, September 22, 1973

Were the power of public discourse alone sufficient to win elections, then Harvey Milk would have triumphed in his first bid for Board of Supervisors. However, most San Franciscans, including a large number within his own GLBTQ community, ignored or wrote off or deliberately opposed Milk's candidacy. Thus it was Milk's challenge not only to argue for his populist vision, but to argue for a platform itself, to use rhetorical artistry in order to attract audiences, to register and circulate in the minds of voters. Getting heard, Milk instinctively knew and better understood in 1973, was more complicated than slapping "soap" on the side of a box in the Castro and delivering a speech.

But Milk's political talent made him a quick study in the arts of publicity: putting Mayor Joseph Alioto on the spot, for instance, rather melodramatically, regarding fundamental democratic principles and electioneering. The irony of beseeching Mayor Alioto surely was not lost on Milk. Alioto, a socially conservative Italian-Catholic Democrat, had, during his mayoralty, vetoed legislation that would have legalized private sexual activity between consenting adults. He also had been responsible for the homophobic police crackdown on public sex in recent years that had resulted in arrests of thousands of gay men, causing the ruination and death of many. When Milk decried government's moral intrusions, Alioto might well have been his poster boy; he thought of him in the most derogatory terms, namely Nixonian. Alioto was a "machine" political official, a great champion of downtown corporate and tourist industry development, which Milk diametrically opposed. Just days before, in bitter denunciation of the proposed Yerba Buena Center, Milk called for a "DECLARARTION OF WAR to rid the city of pockets of poverty and crime and to give the people a real chance to learn skills and trades that would make them self-sufficient, which in turn would reduce the unemployment rate, lower the crime rate, and thus bring about a lowering of the cost of government. This, indeed, would be a very real reason to bring tourists to our city." A year later Milk, in his "Waves from the Left" column in the Sentinel, *would impugn the mayor, who had hired a "Director of Information" at a salary of $25,000 while "unemployment rolls remain high," of harboring "CONTEPMT for San Franciscans." During the police strike of 1975, Milk filed an unsuccessful class-action lawsuit in U.S. District Court against Alioto and SFPD officials for endangering the lives of the city's citizens by not providing for their protection.*

. . .

Dear Mr. Mayor,

The San Francisco Council of Democratic Clubs suspended democracy at their convention on September 21st. Their blatant disrespect for their own stated policy on speaking order was just rudeness . . . what makes me angry is *their* democratic system of voting. They "conveniently" encouraged their delegates to cast their votes early in the evening; before any of their "unfavorite" candidates were allowed to speak. At any convention I have ever attended, the delegates may have already made up their minds before they arrive, but they always listen to all speakers before they cast their ballots. Not so with these people. They invite you to speak . . . give you five minutes to declare your positions, presumably in order to make some kind of judgment. (The incumbents have had four years to make their comments.) Yet, they have this blatant disrespect for democracy by asking people to vote before any of the challengers are allowed to speak.

Contrary to the very principles of Democracy upon which these organizations are formed to support, the vote was being called for. Evidently, they care about democracy as much as John Mitchell cares about Justice! Why is it even necessary to have candidates come to speak before them, if they are going to treat candidates with this mockery they call "democracy"? And, I, as a life-long Democrat, had to wonder as I watched democracy grinding to a halt.

The San Francisco Black leadership Forum, The Chinese-American Citizens Alliance, and San Francisco Tomorrow are all out of the same mold . . . a few people controlling the representation of the many for their own power plays. They embarrass me. They make me ashamed to call myself a Democrat. They turn the very word, democracy, into a sham, a hoax, a lie.

Mr. Mayor, at a time when this nation so desperately needs honesty, it is sad to see the people of our city languishing in a sea of unfairness, especially from the hands of those who themselves call out for equal treatment. You seek to lead . . . (it is said you want to be Governor) . . . I ask you, in all seriousness: Will you walk with these clubs, clubs which are a mirror of back-room political prostitutes, clubs which use the name of democracy for their own corruption, or will you walk with the people?

5

"MUNI/Parking Garage"

Press release, September 27, 1973

The San Francisco Municipal Railway, known as MUNI, was, during Milk's residency in the city, the agency in charge of multimodal transit services. The "Transit-First Policy," passed by the City Planning Commission and Board of Supervisors in this same year of Milk's first campaign, aimed to prioritize investment in public transportation as part of the city's development. Such a policy would have fit well with Milk's drive to achieve paramount quality of life for all San Franciscans. However, word and deed are not always aligned, as apparently had been the case with this policy for decades. Milk fought to ensure that the experience, and thus loyalty of MUNI passengers, would be valued, and their justified complaints addressed. If those bureaucrats and politicians were to make decisions that affected the lives of city residents to live among them rather than in the suburbs, and commute with them on MUNI rather than gridlocking the city by driving to work and parking in those multiplying downtown garages, then all their lives might improve. Here MUNI constitutes another component in Milk's grassroots configuration of the stakes for San Francisco's future. In addition to this press release, Milk publicized the MUNI issue by collaboratively staging one of many public rallies, street performance that would become a staple of his rhetorical repertoire.

Milk himself walked the walk, or rode the rails as it were, of this policy position, most notably during his commute to City Hall in 1978.

On October 28, 2008, according to the Web site of the San Francisco Municipal Transportation Agency (SFMTA), streetcar No. 1051 was dedicated to "the memory of human rights pioneer and transit advocate Supervisor Harvey Milk. Supervisor Milk was the first San Francisco Supervisor to regularly use a Fast Pass."

. . .

HARVEY MILK, Candidate for Supervisor, will continue to take his campaign to the people, holding the first of many planned street rallies *Friday at 5:30, at CASTRO & 18ᵀᴴ STREETS.*

Candidate MILK will attack the present MUNI service and will call *for a CHAPTER AMENDMENT requiring the mayor, all MUNI inspectors, and especially all 11 Supervisors to ride MUNI every day to and from City Hall.* At rally time, petitions will be initiated seeking the enactment of such an amendment. MILK feels that this seems to be the only way that the people of San Francisco will ever get better service from the present supervisors.

Candidate MILK will further state that the recent voting record of the present Supervisors has been for the creation of even more garages in the downtown area. MILK contends that this will increase the number of cars entering the core area thus competing with MUNI for space on the already congested streets. *This leaves little doubt in this candidate's mind as to where the present Supervisors have placed their loyalty: The garage owners once again triumph over the MUNI rider.*

Harvey Milk for Supervisor Headquarters: 575 Castro Street/ 864-1390

6

"Alfred Seniora"

Press release, September 28, 1973

Harvey Milk likely concurred with William Shakespeare and Charles Dudley Warner's familiar notion that "misery and politics make for strange bedfellows." Angered by the common practice in some San Francisco political clubs of voting for endorsements before all the candidates, especially minor candidates, had had their opportunity to speak, Milk sought to outfox his enemies; score a little retribution; and, most of all, get his platform heard by aligning, if only for purposes of the press spectacle, with a similarly "silenced" Republican counterpart, Alfred Seniora. As Milk dramatized in this and another press release, ideological differences can be put aside momentarily for the sake of fairness and justice in democratic process. Mr. Seniora proved to be not only an ironic juxtaposition and useful "straight man" in Milk's political theater, but something of a brief political boon when he "borrowed" and publicly espoused and circulated the "gay candidate's" campaign materials, and positions, as his own. Amid muddy criticism throughout the campaign that he wasn't serious, or was too gay, or was not gay enough, Milk must have felt somewhat vindicated by Mr. Seniora's rhetorical theft. Either way, his clever exposé evidenced the resonance of his candidacy, even for a neophyte with liabilities canvassing uphill in blustery political winds.

. . .

One of the great compliments of the current Supervisorial campaign was paid this week to HARVEY MILK by another candidate. ALFRED SENIORA printed, in the Wednesday issue of the SAN FRANCISCO PROGRESS, a 2/3 page advertisement using as copy, almost verbatim, a letter that MILK sent to the Mayor on Monday and then signed his (SENIORA'S) name to that letter . . . *He further paid the additional and more important compliment to MILK by also printing in the ad most of MILK'S platform positions in the form of a "box score" flyer which MILK created and has been using for almost two weeks.*

The fact that MILK, a Jewish Democrat, now has his platform being used, almost intact, by a Republican, buries the issue of MILK'S homosexuality. For if this conservative Republican is willing to put his name on almost the same letter that MILK mailed to the Mayor and also put his name on MILK'S platform, *then the Republican must feel that the issues are indeed far more important and that the need for a new direction in our leadership is far more important than MILK'S homosexuality.*

MILK feels that, even as a non-monied candidate, *if he has already made this kind of bridge in ideologies, that he does in fact, offer the people of San Francisco a strong leadership that will bring together people of different backgrounds and life styles.*

HARVEY MILK FOR SUPERVISOR HEADQUARTERS: 575 CASTRO ST. / 864-1390

7

"Who Really Represents You"

Campaign flyer, September 1973

Milk's impressive if unsuccessful performance in his first campaign for supervisor, garnering 16,900 votes and finishing tenth in a citywide field of thirty-two candidates (had Milk's desired implementation of district elections occurred, he would have emerged victorious; Proposition K failed by a two to one margin) must be attributable in some significant sense to his tireless canvassing of the city. Well beyond the more familiar environs of his Castro neighborhood, on sidewalks and buses, in shopping centers and throughout the financial district, Milk sought out the electorate in an embodied way, to look a voter in the eye, to have a conversation, to debate an issue, to make an impression that might belie homophobic abstraction and perform his populism. Such hand shaking, stumping, and photo opportunism are, of course, the standard currency of political exchange in a campaign season. However, insofar as Milk's person and platform veered from such straight and narrow paths, by temperament and necessity, his polling of voters appeared to take a different cast; his interest in "your view," solicited directly and in campaign fliers such as this one, was meant to be constitutive of voter agency and his own voice as a legislator. Milk castigated incumbent Supervisors, all victorious, for election-year lip service to peoples' concerns, only to baldly contradict them in subsequent votes, as their records evidenced. He saw himself enacting, as he told the Advocate, "Jeffersonian democracy as stated by Lincoln: Of the people, by the people, for the people, and not a Nixonian philosophy that stands for a government of the few, by the few, and for the few."

. . .

CHECK WHERE YOU STAND . . . WHICH ISSUES ARE MORE IMPORTANT TO YOU?
WHO COMES CLOSER TO YOUR OVERALL STAND?

The Issues . . .	Harvey Milk	Your View	Present Supervisors
SUPERVISORS BY DISTRICTS	FOR		AGAINST
CRIME & POLICE	To cut crime we MUST attack the drug problem and rehabilitate the people in jails . . . We MUST put all the police force in uniform and most of them on the streets at night . . . All police MUST live in the city!		More money for police, without questioning the usage.
YERBA BUENA	Strongly against the present method of financing . . . Wrong sense of priority for public funds to be spent on . . . Alternative should be on "OPERATION BOOTSTRAP" to help San Franciscans.		FOR
MUNI & TRAFFIC	Free service . . . More and better MUNI . . . Banning all autos in downtown area . . . create a rapid shuttle system in the downtown area.		Build more garages downtown.
CITY EMPLOYEES	ALL without exception must live in the city!		Present System.
PERFORMING ARTS CENTER	Neighborhood arts centers must be first!		Build another downtown center.
VICTIMLESS CRIME LAWS	Repeal all such laws!		Citations for arrests.
CHILD CARE CENTERS	FOR		No comment.

(continued)

The Issues . . .	Harvey Milk	Your View	Present Supervisors
"RESPONSIVENESS"	Regular scheduled district Town Hall meetings.		They already consider themselves fully responsive.
PLANS FOR THE FUTURE	Less dependence on tourism as a means of city income.		More dependence on tourism.

Who really represents YOU?

Why MILK? Why NOT!

. . . Owner of a camera store on Castro Street.
. . . 8 years as a stock market analyst for major firms.
. . . Asst. to producer and director of several plays and musicals on New York's Broadway.

AT LAST YOU HAVE A
CANDIDATE FOR SUPERVISOR!

1. I understand that Harvey Milk needs financial help. . . . . .

    I am sending a check for $1.00
$5.00 $10.00

2. I will wear a Harvey Milk button.
3. I will put up a Harvey Milk campaign sign . . . I'll make my own!
4. I understand the Harvey Milk needs campaign workers . . . I'll help!
MAIL TO:

HARVEY MILK FOR SUPERVISOR
CAMPAIGN HEADQUARTERS
575 CASTRO STREET
S. F., CA 94114

OR BETTER YET, STOP BY!!!

8

"Milk Note"

Column, *Vector*, February 1, 1974

A month before his defeat in the fall of 1973, Milk reasserted in the pages of the Advocate *his vision of a gay candidacy and its significance. "To see and hear a gay legislator argue for people and individual rights changes the images overnight and brings respect to all Gays." From his perspective, those gay establishment politicos in the Alice B. Toklas Memorial Democratic Club and elsewhere who aggressively worked to thwart his campaign—those who in this editorial for SIR, of which Milk was a member and served on its publicity committee, he would memorably dub "Aunt Marys," that is, sell-outs or traitors in toady-ing complicity with oppressive power—errantly believed that patient and loyal electoral support of heterosexual liberals would better the lives of GLBTQ people. After all, candidates and the media during the campaign recognized the influential presence of the "Gay Vote," and a number of politicians courted it by attending events hosted by Toklas, touring gay bars, and commenting on gay issues.*

In this case, according to this political logic, Dianne Feinstein, whose vote total returned her to the Board presidency and who acknowledged GLBTQ contributors as her largest, would be relied upon as an ally to appoint liberals to key Board committees with the power to advance gay rights in material ways. By contrast, Milk saw in straight politi-cians only empty pledges, forgotten promises and half measures, mere "crumbs" for the price of votes, donations, and dignity. Echoing the Civil Rights Movement, as he often did, Milk rejected gradualism for the immediatism of freedom, achievable if only his community would empower itself by coming out and coming together to elect their own, to use its voting bloc and economic might as political influence, and to forge deeper solidarity with each other and in coalitions with other groups. In response to San Francisco Chronicle *columnist Herb Caen's sardonic question, "What do these people WANT?" Milk exclaimed, "I want freedom for gay people. . . . I reach out to my gay brothers and sisters. I reach out so we can grab each other's hand and fight for what God and the Constitution has given us and man has taken away from us."*

That Milk's vision would remain consistent into 1974, through the postmortem of his first campaign (he was already planning his run in 1975), indeed throughout the remainder of his political career and life, tells us much about his fortitude and optimism, his determination and drive, his unshakeable belief in GLBTQ freedom that would yet come.

. . .

January 9 marks the anniversary of the birth of Richard Nixon. January 15 marks the anniversary of the birth of Martin Luther King, Jr. One man has divided a nation—he lives. One man united a people—he was killed for that! The irony.

Dr. King was much criticized for "moving too fast." His answer to that was total dissatisfaction with the "halting and inadequate attempts of (this) society to catch up with the basic rights of membership in the human family . . . (that black people were) no longer tolerant of or interested in compromise."

He saw that the only way the blacks were to gain/win their rights as citizens was to seek not mere survival but full success . . . full citizenship. The implication was broad . . . with the incorporation of blacks into national life, not only were blacks free to offer their full creative contribution to society, but the whites were challenged to reconsider the roles by which they lived. He was uniting the blacks to wield the strength of their numbers in evident blocs of consumers, audiences and votes!

The longest and most deeply suppressed of all groups refuses to learn from history. In order for homosexuals to win our right to self respect and equality, we must first assert our full existence and then its strength. One of the major differences between homosexuals and other suppressed groups is identification . . . the blacks cannot hide. . . . the homosexual can melt into society. Open avowal of homosexuality is necessary for gays in every walk of life, most significantly of homosexuals in respected and necessary positions. Most homosexuals live in constant fear of discovery . . . the only way to combat this form of oppression is to seek success . . . to join with all other homosexuals and to identify oneself as oppressed . . . the open homosexual opts for full citizenship!

The black was never to gain freedom while he was lead by "Uncle Toms." The homosexual will never gain freedom while he is lead by "Aunt Marys." These are the people who, for whatever personal reasons, tell us that "we never had it so good" and brag about the "crumbs" thrown to homosexuals. They talk about these "crumbs" as if they were the Bill of Rights. They disregard the fact that oppression, real oppression, remains rampant and we remain "criminals" under the law. They brag about the "crumbs" given to homosexuals when the issue is FREEDOM. As soon as the gay community gets rid of the Aunt Marys and puts together their strength in blocs of consumers and votes, as Martin Luther King was doing with the blacks, we will remain oppressed and used.

But the gay community remains ineffective because of the Aunt Marys and those who remain hidden in their closet and opt to win their rights as citizens by living in constant fear of discovery. The blacks because of their color had no choice . . . remain oppressed or band together so that they ALL could win respectability. The gay community remains oppressed! The Aunt Marys and "those who never had it so good" keep it that way. The answer is for those who *really* want to win respectability, not only for themselves but for *all* homosexuals, to fight much harder. To use their influence to combat not only straight oppression but the sell-out by so many gay "leaders." Someday, somewhere a gay consciousness will take hold and true "gay power" will emerge . . . it will take time, it will bring inconveniences, it will bring bitterness, it will bring hardships, it will bring FREEDOM.

9

"Anyone Can Be a Movie Critic:
How Not to Find Leadership"

Editorial, *San Francisco Crusader*,
February 1974

Harvey Milk was far from a political dove toting an olive branch in the wake of a deluge of gay establishment animus that surely cost him votes in 1973. After all, the title of a commentary by radical gay rights activist and publisher Ray Broshears, in the previous issue of the San Francisco Gay Crusader, *suggests reason enough for retributive motive: "Why Milk Lost: Our 'Milk' Wasn't Delivered on Election Day . . . Some Gay Blades Cut the Cartons Open!" Milk and Toklas leader Jim Foster would remain political enemies throughout his career; in his tape-recorded political will, played after his assassination, Milk delivered a posthumous come-uppance by smiting Foster as a potential successor with the damning judgment, "The Jim Fosters never understood the movement." Harvey, like any politician, certainly knew how to get even.*

However, because Milk did understand the movement, he managed time and again to accommodate political ill will and opposition, especially among his own people, keeping his eye on the prize. As he recounted in an interview the same month that this editorial in the Gay Crusader *appeared, "About a month ago a respectable middle-aged man told me, 'I voted for you but I hate your guts.' He is a businessman who conceals his homosexuality. I made him think about that. He wants to help me if I run again. . . . when some young kid comes up to me and says, 'Thank You,' that is the most important thing." For Milk, who had already begun to look forward to the next campaign the following year, leadership required that one overcome the slights and carping and get on with the business of political transformation. As this editorial argues—and similar appeals appeared prominently in his* Sentinel *and* Bay Area Reporter *columns during 1974—debilitating jealousy, bitterness, and hate, focusing on others' shortcomings, and undermining the efforts within the GLBTQ community, would only enable those homophobic forces that oppressed them. Turning toward rather than turning on each other, achieved through able leadership, was the key to this or any movement: "If all that negative energy was united and turned into a positive force there would indeed be heard a cry that would lead to freedom."*

Surely this idea of opposing the "real enemy," to use his phrase, and not one another, must have been on Milk's mind as he picketed the film Laughing Policeman, *starring Walter Matthau, for its homophobic representation of gay male villainy, a protest action organized by the Gay Activists Alliance—the impetus for this editorial.*

. . .

One hundred people seeing the same movie can come out with one hundred different views. If those one hundred people are negative people there will be one hundred negative comments on that film. If they are positive people there will be one hundred positive comments on that film. For every film ever made has good points and bad points. The negative mind will search out and find the faults. The positive mind will search out and find the good points. That makes the film neither good nor bad. It only makes the film good or bad to each viewer based upon his or her own reference towards life in general. Those who search for the bad point, the fault, the error, the mistake, will never let anything sway them from emphasizing what is wrong. The opposite is also true. People are generally either positive or negative and when we hear their comments we usually take that into consideration and automatically discount some of their comment.

Yet, when a person talks about a "leader" we somehow do not discount the frame of mind of the "viewer." And a person/leader is a lot more apt to make mistakes than any movie . . . for no one has the chance to edit over and over his actions and speeches the way a film is edited before it is released. We somehow expect a human being to be more perfect than a film. We allow a play to have weeks of out-of-town showings before it moves to the big city, yet we hang on every word and action of our leaders and allow them no margin for human error, for correction. When a person comments upon a leader, we never say to ourselves, "That person is a negative force and will naturally find the mistakes of the leader and harp on it." Nor do we say that the person is a positive person and will look only at the good a leader does and overlook all faults. One reason why so many people in this nation today accept Nixon as a good president is that they are people who will only search for the good that he has done and overlook all his faults.

What must be done is to look at both the good and the wrong a person does and weigh it out. For them, there are no "perfect" leaders . . . no Christs . . . no Gods leading us today. We must find for ourselves what we want and who represents us "best" and not try to find out who represents us "totally." For in the end, the only person who fully and completely represents us is ourselves. If we expect to find one other person who is exactly like ourselves, we are in for trouble. We are in for 1984!

When we find this and that wrong with anyone who could lead us where we want to go, the final result is that we end up in the wrong place, for we drive away many potential leaders by asking them to become all things to all people. How can one person represent all views at the same time? And yet we chastise the leader for not being exactly like us. In a small community there can be a true "town hall meeting," but in a city, a state, a nation it is impossible . . . and we seek the impossible. Maybe the church is to blame for telling us that only GOD can lead us and then putting mortals in positions of leadership.

For whatever the reasons may be, there always seems to be more infighting, bitching and rottenness among gay brothers and sisters than among our straight neighbors. Maybe the rejection of homosexuals by the straight world causes homosexuals to try to be superior to other suppressed people . . . and thus comes the rejection of homosexuals by homosexuals. The snobbery, the attitudes, the comments made by gays about other gays is not to be found in any other suppressed group. The jealousy, the enviousness that gays have for other gays is incredible. It is all negative force. It is the tearing down rather than the building up. This gay "leader" is jealous of what that gay "leader" is doing, and he in turn is bitchy toward others. Rather than for all to lead and encourage others to lead so that we all can win what we want, we spend more time and effort in fighting each other than in fighting the forces of oppression. If all that negative energy was united and turned into a positive force there would indeed be heard a cry that would lead to freedom.

The first step towards this must be at the very least a cessation of bitterness towards leaders and groups that have differences from each other. Picture every straight club, church, society and organization spending most of their time fighting and bitching [at] each other. There is indeed always room for different views . . . different thoughts . . . different opinions. No one person, no one group, is wrong. The idea is for all to be able to express their own views . . . to do what they feel must be done . . . for there is only one way to go, and that is to gain freedom. Any energy spent looking for the negative in another person or group is energy wasted from gaining freedom for all homosexuals. It is easy to hate. It is easy to bitch. It is easy to find fault. It is hard to find the strength to love.

Leadership is needed. Joint leadership is needed. Many leaders are needed. Bitching is not needed. Jealousy is not needed. Hate is not needed. We are still a long way from freedom. Until we get freedom there is no room for self-destruction. The goal is freedom. Anyone who fights for that is needed; no matter how he fights, just as long as he fights the suppression! If he is so busy fighting other homosexuals, then HE is keeping us from attaining freedom just as much as the straight oppressor is.

A new era must take place. If joining of arms unfortunately cannot yet be achieved, then at least the stopping of self-destruction must take place. The greatest weapon, the greatest tool that our straight oppressor has to keep us oppressed is the incredible energy spent by homosexuals tearing each other apart. Some one leader, some one group must start by turning the other cheek and finding the strength of love rather than the need of hate.

10

"Letter to the City of San Francisco Hall of Justice on Police Brutality"

Public letter, February 14, 1974

Homophobic discrimination and violence by the police department, of-
ten fostered by malignant political aspirations, are as old as the history
of GLBTQ San Francisco itself, recurrent and predictable as the ebb
and flow of tides. It is also the case that such state-sanctioned bullying
and bashing in the city spurred some of the earliest developments in
GLBTQ activism and movement anywhere in the United States, from
the political nascence of Jose Sarria to the founding of the League for
Civil Education, Society for Individual Rights, Council on Religion and
the Homosexual, and the National Transsexual Counseling Unit.

Recent years had been noticeably turbulent, owing to GLBTQ
migration into Most Holy Redeemer Parish, as well as Mayor Alioto's
self-aggrandizement by means of catering to the homophobic bigotry of
the Catholic Church. The year 1974 was particularly bad, with its rash
of raids and trumped-up charges for public sex and drunkenness, drug
possession, blocking sidewalks, and then, after the beatings, resisting
arrest. The harassment crested with a bloody clash between a crowd
of gay men and police (with their badges deliberately and cravenly ob-
scured) outside Toad Hall bar during Labor Day weekend. Those who
would be dubbed the "Castro 14" defied their indictments, and Milk's
public efforts at raising a defense fund and organizing outraged com-
munity response, through his Sentinel *and* Bay Area Reporter *columns*
and personal conversations, forged more deeply his commitment and
status as a gay and neighborhood activist. His rally cry, "I pay taxes for

police to protect me, not persecute me," amplified his now frequent call for GLBTQ Political Power. In this open letter from earlier in the year, Milk deployed the Holocaust trope—used by the previous generation of GLBTQ activists and which would become one of his own favored rhetorical frames in future fights with Anita Bryant and John Briggs—to dramatize homophobic police brutality and seek solidarity with those heterosexuals who might also become victims of licensed governmental assault.

. . .

There are those in our community who claim that police brutality does not exist . . . that police harassment of gays does not exist . . . and I ask why? Why in the face of facts do they maintain that posture? The answer is that they do not want to know that it exists because once they accept its existence they then have to condone or commend police brutality! And, since they want neither to come out in favor of it nor to attack the establishment, they have to become the ostrich and stick their heads into the dirt—and see no evil. That is exactly what happened in Nazi Germany in the '30s. The German people did not see what was happening to the Jews, for, if they admitted that it was happening, then they would have had to take sides. So, the Germans did not know for they did not want to know. Unfortunately, after Hitler eliminated the Jews, he then eliminated the gypsies, then the Catholics, and then one group after another until he had turned the entire nation into a police state where the children were turning their parents in for just talking about the establishment. It had gotten out of hand, those people who would not acknowledge police brutality against the Jews found that they themselves ended up on the list because once the cancer festered, it spread. There were not privileged people or classes. The same can happen in this nation. If police brutality against homosexuals is allowed to take place it will spread to other groups until a police state exists . . . no one will be spared. In Nazi Germany many people said that police brutality was just against the Jews who were undesirable anyway . . . in San Francisco many people say that the police brutality is only against the homosexuals who are undesirables anyway. In Germany after the Jews were beaten brutality became unchecked and group after group fell victim to its force. Once we allow the police force to release hostility against homosexuals by violence then it will soon spread to other people . . . the police state will be evolving . . . the Nixonian philosophy as expressed by the corrupt former Attorney

General Mitchell will take hold. We must learn from history . . . the Germans who hated Jews and allowed the Jews to be beaten should have fought for Jewish freedom. For in fighting for the Jews they would have in reality been fighting for their own freedom! When they did not, they gave up their own freedom! The people of San Francisco who hate homosexuals must fight with the homosexual against police brutality. If they do not they are allowing their own freedom to be encroached upon and they will in turn one day find that they too are becoming victims of the police state. But, it will be too late, for there will be no one to help them. As long as we are able to fight now, we must all band together to fight for common freedom before the police silences us one group at a time. It is not a case of police brutality against homosexuals—it is a case of police brutality! It was not just a case of Hitler against the Jews—it was a case of Hitler against humanity. There is no way that the straight can say there is no police brutality just because they do not want to become involved. They must read history books on Nazi Germany. It is a fight against the festering disease that encompasses all people, whether they wish to be involved or not.

II

"Where I Stand"

Article draft, *Sentinel*, March 28, 1974

To be a maverick is, in political terms, to be ungovernable, demonstrably independent in perspective and platform, beholden only to one's own principles, and rhetorically unfettered. Although with eventual success four years on (some have argued throughout his campaigns), Milk, like all elected politicians, would become constrained by the very system he hoped to transform, during his political ascendancy, always a struggle, Milk unabashedly and unapologetically embodied the maverick. Of course this had earned him the political ambivalence if not enmity of groups as diverse as the moderate Alice B. Toklas Memorial Gay Democratic Club and the radical Leftist organization, Bay Area Gay Liberation, not to mention the rest of the Democratic Party, prefiguring the larger-scale showdown in his 1976 bid for the California Assembly, which he advertised as "Milk vs. The Machine." Such a political and rhetorical modality, as Milk articulates in this editorial, allows for seeming contradictions, standing on the Right and the Left, depending on the issue, guided not by party lines but rather abiding the line by line of trusted political philosophy and founding documents. One might, for instance, cite a papal denunciation such as Defensor Pacis *while endorsing for State Assembly an activist Catholic priest who had welcomed the Black Panthers into Sacred Heart church in the Mission District and marched with Martin Luther King, Jr., and Cesar Chavez, while also publicly criticizing the Catholic Chavez for his homophobia. Milk's sensitivity here to the freedom of speech, to the limits of representation*

and the pitfalls of ideological certitude, bespeaks the virtues of indepen-
dence that makes a maverick at once so alluring and appalling, political
boon and bane.

. . .

An explanation is needed . . . "Waves from the Left" . . . "On the Right
Side." What do they mean? Far Right? Far Left? Left of Center? etc.,
etc. To the dictator, American conservatism is from the Left, and, likewise, to the pure Communist, American socialism is from the Right!
The people who feel that only they can represent the Left or the Right
are the same types who are for freedom of speech as long as it is speech
that they agree with. Witness what took place at a recent Board of
Supervisors meeting . . . when one supervisor, who is well known for
his "views from the Right" verbally pinned a "liberal" spokesman up
against the wall for a letter written and signed several years ago, the
"liberals" in the back of the chambers hooted and yelled and exercised
a lesson in childish or revolutionary behavior. All regards for equality in
freedom of speech went out the window. After all, they lost some points
in the argument and thus, rather than resort to intelligent answers, took
up the "drown 'em out" philosophy . . . Yet these same liberals who
would not allow freedom of speech are the first to complain about
unrepresentative government. To this group, anyone who does not see
eye to eye with them is from the Right. They probably would rather not
win than to give in and work through the government. They sometimes
appear to want to be on the losing side, so they can be martyrs. Thus, if
winning seems possible, they will even come up with the expression . . .
"we are not ready for victory. What happens if we win?" Unbelievable
as that may be, that was not the stand taken. There are some people
who would rather be for a losing cause, for winning does not satisfy
their needs. I do not belong to that school of thought. That's why to
many of those people I am not from the "Left." Extreme Left I am not, I
am from the Left as was Truman and Stevenson. I believe in many of the
same things that those on the extreme Left believe in. Our methods of
gaining them differ. I believe in many things those on the Right believe
in. Our methods of gaining them differ.

Those who claim to speak from the true Left or the true Right are
usually people who are not committed to wanting to win. For the only
way any extreme group has ever won is by revolution and I'm not ready
for that yet . . . try as hard as Nixon does to make me lean that way.
There have been very few revolutions that were successful and most of

them were in an age long gone. For those who represent the extreme Left and Right, I suggest that they read MARSILIUS OF PADDUA— The Defender of Peace. He lived in the early 14th Century.

I cannot regard myself as from the extreme Left. I stand with the conservative in this nation who is for freedom of individual! The true conservative—politically, not morally—is for the end of victimless crime laws. I stand in agreement with that. Where does the extreme Left stand on that principle?

The "liberal" that I run into so often wants the government to do everything. I disagree. I think that the government does too much. The government started a war in Viet Nam. The government spends millions of dollars in the war against dope. The government spends millions of dollars to put homosexuals in jail for sex crimes. The government runs computer checks on its citizens. I have had enough governmental control in many areas. If that makes me not so far from the Left, well, so be it. Let those on the Left stand up for big daddy doing it all. When you allow the government to get too powerful there are always encroachments. I think that the government should spend more time caring about hospitals, schools and homes and less time caring about the books we read, the movies we go to, the things we put into our own bodies and the acts of sex we may commit. I think the government has long lost its way from being what a government should be . . . I think that everyone in government from those on the Left to those on the Right, and especially those in elite office should reread the Declaration of Independence and the Constitution. Then read the papers that went into the arguments on the Constitution. Next they should skip to today and see what they believe in. If that happened, then we would not find "liberals" shouting down Supervisors and, more importantly, we would not find Supervisors being in the position of causing themselves to be shouted down. I think our government is deficient . . . I think that almost all our "leaders" are deficient. I think that we need people in our government and not politicians, and certainly, we don't need people in office who so quickly resort to name calling and who are only willing to accept their own personal views allowing no others. How can any one person "represent" all people? Looking for that, we arrive at 1984. There are people from the Left and people from the Right living in each and every city and state. There is no way that only one person could represent both views on all issues. To demand only your view is wrong. To remember what government is about is primary. To lead is needed. We will never be able to achieve what we indeed can achieve if we insist on only "our way."

So where do I stand? I stand about as far Left or as far Right as you see me, depending upon where you are standing. I stand with Stevenson and Truman on many issues. I stand with the spirit of revolution that took place about two hundred years ago. I stand disgusted with most of our political "leaders" . . . the Nixons, the Reagans, the Aliotos, the Forans. That is why I turn to people like Father Boyle. I stand for a government which regards the human being as more important than a highway, which regards a hospital as more important than a bomb. Maybe I'm on the Left. Maybe I'm on the Right. Read Marsilius. Read the Constitution. But no matter where you think I stand . . . I stand for winning and that is an important difference between an extremist and myself. The blacks won the right to ride anywhere on the buses in Birmingham for the wrong reasons . . . but they won!

12

"Where There Is No Victim, There Is No Crime"

Press release, April 1, 1974

One of the noteworthy aspects of Harvey Milk's political career was the consistency with which he held, developed, and stumped on behalf of issues he believed mattered and the larger vision that encompassed them. Milk's outrage about the corrupted priorities of elected officials was no mere provocation for a solitary campaign season. Milk repeats here in part verbatim and extends his arguments about the true victims of miscreant morality merged with politics, and those officials divorced from the lived experience of the city who regulate it with their wasteful and costly policing and prosecution. Milk had a rhetorical talent for damning juxtaposition, creating perspective by incongruity through figures such as cowardly officer O'Shaughnessy and those "deviant" prostitutes, pot smokers, and queers he harassed, all the while on vacant police beats throughout the city it was open season for burglars, rapists, and murderers. Such framings challenged a cheap and vicious moral economy heavily bankrolled by tax dollars and governed by compromised bureaucrats, and they reconfigured the conditions and enactments of justice.

Milk would never abandon his fight against the criminalization of homosexuality (or other victimless "offenses"). Surely his advocacy, richly exhibited in this press release, contributed to the momentum that resulted in the 1975 passage of Assemblyman Willie Brown's hard-won California AB489, Consenting Adult Sex Law, which repealed the state sodomy law. He also influenced State Senator George Moscone, who ensured AB489's success, and who would institutionalize the curtailment of prosecutions for victimless crimes when he became mayor in 1976.

. . .

We have heard a lot this afternoon about the high costs to all taxpayers, especially the homeowner and renter, of police enforcement of victimless crime laws. There is another high cost that cannot be "statistically" computed. Not too long ago, several members of our famed vice squad rented rooms in the Hilton and called up prostitutes from East Bay. They made a great deal of busting these women. We can compute the cost in policemen hours, hotel rooms, and so forth that went into this great act of police heroism. What we cannot add up in dollars and cents is the cost to a young woman who, at the very same time, was raped on Castro and 20th street because there was no police on patrol. While viceman O'Shaughnessy was "protecting" our city from crime by drinking in the Hilton and calling up East Bay prostitutes, one of the citizens that he was supposed to be protecting was raped in our city streets.

How many homes are burglarized while our vice squad hunts prostitutes in hotel rooms? How many cars are stolen while our vice squad spends hours lurking in men's toilets? How many elderly are mugged while our brave police are beating up homosexuals? What is the cost in stolen property? Stolen cars? What is the cost in increased insurance rates? What is the cost in increased burglary alarm equipment? What is the cost in added private security policemen? And, all because we allow our police force to spend hours after hours pursuing crimes where there is no victim. How many men do we have tracking down homicides? All of 17! How many do we have in the Hilton and men's toilets tracking down homosexuals! Our great defenders of peace and law and order. Ask the wife of a murder victim if this is a proper use of our police!

What is the cost in the new fears of mugged victims? What is the cost to the women who have been raped? All because [people] like O'Shaughnessy feel "safer" busting gays than going after real criminals who might, in turn, show him that he is nothing but a coward.

And why does all this happen?

One: the police apparently don't want to, or can't catch real criminals for they are basically afraid to walk the beats at night in crime areas. Afraid that they may have to come face to face with a criminal in carrying out their duty to protect the city and its people. Thus, in order to get their statistics of arrests high enough and to "prove" to themselves how brave they are, they resort to the manly and dangerous acts of busting prostitutes and entrapment of gays.

The second reason is because of our leaders. Our political, ministerial, educational, and parental leaders all have failed in their efforts to teach morality and make themselves moral examples. Because some "influential" people have families that are unstable, because their own church has failed its mission to install decency, because their chosen politicians have failed to prove themselves worthy of emulation, these modern day moralists are attempting to make the police guardians and ministers of morality while serious crimes against victims continue unabated. Our modern moralists are like their cousins of the '20s, revitalizing crime: organized crime! For out of the moralists who forced prohibition on us was created the greatest crime waves and crime syndicate this nation has ever known. In the name of morality the prohibitionist created Murder Inc. Today we have the same thing happening. And this false morality violates the freedoms guaranteed by the Constitution—the separation of church and state!

If these moralists do not like the Constitution, let them amend it in a legal manner. Let them scrap the Bill of Rights and, in turn, let them go back to God with their morality and become ministers—true ministers. Instead of spending time trying to get the death penalty passed, let them remember the Ten Commandments. Let them teach the Commandment: Thou shalt not kill. Where is the commandment that says: Thou shalt not smoke marijuana? Where is the commandment that says: Thou shalt not read dirty books? Where is the commandment that says: Thou shalt not be naked? Why are these moralists so zealous in the application of man-made Commandments and so strangely apathetic when it comes to the Commandments of God?

Let my tax money go for my protection and not my prosecution. Protect my home, my streets, protect my property, protect my life. Let my minister and not some policeman worry about my morality. Let our mayor worry about gun control and not about marijuana control. Let our mayor worry about dental care for the elderly and not about what books others may want to read. Let our mayor worry about becoming a human being and not about how to prevent others from enjoying their lives. Where there is no victim there is no crime! The gays who are entrapped have to pay the costs of Alioto's false morality. Where there is no victim there is no crime! Our leaders' sense of priorities is out of order. Alioto, Scott, O'Shaughnessy and all the others should become ministers if they are so worried about morality. Let us have a real mayor, real police who want to stop crime against victims. Where there is no victim there is no crime!

13

"Political Power"

Article draft, *Sentinel*, May 23, 1974

Although Milk himself was not running for office in 1974, that season's races provided an opportunity to expand upon his political vision for the GLBTQ community. As he had argued during his supervisorial campaign the previous year, if only GLBTQ people would overcome their differences and infighting to align in solidarity against those who prevent their full equality, to vote as a bloc to influence elections and thereby make a statement, to elect their own, to use their economic capital, then they would see the expansive rewards of political power. Milk repeatedly pointed out that heterosexual politicians, exemplified by Supervisor Dianne Feinstein, courted the "gay vote" at campaign events but once in office predictably failed to live up to their progressive lip service. The impending vote in the 16th Assembly District heightened Milk's agitation in this regard, and he challenged the sincerity of candidate John Foran's sudden interest in gay rights after having not supported Assemblyman Willie Brown's Consensual Sex Act, which would repeal the century-old statute criminalizing sodomy. In order to deliver a bloc vote, and pointed message, against ballot-weather political "friends," the GLBTQ community needed first to mobilize. Thus Milk's call for political power included a battle plan for volunteerism, voter registration, and consolidated endorsements and votes that would not only make a difference in this election but in future elections, gesturing toward his own campaign in 1975. Three such editorials appeared during this week, here in the Sentinel *as well as in the* Bay Area Reporter *and in* The Voice of the Gay Students Coalition *at San Francisco State University, for whom he entitled his article, "One Hour a Week, For a Year, To Win Our Rights."*

. . .

On Tuesday, May 7th, Officer Fernandez of the Mission Street Police Station came into my shop and told me that if the gays have any complaints about anything, the only way that such complaints will be heard is if we use POLITICAL POWER.

On Wednesday, May 8th, at a meeting of concerned citizens in the Eureka Valley area which centered around the issue of "straights" vs. "gays," one of the most vocal leaders of the parents' groups called for getting rid of the "gay problem" by forces, or, if need be, by use of their POLITICAL POWER and that they, the straights, had the muscle to use such POLITICAL POWER.

We are told that if we want anything, we need POLITICAL POWER. We are threatened that if we don't mend our ways, POLITICAL POWER will be used against us.

The time has come for the gay community to answer. In the past, we have helped elect people to public office, and, once elected, they have not come to our aid one bit. We have been wooed with pretty words and gotten only pretty smiles in return. The time has come to take the advice of the straight community and show our POLITICAL POWER.

POLITICAL POWER can be shown only in a real vote—a joint vote of all gays—upfront, closet, liberal, conservative, Republican, Democratic . . . all gays once! If we show our total vote strength once, we never have to do it again. We can then return to our many splinter positions. But for once we must drop all our differences and join together and show the actual power we can muster if need be.

Based upon surveys, only about 40%–55% of the gay community is registered to vote. We must register the remaining percentage. We must do it now.

If we do that, we then can use that huge bloc of votes, added to those who are already registered, as leverage. We will then have what we are told we need, POLITICAL POWER.

How can we do this? We need a small army of registrars— approximately 100 gay persons—who are willing to devote all of one hour per week for the next year, to go out and register our gay brothers and sisters. What a price to pay: about 50 hours of work spread over one year. What a small price to pay for so large a gain! And, for the most part, we will even be paid for doing that registration!

Thus I call upon all in the gay community who want to help achieve a voice that indeed will be not only be heard, but listened to, to meet at 7pm on Wednesday, June 5th, at my shop— 575 Castro Street. That is the day after the primary election. What a perfect time to start.

We are told time and time again by the straight community that we have to achieve POLITICAL POWER if we want anything. I'm for so doing. I ask you to help form a working task force. If you are willing to help in any way . . . if you are committed to Gay Civil Rights . . . if you believe . . . then the time has come . . . it is long overdue.

We can help somewhat in the coming primary on June 6th by voting for those who are running and have taken outspoken stands on Gay Civil Rights . . . the race for governor leaves only one person among the leaders who has taken such a stand: Bob Moretti. The race for the 16th Assembly leaves only one man: Gene Boyle. Also, consider I ask you to stand by Ed Cragen for Superior Court Judge.

14

"Letter to the *San Francisco Chronicle* about Anti-Gay Editorials"

Draft, July 1, 1974

The post-Stonewall annual ritual of marking "gay pride" and the gay rights movement began in San Francisco on June 28, 1970, with a small march by transsexuals down Polk Street, followed that afternoon by the Christopher Street Liberation Day (after its namesake in New York) "gay-in" by hundreds in Golden Gate Park. The theme that year was "Gay Freedom Revolution," and after a year's hiatus the Gay Freedom Day festival and parade returned for good in 1972. The theme for the festival in 1974 was "Gay Freedom by '76," attended by an estimated 60,000, with a parade wending through Grant, O'Farrell, and Polk Streets, culminating in a celebration at the Civic Center. Best known is Milk's appearance and speech during the 1978 Gay Freedom Day, as well as that iconic image of Milk on the parade route, holding a sign saying, "I'm from Woodmere, N.Y."—a sign he encouraged everyone to bring that year, as he put it in his "Milk Forum" column in the Bay Area Reporter, so as to "come out to your hometown" and prove that GLBTQ people are from everywhere in the United States. But Milk had long enjoyed the festival and understood its political importance. He also knew well the value of the media and proved from the beginning of his political career to be savvy and skilled in the art of enticing, provoking, and manipulating the San Francisco press. Milk was unafraid to throw down the gauntlet with the San Francisco Chronicle, *a challenge amplified here by his personification of the paper, indictment of the offending reporter, and patriotic framing of both the event and its homophobic rendering. Milk also knew that such a clash would make good copy.*

. . .

Dear Editor,

The fourth of July celebrates an event that, to many people, not only in this country, but throughout the world, stood for the shedding of oppression. The homosexual community is the last minority group in this country that has received no Civil Rights. Last Sunday, we marched not only on the streets of San Francisco, but in many cities in this nation from New York to Anchorage. We marched for several reasons: to show other homosexuals that the time is now for them to come out and to show our straight oppressors that the time is now for them to no longer deny our civil rights.

The news article written by your person on the parade here in San Francisco was not a news article but an editorial. How can that writer know what the parade means unless he is homosexual? How can that writer understand oppression unless he is homosexual? How do you allow news articles to become editorials? Does that article mean that the *Chronicle's* editorial position stands for a continued put down of homosexuals? Does that article mean that the *Chronicle* still regards every homosexual as a criminal? Does the *Chronicle* stand for continued repression and oppression of homosexuals?

The time is now for the *Chronicle*, the political leaders if this city, the "moral" leaders of this city, the business leaders of this city, and the people of this city to either end their discrimination of homosexuals or have the "manly" guts to come out and say that they remain bigots.

There may have been fun in the parade, no more or no less than in the Shriners Parades . . . there may have been too much fun for some people . . . but I'll opt for that anytime given the choice between that way of life and the way of life that the *Chronicle* has so strongly endorsed . . . the election of Richard Nixon.

If the *Chronicle* wished to know what the parade meant, it shouldn't have sent some uptight bigot to editorialize it . . . just ask the many who carried American flags in the parade. The bearing of the American flags and the demand for Gay Civil Rights was apparently too much for your reporter's narrow mind.

I repeat: does the *Chronicle* stand for Civil Rights for all Citizens or does the *Chronicle* stand for the continued prejudice of homosexuals?

15

"Library or Performing Arts Center"

Press release, December 4, 1974

This press release advocating on behalf of the public library was printed on Castro Village Association letterhead, signed by CVA President Harvey Milk. Although this was not a campaign year for Milk, it was politically significant for his successful effort at mobilizing the GLBTQ community under his self-crafted banners of "Buy gay" and "Vote gay," or "Gay power." Snubbed by the Eureka Valley Merchants Association, a dozen GLBTQ merchants led by Milk formed the Castro Village Association in 1974, in the back of a pizza parlor, as Randy Shilts tells the story in The Mayor of Castro Street, *an organization designed to protect and amass and consolidate economic might and therefore increase its political influence. That August, CVA sponsored its first Castro Street Fair, drawing an estimated 5,000 people. By year's end CVA had more than 50 members, including 20 straight merchants and the initially resistant Bank of America and Hibernia Bank, with aspiring politicians in attendance at its meetings.*

In a column for the Bay Area Reporter *the same month, Milk noted that some fractious GLBTQ people had criticized the CVA as a means to achieve gay rights. Milk, however, believed it not only to be a means of developing community and resources, a site of gay rights and a platform for his passionate voter registration drive, but as a means of "forming a bridge between the communities." As Milk had clearly articulated during his first campaign, his populist vision of a city of interdependent neighborhoods sought to make life better for all San Franciscans, even as he was emerging as the champion of GLBTQ San Franciscans. Fighting for the public library exemplified Milk's call for interconnectedness. That he himself was an aficionado of high culture, especially the opera (Harvey Milk, An Opera In Three Acts, was staged in his memory in Houston, New York, and San Francisco in 1995–1996), made his juxtaposition of the public library and the proposed performing arts center all the more poignant and powerful. In a passage that should be repeated in our own time, Milk averred, "More than any of our other cultural assets, it is the library that currently suffers from neglect. It gets neither publicity nor applause, even though it serves in silence the needs of all and asks no price for services rendered. It provides fantasies for the young, solace for the old, and information for all who seek it."*

. . .

San Francisco is justly famed for its cultural heritage—a symphony hall orchestra, a ballet, and an opera that are not only well known and well beloved by its inhabitants but are world-renowned as well. Newspaper and television coverage of their troubles and their triumphs is extensive. Their patrons number not only San Francisco's own "four hundred" but students from universities both in the City and across the Bay. All of these cultural activities run deficits that are made up for by the generosity of the wealthy—as well as by the prices charged for both box seats and those in the balcony. There is no question but that the symphony and the opera and the ballet cater to the affluent and the culturally inclined: there are no free performances.

As a frequent patron of all of these cultural events, I am quite fond of them. But not too far from the center of these activities, in a building that should have been renovated and enlarged years ago, a different sort of performance is held daily from nine in the morning until nine at night. There are no stars and there is no music. The attendees are not the affluent—though they're not excluded, nor necessarily those with a taste for culture—though culture is high on the agenda. The patrons include both the poor and the rich, the students and the entertainment-starved, the blue collar and the executive, the very young and the very old. The performances are held in silence and the performers are tiny black figures on white pages. There is no charge: it is free to all.

I do not know the total attendance at the opera and the ballet and the symphony. Whatever the figures are, they're dwarfed by the number of people who daily use our library.

A Performing Arts Center represents the ego of a great city, the public library represents its heart. More than any of our other cultural assets, it is the library that currently suffers from neglect. It gets neither publicity nor applause, even though is serves in silence the needs of all and asks no price for services rendered. It provides fantasies for the young, solace for the old, and information for all who seek it.

We can live, though perhaps not so richly, without a Performing Arts Center. Without an expanded, functioning library that serves the need of everyone—the masses as well as the elite, the poor as well as the wealthy—we suffer an impoverishment of the spirit and the City dies a little.

PART TWO

The Grassroots Activist Becomes "The Mayor of Castro Street"

16

"Au Contraire . . . PCR Needed"

Column, *Bay Area Reporter*, February 9, 1975

Given Milk's outspoken moral outrage regarding homophobic police harassment and violence, especially in the wake of the Castro 14 confrontation the previous September, the conciliatory position he here takes in his Bay Area Reporter *"Milk Forum" column, encouraging a positive attitude and public friendliness toward police and endorsing the Police Community Relations (PCR) Department and its seminars, may come as a surprise. Just months before, he had railed against what he called "police sickness," asking publicly why "police officers were allowed to make wanton assaults against citizens"; why crowded sidewalks outside bars in the Castro were targeted, but not those in front of the city's elite theaters; and why there were no openly gay members on the force. At the time he had been criticized for his attacks on the Police Department by Thomas Edwards, gay rights activist and District Chairman of the PCR, which Milk argued was merely another symptom of errant accommodationism and tokenism by so-called "gay leaders." Thus Milk's desire and capacity to seek workable solutions to the city's problems, regardless of deep differences and animosities, is noteworthy.*

It is also worth noting that soon after this column was published, Milk announced his candidacy for supervisor. During the 1975 campaign, Milk's political presence and public record criticizing local government and downtown interests forged stronger bonds with some unlikely constituencies, namely the unions. Milk gained the endorsements of the

Building Construction Trade Council, Beer Truck Drivers local, and the Fire Fighters local. He didn't get the support of the police union, despite the fact that he was one of only two candidates to oppose the incumbent Board of Supervisors in support of the August police strike pursuing a wage increase (though he also filed a class action law suit in District Court against Mayor Alioto and SFPD officials for failing to protect citizens during the strike), and in the strike's wake to fight against Board-sponsored retaliatory initiatives on the ballot. In an exchange politico Michael Wong recounted, he wanted to support the ballot propositions to get even with the Police Officers Association, but Milk objected: "The Supervisors fucked the union and refused to meet with them . . . they had no choice but to strike. You cannot hurt labor . . . we need them. . . . the rank and file are decent working people like you and me." Decent working people like GLBTQ residents, whom Milk urged here to set aside deep hurt and legitimate rancor for the sake of protection and progress in the city's neighborhoods, for themselves and for everyone.

. . .

Some people argue that there should be no need for an organization such as the Police Community Relations. They say that the fact that it exists means that something is amiss. They say that there should be no need for a group to improve relations between the police and the community. They are right. But if they were to continue their logic one step, they would also have to say that there should be no need for police. The very fact that there is a police force means that something is amiss. They are right.

But things are not as they should be. People do steal, rob, mug, kill, rape, etc., etc. Thus, there is a need for the police. And because of some police, there is a need for improving attitudes between the police and the community. Because of the nature of man, we need police. Because of the nature of man, we also have come to need Police Community Relations . . . but a meaningful PCR and not tokenism. Things must change. Man must stop his robbing, his killing. The police must stop their misuse of power, i.e. their attack on last week's anti-Viet Nam demonstrators and the press, the Castro Street Sweep, their harassment of gays. It adds up that on both sides, there is a percentage of people who abuse the rights of others. The question is what can be done to help change the thinking of the percentage of the people?

There always will be some who will not play by the rules. There always will be someone who will take advantage of others. There will

always be some who, for many reasons, will create an unsafe atmo-
sphere. There are deep rooted reasons for this . . . lack of education,
lack of of job opportunities, frustrations, etc. These are paramount
problems that will only be solved when our elected leaders get the guts
to attack the problems instead of the crises. No PCR unit can hope to
solve these deep rooted problems. What a PCR unit can solve is the
attitudes on the surface and the attitudes that exist for lack of understanding on both sides. The PCR can bring their various communities
together and work on improving attitudes. It is no easy task. There will
be no fast solution. The Eureka Valley PCR is correct in trying to solve
some of the local problems before trying to solve the citywide problems.
If you can not improve your own area, how can you have the ability to
solve things on a larger scale? A great opportunity to improve relations
has been formed—the local seminar. It will offer the police the chance
to explain in detail the problems that they face—and they do have problems. If the gay community is able to get a fuller understanding of the
police, maybe some of the confrontations will lessen. The burden will
then be transferred to the police to understand the life style and the
frustrations of the gay community. If that happens, we might see less
and less police harassment and less and less instances of police beating
up gays.

The end result is what we are after. We wish to live and work in
harmony. In order to do that, many of us will have to improve our
attitudes towards the police. Few among us, including myself, have
never yelled, "pig." That must change. Instead of making faces at the
police, we must start to smile and be friendly. We must welcome them.
That may sound strange coming from this pen, but I look to the end
result. If the gay community welcomes the police and makes friends
with them, we can then expect the police to respect us and our rights.
It has to be a two-way meeting and I have no hesitation to take the
first step. I will take that step, but, I in turn want to see the police take
the next step!

Last Saturday night in front of the Regency theatre there were about
500 people waiting to get into the movie. The sidewalks were blocked.
Even though you could not pass, there were no arrests for "obstructing
the sidewalks." Last week at the Hilton, there was a Photo Show. In all
the ads there was mention of a holographic exhibit. The center of that
exhibit was a hologram of two naked women kissing and licking each
other's breasts. Even though there were no warnings and even though
children were watching, there were no arrests for "obscenities." The

"double" standards against the gay community must stop. Gays must not be arrested on made up charges. Gays must not be arrested for doing the same things straights are doing. Gays must not be beat up by the police . . . (we have on file incidents of that happening).

Once there are steps taken, then the next step can be taken. That is where the entire community, gay and straight, can help the police. Last year in this city, 40,000 serious crimes were reported. Over 100 per day! Add to that [the] number of serious crimes not reported. Something has to be done to lower that rate rapidly. While police are busting gays for obstructing the sidewalks and while gays are yelling "pig," people are being mugged, robbed, and murdered. All that negative police energy, not to mention the tax payer's money, being spent in harassment of the gays must be turned into a positive force against serious crime. Instead of looking for a gay to beat up, the police should be looking for criminals. The gay community can be of help. The upcoming Eureka Valley PCR seminar can open the door for the gays who have been victims of the police and for those police who hate us. But it is a step that must be taken. The end result will be not only an ending of harassment, but also a lowering of serious crime . . . all benefit.

With the end result in mind, I ask the gay community to continue to take a very active role in all local PCR units. To attend the Eureka Valley PCR seminar with a positive approach rather than a disruptive approach. The problems will not be solved overnight. Hatred has taken years to build. It will take time to overcome. But if the gay community takes that first step and makes it positive, friendly, and warm, then maybe those police who have abused their authority will take the next step. We have questions about some of the police leadership. We may even have hate. We have to bury that, not only for our own sake, but for those gays who will follow us in the years to come. We have the opportunity to show not only this city, but the nation, how to bridge the communities. It would be a shame if we don't make the most of it.

17

"Harvey Milk for Supervisor"

Campaign letter, February 26, 1975

Politico Michael Wong observed in his diary that "Harvey did not change his platform very much" after the 1973 campaign. "He was a better speaker and his statements were more refined." Indeed, Milk's populism again underwrote and punctuated his platform, as his campaign brochure made plain with this series of questions: "What have you got in return for past increased taxes? Better police protection? Better Muni service? A more efficient purchasing department to save taxpayer's money? Why didn't the present Board of Supervisors ever give you a chance to vote, either way, on the Yerba Buena Project? Why did the Supervisors allow $100,000 to be spent on an 'I Love Muni' campaign when a lack of money for spare parts idled up to 100 vehicles at a time? Do the Supervisors ride Muni themselves? What have the Supervisors actually accepted for our ever increasing police budget? Police who arrest senior citizens for playing poker? In the recent police and firefighters strike, why did the Supervisors start negotiations so late? And why did they admit they were 'powerless to do anything' before the strike—but can now find a dozen ways to 'punish' police? AND WHAT ABOUT TAXES?" Milk's now-familiar "us vs. them" trope found its surest configuration in this race against the incumbent supervisors he hoped to unseat—or at least one ("I ask for just 1 of your 6 votes for Supervisor."). "I accuse the present Board of Supervisors of creating an atmosphere that has led to municipal strikes, poor city services, an *out of hand city budget, and a City Hall that yawns at the plight of the neighborhoods." Although once again Jim Foster and most other powerful members of the gay establishment opposed Milk's candidacy, his support among GLBTQ voters flourished, and he garnered a remarkably diverse array of endorsements, including the San Francisco Black Political Caucus, The Democratic League, San Francisco Tomorrow, Homeowners of Western Addition Association, Citizens for Justice, Harry S. Truman Democratic Club, Associated Democratic Club, Citizens for Representative Government, Frank R. Havenner Democratic Club, National Women's Political Caucus, People's Democratic Club, San Francisco Building and Construction Trade Council, Seniors Union for Social Justice, and the Union Labor Party.*

Nevertheless, Milk lost for a second time in the 1975 election, finishing seventh behind six incumbents, with 53,000 votes—once again proving that had there been district elections, he would have been victorious. Milk's optimism for deepening and expanding GLBTQ power never faltered; he always urged his supporters to discover their political and economic agency in the interest of redressing material grievances by exercising their votes, opening their wallets, and finding their voices, which he exemplified. His passionate voter registration drive had made a difference, if not in bringing him to the Board, then in bringing GLBTQ people into fresh and consequential focus for those coming into power, including George Moscone, whose mayoralty would mean change for minorities throughout the city.

. . .

Dear Friends,

It probably comes as no surprise to most of you, but I am going to run for Supervisor again this year. One of the more important reasons for venturing into the political arena once again is to let the 17,000 people who voted for me last time know that my attempt at political office wasn't a one-shot affair. To have won the first time out, with limited funds and limited experience, would be to have expected a miracle. This time, it's a whole new ball game.

Winning an election requires both financial support *and* lots and lots of hard work, along with the cooperation of others. That is why we've turned Castro Camera into a voter-registration headquarters for our neighborhood—Senator Moscone perked noticeably when he discovered that we registered more than 2,500 people for the Governor's race last November. We have just begun to get this year's drive rolling again.

But that's only part of the overall picture. To expect to carry an election on the Gay vote alone is wishful thinking. The Gay vote *is* powerful, the Gay vote *can* make a difference. But it is the tremendous straight vote which makes the real decisions. With this fact in mind, I've gone into the straight community—at many functions I've been the "token" Gay. I've tried to build a bridge between "us" and "them" because I believe that contact with the straight community is a two-way street and it is only by it that we can gain what we *all* want: equality and acceptance. This is exactly what we have attempted to do with the merchant's group in the Castro neighborhood. The Castro Village Association started with twelve Gay—and one straight—merchants about a year ago. Through hard work and sustained effort, we now number more than 55 members, many of them are straights, including the banks. We're trying to make our neighborhood a place where the two diverse communities *can* live and work together. We want it to become a model of economic strength within the City. We have moved in the right direction.

. . . In this campaign, I am not going to be a "one issue" candidate. There are too many problems which desperately need solving to indulge in a simple one-issue campaign. I intend to fight for a better sense of spending priorities in city government, calling upon my own financial background. As a small businessman, I intend to fight for the needs of small businesses rather than solely for the interests of "Downtown." I will call upon my work with the police department, and my experience with top police officials, to recommend more successful ways of fighting serious crime. And, finally, I will draw on my daily contact with our community to fight for the needs of all people in The City. This campaign will be conducted on several levels but perhaps it can best be summarized by saying it will be a "populist" campaign.

With all this in mind, I fully realize that I am going to need a hell of a lot of positive help and criticism. Thus, I am inviting you to an open meeting to help set some guidelines and get a more rounded and united viewpoint from our community [in order] to put our campaign together. Win or not, the fact that we're willing to wage a hard, uphill fight for what we feel is right will provide help and courage to others. While on my various speaking engagements, both here and away from The City, I've found that young Gays, especially, as well as those just emerging, derive encouragement and strength from our battle for equality and acceptance.

I regret that this is a form letter and not the individual one I would like it to be. But there are so many different people and so many varying viewpoints and I want to hear from them all. I hear a great deal from the people I meet on the street, in the shops, in the bars, and at the many meetings which I attend. Now I want to hear from you!

Please join me on Sunday, March 9th, at 2 P.M. at Castro Camera, 575 Castro.

If you are unable to attend but would like to join us in this important campaign, please give me a call at 864-1390 or stop by the store at your convenience.

Again, my thanks for taking the time to read this.

All my best,
Harvey Milk

18

"Statement of Harvey Milk, Candidate for the 16th Assembly District"

Campaign material, March 9, 1976

George Moscone's election as mayor would seem to have portended a new era for GLBTQ people. Moscone had played a key role in overturning the state sodomy statute and appointed Milk, along with many other minorities, to posts in his new administration. Milk's position as commissioner on the influential Board of Permit Appeals consummated his long-standing call for GLBTQ people themselves to serve in office rather than relying on the good will and patronage of those liberal heterosexual allies, who always disappointed, as he had long argued. Why, then, did Milk's tenure in city government last only from January to March 1976? Hubris? No, Milk contended, he was simply responding to the recently exposed deal struck in 1974 among a number of prominent California politicians—then State Senate Majority Leader Moscone, Assembly Speaker Leo McCarthy, Congressmen Phil and John Burton, Assemblymen John Foran and Willie Brown—to fill the recently vacated 16th Assembly District (AD) seat with McCarthy aide Art Agnos. On the day Agnos announced his candidacy, Milk leaked his potential interest in a run, and Mayor Moscone made public his intention to fire Milk if he did so, only exacerbating the media frenzy over alleged bossism. That was precisely what occurred shortly after this announcement address, and with it emerged the memorable campaign slogan, "Harvey Milk vs. The Machine." According to that now-familiar coded map hanging at campaign headquarters, otherwise known as Castro Camera, Milk surmised that his vote count in 1975 exceeded the number of votes John Foran had garnered in winning the 16th AD seat in the last election. That analysis would prove to be inaccurate three months later, but for reasons that only substantiated Milk's accusations regarding machine politics in California, in a losing campaign that would transform Milk into a national politician.

. . .

I would like to announce that I am a candidate for the office of Assembly from the Sixteenth Assembly District. I would consider it a great honor to be allowed to represent the people of this district.

I know the people of this district; I know their problems. I live in the Sixteenth Assembly District. I'm a store owner in this district. I serve on many neighborhood boards within this district, most of which have worked for years to improve the living and working conditions of the district.

Few people are more aware of the painful problems of the district than myself. Our rate of unemployment is obviously higher here than in any other district in our city. That unemployment has been fed by the closing of the Hunters Point Shipyard, by the failure of Yerba Buena. You can see the results of that unemployment in the beaten faces on Third Street, on the streets of Chinatown and among the Senior Citizens of the Tenderloin. Conditions are bad.

The political figures and their patronage system that worked in the past have failed in the present. It is a different ball game, and we need a different team. The old catch phrases, the old faces, the old loyalties, are not putting bread on the table, are not producing gainful employment. The vision that our political figures may have had at one time has vanished. We need people who understand, who understand money, who understand the value of a dollar, who realize that bread costs over fifty cents a loaf and milk forty cents a quart, and if you don't have that forty or fifty cents, your kids don't eat. We need people who understand that jobs mean more than welfare, that a job means pride, and, that for many people, handouts mean humiliation.

This district doesn't need politicians who are skilled in the practice of pay-offs, log-rolling, and political trade-offs. We need people with a concern and awareness of the problems of the people of this district: the poor people, the little people, the people who pay the taxes and who contribute to the quality of life that is so prized in this district. In every race that I've run, every board that I've ever worked on, my aim has been to help these people.

Recently, politicians and candidates for political office have apparently decided that the way to serve the people of this district is through the creation of a political machine. Political machines do not *serve* the people—they *reward* the people who serve *them*. Everybody is agreed that San Francisco must not become a New York financially.

I think we are also agreed that San Francisco must not become a Chicago politically.

Does a machine exist? Dick Nolan, of the *Examiner*, articles in the *Sacramento Bee*, the *Bay Guardian* and the *Sunset Journal* have all referred to a power play taking place by San Francisco's newest political machine. The President of the Board of Supervisors has even termed this machine an "Unholy Alliance."

Before making up my mind to run for the Assembly, I walked the streets of the Sixteenth Assembly District and asked hundreds of people who lived here if they thought I should challenge this machine before it took control of our district. The vast majority said yes and urged me to run.

With the support of the people, and knowing all too well the limited funds available to us versus the immense financial support the "Unholy Alliance" will give to their machine candidate, I am entering the race. *I think representatives should be elected by the people—not appointed.* I think a representative should earn his or her seat—I don't think the seat should be awarded on the basis of service to the machine.

The overriding issue is simply: do the people of the neighborhoods that make up the Sixteenth Assembly District have the right of political self-determination—or, can the machine take that right away? Machines operate on oil and grease; they're dirty, dehumanizing, and too often unresponsive to any needs but those of the operators.

It's therefore my intention to challenge the machine and the legacy of neglect that it has bequeathed to the voters of my district.

19

"Reactionary Beer"

Column, *Bay Area Reporter*, March 18, 1976

Harvey Milk himself was not a drinker, but beer played an important role in his political career. Although not typically featured in the standard narrative of the Coors Boycott, often dated to the nationwide effort begun by the AFL-CIO in 1977, its roots are traceable to Teamster and California Coors Boycott Director Allan Baird, who sought out Harvey Milk and Howard Wallace in 1974–1975 to gain GLBTQ support, along with Arab and Chinese grocers, of the beer drivers' strike against six distributors. Memorably, Milk in return had asked for union jobs for his own people, not Baird's endorsement for his supervisorial campaign. And with the exception of holdout Coors, they succeeded, leading to an expanded boycott of Coors. Baird was impressed by Milk's "no-bullshit" approach, organizing acumen, and broader vision that included, for instance, equal outrage concerning Coors' discrimination against the Latino community. Milk, in turn, relished "the symbolism of tying gays to the conservative Teamsters union." It is noteworthy that Baird resiliently endured homophobic slurs on the job and in the neighborhood for his work with Milk and the GLBTQ community. We should also better remember gay Teamster organizer Howard Wallace, who formed Bay Area Gay Liberation (BAGL) in 1975 as a response to the coalition boycott against Coors and did much to make gay rights a union issue writ large. That same year, when the national Teamsters' organization muscled local leaders out of the boycott, which Milk thought smelled

of a payoff, he called on GLBTQ people for courage and a show of
political maturity and strength by carrying on the boycott themselves.
Milk, Wallace, and Baird exemplify the bridging, the coalition build-
ing to end discrimination and achieve equal rights, championed in this
"Milk Forum" column. Moreover, the boycott of Coors substantiated
Milk's theory of GLBTQ economic power. In 1977, when gay bars and
their patrons renewed the boycott, responding to Joseph Coors' support
of Anita Bryant's insidious homophobic campaign, Coors instantly lost
its stronghold as California's best-selling beer.

· · ·

This past week there was a fundraising event for aid to some Native
Americans. Attending was a cross section of San Francisco. Some of
our local unions are working with neighborhood associations, some
local unions lobbied for gay rights last year in Sacramento, the list goes
on and inter-winds. In issue after issue, we see different groups coming
to the aid of others. The bridges between the many communities and
people of the city are being built. Maybe out of necessity, but the exciting thing is that they *are* being built. The combined effort can put an
end to the insensitivity of government.

Several years ago the Gay community took a step in working for others in their fight (in reality, our fight too) by participating in a boycott
against Coors Beer. In many areas of the state and in the nation, the
boycott continues. It has not been as active locally, lately, even though
it still remains effective. Last week a woman came into my store, who
had just driven across the nation. Like many others, she stopped off at
the home plant in Golden, Colorado. She stopped there, for, like many
people from the East, Coors has some sort of mystique. She was excited
about taking the tour. Then she drifted off the tour and her eyes were
opened. She is now a vocal part of the boycott.

The reason for the boycott comes from two basic points. One, a
company that has an attitude towards its employees that can not only
be called discriminating but also downright humiliating. (The discrimination of gay people in the work field is well known to all of us. It
could be a major step in the gay movement if we started to join tighter
forces with other groups to fight any and all discrimination by any
and all companies.) In this case, the company has been brought before the Federal Equal Employment Opportunity Commission and the
Colorado Human Rights commission more than once. A second reason

for the boycott comes out of the paternalistic attitude of Coors towards its workers and a very poor labor relations history.

WHAT ABOUT JOE COORS?

Yet there is still another side to the overall picture and that is Joe Coors himself. The number of articles written about him fills a book. Not just the local Denver papers or our San Francisco press. It reaches even to the Sunday *New York Times*. The ideological views of Joe Coors are right there with the John Birch Society—he is a good contributor to that group. His attempt to manipulate the media, his involvement with the philosophies of Reagan, his dislikes of the "pleasure-loving parasites," and well, we have all heard it all too often, all too many times.

Joe Coors was a regent at the University of Colorado. Another regent at that time, the highly respected Republican, Harry Carlson, said that Coors was a "super patriot who believed in interpreting the First Amendment to suit himself." Coors fought against "permissiveness" and "strongly attacked the practice of giving birth control advice to female students." Joe Coors has a long record of more of the same. It is thus easy to see where his company's policy of discrimination comes from.

Months ago, I talked with one of the distributors of Coors in the Bay Area. He was going to set up a meeting with other Coors distributors so we could discuss the problems. He never did. I offered to go with several of their company officials to Colorado and tour the plants, just to see who was working there and at what types of jobs. The offer was turned down even though I offered to pick up the entire cost of the trip for all of us.

Here is a way that the gay community could show its economic power. It is not too hard to switch brands of beer. (After the second one, not too many people can really tell the difference between brands, and blindfolded, very few people can even tell the difference on the first beer.) The point: if the gay community continues, even leads, the boycott, then the Spanish and labor groups fighting Coors will understand who their friends are and what it means to join together in fighting for a common goal, ending discrimination. The point: we will also be building bridges with others who in turn will aid us in our fight for equal rights. The combined effort could then trigger other groups and communities to joining in the struggle. The time is here when all who are discriminated against in any way should join forces—it's a common battle, Coors beer might have a good taste, to some people, but the company's policies have a very bitter taste.

20

"Nixon's Revenge—
The Republicans and
Their Supreme Court"

Column, *Bay Area Reporter*, April 15, 1976

On March 29, 1976, the U.S. Supreme Court in a 6–3 vote summarily affirmed a lower-court ruling upholding a Virginia sodomy statute that made private, sexual activity between consenting adult members of the same sex—"homosexual acts"—punishable by up to five years in jail and a $1,000 fine. The anonymous plaintiffs in Doe v. Commonwealth's Attorney for City of Richmond, *(E.D.Va., 403 F.Supp. 1199, affirmed,— U.S. —, 96 S.Ct. 1489, 47 L.Ed.2d 751 [1976]) did not enjoy the privilege of having their case heard by the Supreme Court prior to its decision; the Court rendered its affirmation without oral argument or written opinion. Both the National Gay Task Force and the American Civil Liberties Union denounced the ruling on the grounds that it, like such state laws themselves, constituted an "aura of criminality" surrounding homosexuality that facilitated homophobic discrimination in employment, housing, licensing, and security clearances. Milk's hyperbolic predictions in this "Milk Forum" column about the endurance of Nixon's "evil" embodied in the Supreme Court proved prescient insofar as homosexuality was concerned. The Burger Court upheld a Georgia sodomy statute in its infamous 1986 ruling,* Bowers v. Hardwick. *Although* Doe *is not cited in* Bowers, *Nixon appointee Chief Justice Burger may have remembered it when, in his Concurring Opinion, he wrote, quoting Blackwell, that homosexuality is "the infamous crime against nature," an offense of "deeper malignity" than rape, a heinous*

127

act "the very mention of which is a disgrace to human nature," and "a crime not fit to be named."

Milk's enmity for Nixon and his Administration was, to say the least, formative. He cited Watergate as a chief cause of his entry into politics, and he often turned to the Nixon Administration as rhetorical fodder when in need of perspective by incongruity, as when he memorably remarked of Democratic Clubs in San Francisco, "Evidently, they care about democracy as much as John Mitchell cares about Justice!" As reliable as Nixon's negative touchstone, Milk's rally cry that GLBTQ power, exercised politically and economically, must rebut homophobia resounded in this campaign season editorial and throughout his career.

. . .

The recent ruling by the U.S. Supreme Court on Homosexuality brought home something I wrote about a long time ago. "The evil that Nixon brought on this nation will last long after he is gone from public office. His appointments to the Supreme Court will affect our lives to a greater degree than anything else he can do as president. We will have to live with that court and their rulings for too long."

The Nixon court has struck out against all gay people—be they liberals or conservatives. The day-to-day blunders that Nixon gave to this nation can and will be corrected. The decisions made by his court will be on our necks for a long time. Even if you may have liked his foreign and/or domestic policies, as a gay person, you have to regret this decision handed down by his court and we will be stuck with his court for some time.

The Republican Party—on a national level—has long told us that they know how to handle the economy. That they are best with fiscal policies. They have to be given some sort of credit for they have done what most economists thought was almost impossible—given us high unemployment and run-away inflation at the same time. They have once again mismanaged our economy. After seven years in the White House, they have given us long lines at the unemployment offices. They have proven that they cannot handle our economy. All by themselves, they have shattered the myth that they themselves created—that the Republican Party understands money and is fiscally responsive.

With the inability to handle the economy by the Republican Party, and this ruling by their court which will affect the gay movement and the lives of too many thousands of gay people, I can see no reason whatsoever why any gay person could vote for a Republican on the national level. If you care for an end to discrimination and are for the rights of gay people, look at what our great Republican Party has brought down on our backs.

I would like to hear just one solid reason why any gay person should support the national Republican Party—unless you are the type that likes to be discriminated against.

THE DANGER OF SCOOP JACKSON

With that as the record, I feel it is important for gay people to register as Democrats. If you are currently not so registered, then you can not vote in this June's primary. The importance of that is that we have some of the Nixonian thought process creeping into the Democrat Party, and it must be stopped. Scoop Jackson is running for president. His stands, over and over, are just plain anti-gay. If you want to let a person like Jackson into the White House, all you have to do is sit back and do nothing. If, however, you want to prevent Jackson from attaining the position, you must register as a Democrat to vote against him in the June primary. If he wins the nomination then there is no choice for gay people in the November election. It will be Jackson vs. a continuation of the anti-gay Republican mentality.

There are only a few weeks left to change your registration. The last day is May 3. If you are registered as an Independent, "declined to state," etc., you can not vote in the Democratic primary. You may register—if you have not voted in California before—if you live here right now! You must re-register if you moved since the last election. You must re-register if you did not vote in the last two years. The day after election day is too late to complain.

"My Concept as a Legislator"

Column, *Bay Area Reporter*, May 27, 1976

In an interview with the San Francisco State University student paper Zenger's *in November 1976, Harvey Milk was asked if he had any reservations about his campaigns in an era of public suspicion regarding his ilk. "Jefferson, Lincoln, and Truman were politicians. There's nothing wrong with being a politician. But as I got involved in politics I realized that . . . politicians are hypocrites. . . . I just took my stand and lost, unlike other politicians who get involved just to fill their egos and pockets. But I knew the consequence of running . . . it's vital that someone raise the questions." The aura of the stand, principled and last, is prominent in this "Milk Forum" column just a week prior to election day on June 8, the underdog gay neighborhood activist and small business owner against the Machine politician, the bureaucratic "trouble-shooter," flush with campaign funds, endorsements, and chits. As the* Harvey Milk for Assembly Committee *had written in its campaign brochure, "The people of our district have been frozen out of jobs. They've been frozen out of decent schools—out of decent housing—out of decent medical care—out of decent care for the elderly—out of decent care for children. Harvey Milk understands that! After all, they tried to freeze him out of running against their hand-picked candidate. They tried to deny him the right—everyone's right—to run for public office. Harvey Milk is not running as somebody else's errand-boy, or riding on anybody's coat-tails. As a legislator, he'll owe nothing to the power brokers and the big money that keeps them in power. Harvey Milk has already established that he is not afraid to stand up for what is right. Harvey Milk will be able to raise the questions on the floor of the Assembly that our 'experienced' politicians overlook—or are afraid to raise."*

The closing weeks of the campaign had been filled with disappointments as the Machine Milk vilified proved every bit as influential as he depicted it. The press that egged him on did not endorse him, and kindred spirits such as Fr. Eugene Boyle ultimately endorsed his opponent Art Agnos. And then there was that overwhelming direct mail strategy the Agnos campaign launched at the end. The contrast between Milk and the Machine remains stark here, even if perhaps a bit less vibrant than it had been while the prospects on the campaign trail seemed brighter. Yet there is still a twinkle in Milk's description of his political hero Harry Truman, commemorative and comparative, conveying a sense that the fight is worthwhile because the people he hoped to represent mattered so much. Milk garnered 13,400 votes, fewer than he had received in 1975, fewer than he had predicted when plotting the maverick challenge to the Machine, and 3,600 shy of Agnos' total. And yet the numbers as depicted on his map at Castro Camera offered promise despite his third loss in as many campaigns. As the Zenger's *article appeared that November, voters finally approved district elections for 1977. Harvey might be discouraged and in debt, but politically speaking, he was back in business.*

. . .

There is a basic difference in my concept of what a member of the State Assembly should be, versus that which my opponent holds. In my opponent's campaign material, he stresses that he will be a "troubleshooter" for the people, basing this concept on his experience as a wellpaid aide to a member of the Assembly from another district.

My concept is different. I think a legislator should be involved in the root causes of the problems that plague us. He should be involved with enacting legislation to correct these problems, thus doing away with the need for "troubleshooters" in the first place.

If we need "troubleshooters," at the present, it's because so many of our legislators seem to have no idea or plans for solving our problems. In fact, they seem to have given up trying to solve the problems themselves and have merely attended to the symptoms substituting temporary "programs" for real solutions. They avoid the hard, politically unpopular, long-term decisions and rely more and more on the short-term answers provided by their "troubleshooters." It's like putting Band-Aids on a cancer when the logical, though difficult, solution might be surgery.

And so our unsolved problems breed more and greater problems, which in turn breed the need for more "troubleshooters." The bureaucracy continues to do what it does best—create more and more bureaucrats—and we end up with government by "troubleshooting." My opponent even lists as his greatest qualification those of a "troubleshooter"!

I think my opponent lowers the position and importance of a legislator when he conceives of the post as being that of a glorified "trouble-shooter." There is a good reason for this. He has spent the last ten years of his life working for the government—meaning you—at an excellent salary. He has been sheltered in the arms of the System. While he is un-doubtedly aware (at least in the abstract sense) of poverty, the disruption caused by the loss of a job, and the crippling financial blows that steadily mounting taxes can cause a homeowner, for him it's been something of a spectator sport. He's been an observer, not a participant and has never really experienced the daily fight for survival that most of us have to face. I'm not being accusatory here—in some respects, I may be envious. I'm a small businessman and I'm well aware of the uncertainties of the economy, exactly what the "inflationary spiral" means when I'm forced to raise prices to my customers, and how taxes can eat into your earnings.

HARRY S. TRUMAN

Like every politician, I have my own model. My personal hero in government—it's no secret!—is Harry Truman. He was a great President, and I think that one of the reasons why is that he operated a small business prior to going into politics.

Unlike many Presidents, he wasn't born into great wealth. He had to scratch for every dime he made. He never developed contempt for the common man, perhaps because he had personally waited on so many of them in his Kansas City clothing store. Once in public office, he never patronized his constituents, perhaps because he never forgot the time when he had to file bankruptcy.

The people who supported Truman were those who had to sweat for their daily bread, many who may not have been as articulate as others with their tongues, but were loving in their hearts, those who instinctively recognized that no person is born to greatness, but many people rise to it.

Truman was beloved by the people because he was one of them—and they knew it. He was not a devious President and disconcerted many of his fellow politicians by saying what he thought, not by parroting what he knew would be popular. When he retired, he spent his days in Independence giving personal tours of the Truman Library and lecturing to school kids on representative government.

In his final days, Harry Truman always considered himself a representative of the people.

I think that's important. The government doesn't belong to the lawyers. It doesn't belong to the professional politicians, and it doesn't belong to the bureaucrats who, understandably enough, have become wedded to the patterns of thinking that prevail within bureaucracy itself.

The government belongs to the people. And new ideas, as they usually do in business itself, will have to come from the outside—from the people. That's why we have elections as often as we do: to get new ideas and new input from the people.

I can understand my opponent's approach to government and sympathize with it. He wants to solve the day-to-day crisis—it's the only approach he knows. He's a bureaucrat and to be honest, we need some bureaucrats. But we aren't going to solve our problems by electing to public office the aides of those who have already wrestled with those same problems for the past two decades—and lost two falls out of three. We need new input, we need new ideas.

Unfortunately, it hardly seems reasonable to assume that a man who has worked within the bureaucracy for the last ten years is going to have any.

22

"Uncertainty of Carter or the Certainty of Ford"

Column, *Bay Area Reporter,*
September 2, 1976

This was not what you would call an ideal slate of presidential candidates for the GLBTQ community—a conservative Republican or a Democrat who identified as a born-again Southern Baptist. Jimmy Carter, however, had surprised and confounded many on the campaign trail with his un- expected statements on sexuality. Best remembered is the eye-popping Playboy *interview in which Carter admitted that he had "committed adultery in my heart many times." Perhaps not recalled by many is that Carter on several occasions also publicly expressed his opposition to ho- mophobic discrimination. In the San Francisco press conference to which Milk refers in this "Milk Forum" column, Carter pledged to support New York Congresswoman Bella Abzug's bill that would add "affectional or sexual preference" to the 1964 Civil Rights Act, stating that "I will cer- tainly sign it, because I don't think it's right to single out homosexu- als for special abuse or special harassment." However, his perspective on gay rights was ambivalent to say the least, and despite Milk's clever rhetorical turn here on the notion of "uncertainty," it would have been foolhardy to trust Carter's commitment. After all, in that same* Playboy *interview, Carter conceded, "The issue of homosexuality always makes me nervous. It's obviously one of the major issues in San Francisco. I don't have any, you know, personal knowledge about homosexuality and I guess being a Baptist, that would contribute to my sense of being uneasy. . . . It's political, it's moral, and it's strange territory for me . . .*

to inject it into a public discussion on politics and how it conflicts with morality is a new experience for me. I've thought about it a lot, but I don't see how to handle it differently from the way I look on other sexual acts outside marriage." Carter's ambivalence would continue into his presidency, with those campaign pledges unconsummated.

Nevertheless, Milk's comparative analysis had much to be said for it. President Ford's official position was that he had no position on the issue of gay rights. And his actions spoke even more loudly than his silence. On September 22, in San Francisco, Ford narrowly escaped Sara Jane Moore's assassination attempt because of bystander Oliver "Bill" Sipple's selfless effort. Sipple had saved the president's life. Sipple was also gay. That fact should not have mattered to the president, but it did. The fact that Sipple was closeted should have mattered to Milk, but politics mattered more. Milk leaked Sipple's sexuality to the press, and the story of the gay veteran who thwarted Ford's murder made national headlines, and traumatized Sipple and his family. No doubt that trauma was exacerbated by the president's homophobic ingratitude, which, as Milk dramatized, was more egregious by contrast to his magnanimity for those less deserving of his public gesture. Ford's note of thanks that ultimately arrived only after browbeating from the press must have seemed quite hollow to the shaken Sipple. Unaware that Milk had outed him, Sipple gave a copy to the man he had worked to elect in 1975, signed "To Harvey, a good friend."

Most important in this column is Milk's enacted vision of gay power by interpellating and empowering GLBTQ people as agents of change, as a powerful political collective of bloc voters, who could and should cast votes based on the very particular measure of a candidate's commitment to gay rights. The promise of gay power resides in its capacity to mediate and transform the political difference between certainty and uncertainty.

. . .

Facing the reality of it all, either Carter or Ford will be our next president. Some people, especially those who are content with the "way things are," will opt for Ford because they know where he is and can "live" with him. They argue that they don't know where Carter is, and that uncertainty bothers them. Thus, while they are not happy with Ford, they—like many people—will stay with the status quo. Think about Columbus, Marco Polo, George Washington, etc., staying with the "certain" things of life!

Given the fact that this is a problem with many people, let us look at the certainty of Ford and the uncertainty of Carter on one important issue: Gay people's rights. Where do these two people stand in regard to the rights of 5%–10% of the nation's population? Yours and mine.

First let's look at the "uncertainty" of Jimmy Carter. He has stated—not in front of gay audiences to gay press, but right in front of the national press—more than once that he regards as an equal sin—and lumps them together—fornication and adultery! He does not regard a person's being gay any more or less of a sin as—well, I guess, what 90% of the people of the nation do. He then further states that he believes that the government has absolutely no business whatsoever interfering with a person's right to work or live, no matter what their sexual orientation is. He continues with the statement that he would sign Abzug's bill for gay equal rights. In other words, he stands for gay rights laws being passed even though he regards homosexuality as a sin alongside of fornication and adultery. That is more than the California State Assembly or State Senate feels. They never got a gay rights bill out of committee.

Can you "live with" a president that regards you as a sinner but feels that the government has no business interfering with your personal life and will sign into law that point?

On the other hand, we have the "certainty" of President Ford. Let's look at where he stands on that same issue.

During his term as President, Ford was close to being killed twice. Once he was driving in New England and his car was hit by another car driven by a young person. The next day the president called the young driver and personally talked to him to tell him that while that car came close to killing him (Ford), he (the driver) should not worry, etc. Great! Humanitarian at the least. Concerned about another human even though it was one who almost killed him! What a great leader! However, not too long before that incident, Ford was almost killed by a woman here in San Francisco. The police and Secret Service all agree that the only thing that saved the President's life was the action of a person who grabbed the gun and forced the bullet to miss its target. In other words, that person, according to all our experts, by his action saved the life of the President.

And what did our President do about that? After all, if he will call and talk person-to-person to a young man who almost killed him in an accident, you would think that he might even invite the person who saved his life to the White House. Did that person get an invitation to the White House? No. Did that person get a phone call from the President? No. Did that person get a personal letter immediately thanking him? No. Oh, about a week or two later and with much hullabaloo from the press, he did get a letter from the President—similar to letters sent to some of the police who later assisted the hero. Short and almost form letters.

We hear a lot about words vs. actions. I think that the actions that Ford took in these two cases say a lot about the man. Why would he talk personally to someone who almost killed him and almost ignore someone who saved his life? One was gay; one was not. Can you guess which one was the gay person?

Yes, the "certainty" of Ford is that he couldn't even get the (whatever the word is) up to thank a person who saved his life—a person who was gay. Ford might stand for the rights of people—but somehow I'm not "certain" that that does not include gay people.

The point? Well, the worst thing that Nixon did to gay people was his appointments to the Supreme Court. For a long time I have been saying that the most important decisions that governors and presidents make, excepting war, are who they put on the courts. These judges affect our day-to-day life more than anything else that they do; and because the appointees stay on long after the executives leave, the effect lasts and lasts. Look at what Nixon's Supreme Court did in regard to gay rights. They would not even hear the case that was brought up this year! And Ford is more conservative than Nixon.

Ford wanted to impeach Earl Warren! Ford started the fight and led the fight to impeach the best friend we had on the court! What kind of people do you think Ford will appoint to the court? Friends of gay rights? Ford, who pardoned Nixon and lets Connally be his mouthpiece, is no friend of gay rights. (Interestingly, Ford loved Connally's approach to the campaign this past week. Connally is the person who was acquitted in his case of being accused of taking illegal money; but the person who was accused of giving the money was convicted for it! You figure that one out!) Yes, Ford loves Connally. Yes, Ford pardoned Nixon. Yes, Ford wanted to impeach Earl Warren. Yes, Ford would not call the homosexual who saved his life but called the heterosexual who almost took his life. That's the "certainty" of Ford.

For me, I'll take the "uncertainty" of the man who will sign Abzug's gay rights bill. For me, I'll take the "uncertainty" of the man who regards homosexuality as much of a sin as fornication and adultery. For me, I'll take the "uncertainty" of the man who believes that the government has no business in a person's bedroom.

The other issues? We can go into them at another time—however, what good is a great economy of a great nation at a great peace if you are in jail or can't get a job because you are gay?

23

"A Nation Finally Talks About . . . It"

Column, *Bay Area Reporter*, June 9, 1977

There is a concept in social movement theory called "moral shock," an affective, cognitive, and moral surge of adrenaline born of a particularly jolting catalytic event or over-the-threshold moment, the tumult occasioned by the proverbial last straw of accumulated or projected injustice—and the framings and performances that rhetorically configure it. Moral shock, despite being an existential disruption, can culminate in a kind of clarity of vision, vibrantly altered perspective, awakening of agency (what some still call empowerment), and propulsion toward activist modalities. To appropriate the words of an evangelical such as Anita Bryant, moral shock might be called a queer awakening or conversion experience. This exuberant "Milk Forum" column is the voicing of moral shock and its after trembling, the stampede footfalls of movement in the wake of a remarkable catalytic moment.

The extraordinary highs and lows of 1977 surely qualify it as among the most consequential years in GLBTQ history to date, one that began with the wide-eyed vista of a promised land of gay rights geography, mapped by anti-discrimination ordinances in Florida, Minnesota, Kansas, Illinois, Colorado, and Oregon, and those 19 states now free of criminalized sexuality. Then came Anita Bryant, nescient siren thoroughly embraced as the bigot's darling and mouthpiece, fomenting homophobic discourse, legislation, and violence. How easily one might have despaired as that reversal came to pass with the repeal vote on

Orange Tuesday, with the impossible vindication of that devastating canard, "Save Our Children." But Harvey Milk didn't despair or retreat; he saw in Orange Tuesday a moral shock that might just galvanize a national GLBTQ movement in proportion unachieved by the heroic efforts of earlier activists. And, significantly, Milk also knew that circumstance alone was not enough, that he had to frame these vicious happenings, the visceral grief and outrage that he had witnessed in those mass marches through San Francisco, and Anita Bryant herself, as a boon that might be transformative if mobilized for GLBTQ justice and equality.

. . .

No matter which way the vote went in Florida last Tuesday, Gay people won; there was a victory deeper than the actual vote. And it is only the beginning. Too many people look only at the vote count; they do not understand what the vote means.

Without Anita Bryant there would not have been: a cover story in "Newsweek" which dispelled many of the myths about homosexuality; headlines, day after day, in major city after major city, talking about Gay rights and homosexuality; national television nightly covering Gay rights. In short, the entire nation finally opened up and talked about Gay people. Dialogue that had never before taken place became a daily occurrence. The drawing of lines put many of our enemies out in the open where they can be counted and seen. It also brought to the side of Gay people groups like the Dade County Democratic Party (where were the Republicans on this one?). Once people took the stand on the side of the Gay people, they became deeply committed.

AN AWAKENING—AND WHAT IS NEW?

Homosexuality is no longer a taboo subject in the media and in the homes and schools of a nation. The crack in the dam has taken place. While there has been much said and printed against Gay people during the campaign, that is nothing new. The laws have been there for centuries. The hatred has always been there. What was new are the words that were pro-Gay. Never before has so much positive been said and printed. Anita Bryant got in print what so many Gay people for so long have tried to do in vain. She herself pushed the Gay movement ahead, and the subject can never be pushed back into the darkness.

THE TRUE NATIONAL GAY MOVEMENT

The second victory out of Florida was from the statement made by Bryant that she would not take their campaign to San Francisco because "the Gays are too organized there." What that statement said to Gay people all over the nation is: "Let's find out just what they did in SF and how they did it. Then, let's do it here." Anita Bryant told the Gay communities of every city in the nation: GET ORGANIZED LIKE THEY DID IN SAN FRANCISCO! She has, in fact, started what so many of us have talked about—a true national Gay movement.

CALIFORNIA GAY CONFUSION

The result: We in the Gay community should copy the other movements. We must organize beyond our local areas and personal beliefs. We should start with a California state-wide convention next spring of Gay people from all over the state from ALL political philosophies. And we should invite every candidate who is running in all the primaries for all the state offices to talk on one subject only: where they stand on Gay rights and just what they are going to do for Gay people. They should be instructed that at this particular convention there is only ONE issue that we want to hear about. There will be no endorsing. No partisan play. No games. But that their stands and comments will be made public, and that their absence will also be made public.

The Blacks do this on a national level. There is no reason why, in the future, there is not a national Gay convention of Gay people from all political factions asking the candidates for President where they stand and just what they will be doing for Gay people if elected. Then when we look at the candidates on the other issues, we will at least have their Gay rights views up front and not clouded by other issues.

No longer should we allow any candidate (even our "friends") to evade the issue because it will "hurt" them with other voters. If none appear, then none should get our votes. Our votes should go to one of the minor party candidates if any of them show up.

This political action has worked, to a large degree, in SF. It should be now used on a state-wide level and then expanded on to the national level.

Anita Bryant has told us to organize all over the nation as we have done in SF. Thank you for that one, Anita!

24

"Gay Economic Power"

Column, *Bay Area Reporter*,
September 15, 1977

As noted earlier, the idea of economic power—and the independence it wrought and community it inspired—had long been a part of Harvey Milk's politics. The struggles of disenfranchised and marginalized communities had always been situated centrally within Milk's ideological views and his public commitments. Even as early as his 1973 campaign for Supervisor, a San Francisco Examiner *article quoted him as saying, "I stand for all those who feel that the government no longer understands the individual and no longer respects the individual." And, at the same time, he waged multiple campaigns against moneyed downtown redevelopment interests and their political allies.*

In the summer of 1974, just a scant few months after opening Castro Camera Shop, Milk helped organize the boycott of Coors beer throughout the string of gay bars in and near the Castro [see Document 19]. This was done as a showing of both GLBTQ solidarity and blue-collar sensibilities. During his early political campaigns, Milk had also offered unwavering support to San Francisco's unions, while other candidates and elected officials simultaneously balked at strikes planned by teamsters and firefighter unions.

His populist aims of supporting local economies translated, too, into his joining the Eureka Valley Merchants Association, the local guild that protected area business from what Milk called San Francisco's "giants." However, as discussed previously [see Document 15], when this group refused to allow openly GLBTQ businesses to associate with the other Castro burghers, Milk formed the Castro Village Association expressly to promote GLBTQ businesses. This was 1974, a time when Milk used for the first time publicly the expression, "Buy Gay." A brochure, shopper's guide, and Village map that he created in 1973 invited patrons to "Shop and Play" in the Castro. His contention in those early days was that businesses did not just generate dollars, but rather constituted communities and uplifted neighborhoods. Indeed, he would center much of his political campaigning in the coming years on supporting the GLBTQ community; as he noted later, "Gay for Gay. That's my issue. That's it. That's the big one."

The editorial included here is a later representation of Milk's GLBTQ-centered politics, as expressed in economic terms. Following from the tradition of Black nationalism (and immigrant enclave pride), Milk's May 6, 1977, forum piece entitled "Gay Economic Power" served as a call to all GLBTQ merchants to do their part in bolstering their communities. Milk's focus on the "responsibility of the gay merchant" indicated that he viewed GLBTQ economic power transactionally. That is, he first thought that GLBTQ business owners should compete responsibly and equally with "straight merchants" and, moreover, contribute to GLBTQ community causes. In turn, Milk insisted that community members themselves enter into the relationship symbiotically so as to support the GLBTQ businesses. As he said in a June 1977 letter to business owners, urging them to join his Community Guild, "There is more to being a gay business than immediate personal gains. . . . Please reach out and help build your community. It will cost you a lot . . . a little energy, a little time, and a deep concern for your community." Though he conceded that sustaining a GLBTQ economic nationalism would be difficult, what would ease this inconvenience was "Gay Pride." To that end, this document comprises Milk's views on the importance, power, and possibilities of a GLBTQ-centered economy. Importantly, this editorial demonstrates that Milk kept the issue of economics always at the forefront of his political thought. As he prepared himself for his 1977 Supervisor campaign during this month (May 1977), Milk reiterated the need to "Buy Gay"—this would have been a savvy political maneuver, as San Francisco had moved to district elections; District 5, as noted earlier, comprised the Castro and much of the city's GLBTQ-centered and GLBTQ-friendly communities.

. . .

In the last issue I talked about the concept of "Buy Gay." I talked about the fact that we go out of our way to drink at gay bars across town rather then drink at convenient neighborhood bars and the importance of carrying that concept through to other gay business. Why not go out of our way to shop at a gay store rather than a convenient neighborhood store? However, there is another important side to the concept. A side that must never be overlooked. And that is the responsibility of the gay merchant.

If "Buy Gay" spreads and the gay community starts to bring this concept to a high level then there is indeed the responsibility of the gay merchant not to become the rip off. He must offer the product at prices competitive to straight merchants. He must offer competitive service. If his business increases due to BUY GAY then he must not take advantage of the situation. His responsibility goes deeper then giving fair prices and good service . . . he must bend more towards the gay customer. If a person is going to go out of their way to support gay economic power then the merchants must show their appreciation by returning that support. This can be done in one of several ways. Better than favorable prices and service or returning some of the financial gains to the gay community.

There are many gay businesspersons who contribute heavily to the support of gay activities and organizations. There are many gay organizations that need help and as long as they are offering the gay community needed services and do not "demand" help they should be supported. The gay businesspersons who do so must be congratulated for their aid. They are needed and will be for some time.

Then there are the gay business[es] that offer better than competitive prices even though they do not have to. Some of the gay restaurants offer meals that not only are good but are at prices that are below straight competitors. What is sad is the restaurant that makes it on the gay business and then because it becomes an "in" place forgets how they got started and who their supporters were in their time of growth.

Let me also explain what I have done with my camera shop in appreciation of buying gay. There are very few neighborhood camera shops that cut prices on film and supplies. The large camera giants offer discounts to students and professionals. These range up to 20%. But they do not offer discounts to the general public unless they buy in volume. At first I could not match the 20% for my costs. I was only able to give 15%— but I gave that to all. Then I got together with another gay owned camera shop—Eye Food. Together we are able to buy in larger amounts and our costs dropped. Thus I cut my prices on film and supplies across the board to 20% off of list. That makes a price that both of our stores offer to all customers equal to the best that the camera giants offer only to their special customers. Through joint buying we are able to sell to everyone at a price that is equal to but wider-spread than any of the giant camera shops. We do that because we believe that we owe it to the community that supports us.

This type of responsibility . . . passing financial gains on to gay causes and competitive prices is the other side of the picture if BUY GAY is ever to be a reality. It can not be only on the side of the purchaser. In order to make it work in my case I joined my purchasing power with that of another gay shop. More of this can take place. One of the interesting things that is happening is the formation of new gay business associations. The *Community Guild* is only one of these. Their members may find ways to achieve joint buying and to pass the lower prices on to their customers. That association is also committed to helping the *San Francisco Gay Community Building* and the *Guild Foundation*. It is that kind of attitude that benefits the entire gay community.

More merchants must join in the BUY GAY movement by understanding their responsibility. Their profit margins may be lowered but their volume will increase and they will be helping make a stronger total gay community. It is a step towards gay civil rights.

We have to pay our taxes and we are denied our civil rights. One way to help to bring about a change in this is through keeping as much of our money circulating within the gay community. It may be inconvenient to "Buy Gay." It may be inconvenient to get to your favorite gay bar at night . . . but you get there . . . you can also find a way to get to your gay shops. What eases the inconvenience is something called Gay Pride.

25

"You've Got to Have Hope"

Speech, June 24, 1977

As Milk's political career moved into the 1977 race for the San Francisco Board of Supervisors, he stayed true to the vision he had forged through his three previous campaigns. A campaign advertisement from the summer of 1977 noted this vision succinctly: "You know Harvey Milk means it when he says that he will: **Fight** *to save the Gay Community Center from demolition,* **Introduce** *an anti-discrimination ordinance covering all businesses in San Francisco,* **Work** *for gay affirmative action . . .* **Sue,** *if necessary . . .* **Make sure** *that the gay community gets its fair share of City services." As one would expect, Milk never wavered from his position that GLBTQ communities needed an avowed GLBTQ leader in office, and one who was not beholden to those straight liberal "allies" who retreated from their GLBTQ supporters when times got tough. During this campaign, Milk first called for a statewide gay caucus that would mobilize and gather community across political, social, and other lines to create a unified front and influential block designed to test the commitment of any aspirant politician on gay issues. He inspired kids from small towns everywhere where the closet needed to be opened to hold onto "hope"—this became Milk's mantra.*

Milk's vision still bore the marks of the populist, neighborhood activist fighting for "the people" in District 5 and across San Francisco, reaching out throughout the campaign to African Americans, Latinos and Latinas, women, the elderly, and heterosexuals. This was still Milk's

145

signature theme, one that made his call to his GLBTQ family broadly resonant, even in moments of oppression. Recall that 1977 was the year of Anita Bryant's "Save the Children" campaign, a dovetailed effort to smear publicly and occlude legally GLBTQ communities. Bryant and her campaign in Dade County, Florida, succeeded in repealing the City of Miami's gay rights ordnance. Though Milk was not officially enlisted as a leader in what would be called the Orange Tuesday debacle, he became an interpreter of the event for GLBTQ folks in San Francisco. In its June 9, 1977, issue on "The Battle over Gay Rights," Newsweek mentioned that "Bryant is proving to be a catalyst for the gay-rights movement . . . drawing attention to the issue and mobilizing homosexuals to organize politically and raise funds." Part of the backlash of her "Save the Children" campaign was that leaders of GLBTQ communities stepped-up into the breach to lead their respective communities against bigotry and homophobia. Milk was a part of this invigoration of gay rights, and as he mobilized GLBTQ communities in San Francisco, his star began to rise, thereby giving way to his decision to run for the Board of Supervisors in 1977.

The need for a leader like Milk intensified as California State Senator John Briggs announced days after Orange Tuesday that he would campaign to remove GLBTQ teachers from the public schools of California. His smear and bait effort prompted some municipal politicians in California to shut down district elections (which allowed actual neighborhoods to select their leaders through a citywide vote). Importantly, the campaign helped homophobic forces remove GLBTQ-friendly officials from seats of power. If a GLBTQ person was allowed into the political fold at all, she or he was typically conservative—and silenced. As Milk once wrote of gay conservative forces, "The homosexual will never be given [freedom] as long as he is led by what blacks label 'Uncle Toms' . . . maybe we can call them 'Aunt Marys' . . . these are people who, for whatever personal reasons, tell us that we 'never had it so good' and brag about the crumbs thrown to homosexuals . . . [until] the gay community gets rid of the Aunt Marys and puts together their strength . . . we will remain oppressed and used."

Once again opposed by said conservative gay leaders, once again helped by talented young, inexperienced volunteers, and once again outspent (according to the Bay Area Reporter *in November 10, 1977, gay frontrunner for Supervisor, Rick Stokes, spent $50,000 to Milk's $8,000), Milk had finally won in November 1977. And in the process,* *he crafted his most vital campaign speech—one spotlighted in Randy Shilts' book* The Mayor of Castro Street *and immortalized in Gus Van Sant's feature film* Milk.

What came to be called "The Hope Speech" was initially conceived as a stump address, wherein Milk attempted to embolden a strong GLBTQ nationalism within the Castro, while also appealing for an alliance with other disenfranchised groups and straight folks. The speech was delivered at the San Francisco Gay Community Center on June 24, 1977, where Milk announced his third bid for candidacy for City Supervisor. The topos of "hope" was a central theme—a transcendent "hope" that "all will be alright." According to his speechwriter Frank Robinson, the "hope trope" was used because Harvey saw his campaign and success as a synecdoche of possibilities for all. He scripted the promise of GLBTQ, subaltern, and allied communities across his campaign. His election would become the manifest reality, the material embodiment, of that promise by moving the ideal of progress into the literal offices of City Hall, thereby illuminating the way for GLBTQ communities across the nation. Or, as he later said in his victory statement: "I understand the significance of electing the first Gay person to public office and what his responsibility is not only to the people of San Francisco, but to Gay people all over. It's a responsibility that I do not take lightly."

The present version of this speech has been chosen as it represents the first time Milk's campaign address ("You've Got to Have Hope") was delivered. The following version was later revised and used as a motivational speech by Milk following his election to the District 5 City Supervisor seat. Between his swearing in on January 10, 1978, to the time of his assassination on November 27, 1978, Milk delivered slightly altered versions of what is now known in Milk memory and mythos as "The Hope Speech."

. . .

I'm a person of few surprises so it will come as no surprise to you that what I'm about to say constitutes an announcement of my candidacy for Supervisor of District 5. For all I know, I may be the proverbial straw that broke the camel's back for I'm sure by now that the list of candidates is close to equaling the list of eligible voters. The true test of Democracy is when anybody can run for anything and in this case, almost everybody is. Well, they say Democracy is a participatory process so you can't say we weren't warned. . .

I've been running for so many things for so long in this city that I wear a pair of sneakers to work . . . after all, you can never tell when another opportunity will present itself.

What I'm going to say from now on, I should warn you, isn't very humorous. Some of my friends have asked why I keep running, why I keep opening myself up for a bloody nose, why I keep running into debt and, frankly, jeopardizing the financial state of my own business for we all know that it costs a great deal of money to run. Presumably I could retire to the position of gadfly—which costs nothing at all—and let *them* run the city.

Let's go back to the beginning. I am announcing my candidacy for Supervisor of a great City. Think about that for a moment. A city isn't a collection of buildings—it isn't downtown with the B of A and Trans-America Tower, it isn't the parking lots or the freeways or the theatres or the massage parlors. A city is people. In this case, some 675,000. Some 60,000 of them live in District 5. They're Latins and Blacks, whites and Chinese, young and old, straight—and gay.

Each of those people has his or her own *hopes* and aspirations, his or her own viewpoints and problems. Each of them contributes something unique to the life of the city. What they contribute, we call the "quality of life." Friends talking across fences, the baseball players in the playground on Sunday, old ladies tottering down the street hand-in-hand, the smile from a passing stranger.

Buildings have very little to do with the quality of life. They usually go dark at six o'clock at night, concrete hives for the warehousing of workers, monuments to peoples' greeds and needs. They remain desolate and empty until the *people* return in the morning to flick the lights back on and fill the corridors with bustle and activity.

There are exceptions, of course, and we happen to be gathered in one of them tonight. It's one of those few buildings that contribute in a very unique way to the *hopes* and aspirations of a particular group of people. It's not as architecturally beautiful as the B of A or even the TransAmerica. But unlike those buildings, it has a "heart and soul."

Now would you believe this? The city wants to tear it down. For a parking garage. This building—330 Grove—is our Gay Community Center. *Our* Gay Community Center. Because it has meaning to the Gay people of this city, because for us it has both "heart and soul" we've chosen to pass up the larger hotels, those palaces of marble and ice, and have our dinner here.

Consider this Center. Without it, a few nights ago where would those thousand gays who gather in the aftermath of Dade County gone? Where would they have gathered? Where would the people go who attend the multitude of Gay community meetings here? Where would the people congregate who want to take part in the fight to Save Our Human Rights, in Gay Action, in Lesbians United, in the dozens of other groups who meet here?

In the urban wars, this building has already earned its purple heart. It's played a major part in bringing together a divided people. Without 330 Grove, we would never have been able to get it together, as the saying goes . . . And why is it in the shape it is in?

Because our Supervisors want to tear this building down. For a parking garage.

For months this building has served as a focal point for the Gay Community. It's where we meet. It's our own little section of the City's turf. Responsible Gay people have tried for God knows how long to establish a center to which young Gay people can go when they arrive here from the rest of an oppressive America. A place where they can find counseling, friends and most of all, *hope*. Oh, without this Center, there would still be places they could go. The Tenderloin. Market Street. The St. Francis. They'll find counseling, all right. And they'll find friends. At so much per friend. But they won't find much *hope*.

Do you blame me if I accuse the present Board of Supervisors of being unresponsive to the needs of the Gay community? Would you deny it if I said the situation is not unique, that the Board is unresponsive to the needs of other groups, both ethnic and social, as well? What about the desire of the Board to move the pornography "Combat Zone" into the lap of Hunter's Point? Were the people of Hunter's Point consulted? When the Black community objected, they were told "it wasn't planned that way, it just happened!"

A few years ago, they closed the Sears store in the Mission district. The store was originally the doorway to the Mission and our city's Latin community. It provided employment, it drew people from other neighborhoods into the Mission so that the economic outlook of the entire area benefitted.

Today, paradoxically enough, it's being turned into an unemployment office. I don't need to tell you what kind of depressing trade-off that is.

And those are only a few examples.

A long time ago, there was an ancient Christian sect called the Manicheans. Unlike the majority of Christians of the period, they claimed that the sins of omission were greater than the sins of commission. For their beliefs they were, as you might have guessed, exterminated. But they left us a legacy. The opposite of love is not hate.

It's indifference.

There is probably no minority in this city that hasn't been ignored— on the human level— by the present Board of Supervisors. It's no longer the Seniors, the unemployed, the Asian community, the Gay, the Blacks, the Latins and so forth. They're all *US*. It's US against THEM. If you add up all the USes, you'll find we outnumber the THEMS. And yet the THEMS control.

It's the THEMS who benefit when the Gays and the Blacks and the Latins fight amongst themselves. It's the THEMS who want to tear down the homes and community centers of the USes for their special pet projects. It's the THEMS who divide—and conquer. It's the THEMS who are the real outside agitators in our communities. And they've been here for years.

Who are the THEMS? They're the ones who pay the taxes and run the corporations and have large investments in the city.

But who buys the soap, the food, the towels, the shoes, the cigarettes, the beer and the cars that make the profits for the corporations? Who buys the insurance which provides the profits for the THEMS? Who puts their money into the banks so the THEMS can invest in their pet projects? Who convinced us all that somehow people removal was the same as urban renewal?

One of the biggest myths spread by the THEMS is that since it's "their" money to begin with, they should say how the taxes are spent. But it's *your* money. Oh, there's a crumb here and there that's tossed to the different communities. They fund a program, anoint a few "leaders" to run it who then go into the community and shout: "Look what they've done for us!"

The THEMS get most of the pie, the anointed leaders get a few crumbs—and therefore sing the praises of their masters and the community gets a few invisible specks. The anointed leaders are the Uncle Toms—and yes, the Gay community has its fair share. Look at who sings the praises of the government in power and you'll see for the most part people who have been granted position or power or income.

Now let's get personal. Okay, Harvey, you say, enough of the rhetoric—what are *you* going to do? As a supervisor, I will raise questions in public and demand answers. On how the money is raised. And how the money is spent. I will force the other supervisors to stand up and be counted when it comes to the spending priorities of the city. One immediate example: Why money for every other parade and none for the Gay Day parade, the second largest in the City? Maybe the largest. And I will question the lack of priority for other groups and communities. It's true that I've run . . . and run . . . and run. I didn't win, but I sure acquired a long list of questions that need answering. That *demand* to be answered.

What kind of supervisor will I be? Well, the first thing to consider is that while a supervisor represents his district, he also represents the city at large. So let's for the moment ignore where you live. Also, ignore where you stand on any one issue—there's no way I can be in agreement with every one of you on every issue. Frankly, there's no way I would want to—nor do I think you would want me to.

First, the District. Currently, there are 16 candidates running for Supervisor of District 5. Of those 16, only one spoke out *in public* on the problems of Upper Market Street. Should it be a six-lane artery, or should it be a narrower street with the neighborhood in mind—a people-way instead of a highway. A limited number of lanes, some bicycle paths, trees and benches? When it came to public testimony, only one of the 16 candidates got up in *public* and stated the case.

His name was Harvey Milk.

I lobbied the Mayor on this issue, I walked the street with the Mayor and when I found out that the opposition planned on walking with Supervisor Kopp, I walked with them, too. Interestingly enough, several of the other candidates were at the first public hearing and when they heard the testimony of Market Street merchants, they got up quietly and walked out.

Another important district issue was the zoning problem on 24th Street. The neighborhood wanted to restrict second-floor shops, to prevent the street from becoming another Union Street. Aside from one other candidate who owns a 24th Street shop, I was the only other one who spoke out on that issue.

Three years ago I spoke out against the Franklin Hospital expansion. Institutional expansion into neighborhoods. This past year, I've spoken out again at all 4 public hearings. Only one other candidate spoke out, and that was in defense of the particular small street on which he lives.

Where were the other candidates on these and other District issues? Forget the words that they'll now rush into print. Where were *they,* when their words were needed and counted?

On a larger scale, where were the candidates when the problem of airport expansion came up? Again, I was the only candidate to appear before the airport commission. And the question of parking garages, and again, the city's attempts to tear down this community center.

Where were the other candidates?

Where were the self proclaimed fighters, anxious to represent their communities?

Where were our would-be leaders? On issue after issue why were they silent?

There's the touchy subject of the Porno hearings. I attended three different hearings, not arguing the case for or against pornography but pointing out that the resolution was badly worded, that it didn't consider not only what community standards are today but what they might be tomorrow, arguing against the imposing of a pornography "combat zone" on the black community by fiat. What I and other protesters had to say must have been right: the ordinance has always been sent back revision after the hearings.

And so goes the life of a serious candidate. I've been there. From arguing the police budget to protesting high cab fares.

Actions speak louder than campaign literature.

Where were the others? Do we need a supervisor who plays it "safe?"

Is my message clear? Do you understand what I'm saying?

And now, for this particular group, the nitty-gritty. The issue that must not be ducked. One of the reasons why I have fought so hard for public office—and run and run and run. As says the Harvey Milk doll: You wind him up and he runs for public office.

Why?

Because I think there is a tremendous and vital difference between a "friend of the Gay community" and an avowed Gay in public office. Gays have now been slandered nationwide. We have been tarred with the brush of pornography, we have been libelously accused in the Dade County Affair. It is enough to have a "friend" represent us, no matter how good a "friend" he or she may be. The Black community made up its mind to that long ago when they realized that the myths about Blacks could only be dispelled by electing black leaders, so that the Black community could be judged by those leaders and not by black criminals and myths.

The Spanish community should not be judged by Latin criminals and myths.

The Asian community should not be judged by Asian criminals and myths.

The Italian community should not be judged by the Mafia myths.

Neither should the Gay community be judged by its minutely few Gay criminals and myths. Like every other group, we should be judged by our leaders. By those who are themselves Gay. By those who are visible. For invisible, we remain in limbo. A shadowy myth, a person who has no parents, no brothers, no sisters, no friends who are straight, no important positions of employment. A tenth of the nation composed solely of stereotypes and would-be seducers of small children—and no offense intended to the stereotypes.

Well, the Black community is not judged by its "friends" but by its black legislators and leaders. We must give people outside our community the chance to judge us by our Gay legislators and leaders. A gay person in office can set a tone, can command respect not only from that larger community but from young people in our own community who need both examples and . . . hope.

The first Gay person we elect must be strong, a fighter, one who is not content to sit in the back of the bus. He must be above wheeling and dealing. If I had been a wheeler and dealers, I would be on the Board of Permit Appeals today. If I had been content with the back of bus, I wouldn't have broken party ranks. The first Gay person to be elected must for the good of all of us, be truly independent. Unbossed and unbought!

And now we come to the past two weeks.

Where have the other District 5 candidates been? Feelings were running high, there was the potential danger of riots. Where were the other District 5 candidates, particularly the Gay ones from this district? We had our street marches, and they were nationwide. Six thousand here, six thousand in Chicago, nine thousand in Houston, thousands more in L.A. and who knows how many in New York and elsewhere. A nation of Gay people knew that this was our Watts, our Selma, Alabama.

They were angry. Frustrated. They wanted the world to know it. So they took to the streets. I was there every night. And I was proud to be there. I felt it was important to be there to understand and to know the tone of the people in the street. I felt that I might be of some help.

From that first Friday night, it almost did get out of hand. It got ugly. I and a few others talked to the crowd and said what had to be said. But where were our *elected* leaders? Where were the other candidates?

Where were our *Gay* candidates and gay public officials? A public official has the aura of public office. God knows it would have been easier for a public official than it was for the few others and myself.

I think, perhaps, that too many of our elected and appointed leaders forget that their first duty is to lead. And the only way to lead is by example. I disapprove of almost everything that Joe Alioto stood for but I would never deny that he was a leader, that he understood the power of a public office and how to use it to lead.

George Moscone has been a great legislator and understood the power of *that* position. But that is leadership among legislators, it is not leadership among the people. Your mayor and your supervisors, the people elected or appointed to *local* public office, are the ones who front the barricades. And for whatever reason, Moscone has failed to use or understand his present power of office.

And, so hid our appointed Gay leaders. They did not lead . . . It took a group of concerned Gay people to put out a statement warning of outsiders starting trouble in the Gay community. It was a heavy statement—but if you were there you know it was a necessary one. No other Gay candidate signed it. I took a strong position about the tone of the parade this coming Sunday. I made enemies. But I felt it had to be said and since our gay appointed leaders said nothing, I did. And without the power and office behind me like others have.

Leadership was called for and where were the other candidates?

Well, no announcement for candidacy for public office can avoid overuse of the word "I" and I'm as guilty as anyone. And now it's time to tell you why I've run so persistently for public office.

I'll never forget what it was like coming out.

I'll never forget the looks on the faces of those who have lost *hope* whether it be young Gays or seniors or Blacks looking for that almost-impossible-to-find job or Latins trying to explain their problems and aspirations in a tongue that's foreign to them.

I'll never forget that people are more important than buildings and neighborhoods more important than freeways.

I've deliberately schedule this announcement for Gay Pride Week. I've watched a million people close their closet doors behind them and I know they cannot go back.

I use the word "I" because I'm proud of myself.

I stand here before you tonight because I'm proud of you.

I've planned for some time to walk in the march on Sunday because I'm proud of my sisters and brothers.

And I'm running for public office because I think it's time we've had a legislator who was gay and proud of that fact and one who will not walk away from the responsibilities that face such a legislator. I walked among the angry and frustrated after Dade county . . . I walked among the angry and sad gay sisters and brothers last night at City Hall and late last night as they lit candles and stood in silence on Castro Street reaching out for some symbolic thing that would give them hope.

These were strong people . . . people whose faces I knew from the shops, the streets, the meetings, and people whom I never saw before, but who I knew. They were strong and even they needed hope . . . and those young gays in Des Moines who are "coming out" and hear the Anita Bryant story—to them the only thing that they have to look forward to is hope. And *YOU* have to give them hope.

Hope for a better world.

Hope for a better tomorrow.

Hope for a place to go to if the pressures at home are too great.

Hope that all will be alright.

Without *hope* not only the gays but the blacks, the seniors, the poor, the handicapped, the US's give up . . . if you help me get elected, that election. No, it is not my election, it is yours—will mean that a green light is lit. A green light that says to all who feel lost and disenfranchised that you now can go forward—it means *hope* and we—no you and you and you and, yes, you got to give them hope.

PART THREE

Supervisor Milk Speaks

26

"Harvey Speaks Out"

Interview, *Bay Area Reporter,*
December 8, 1977

Following his election in November 1977, Milk agreed to speak with journalist George Mendenhall of the politically important Bay Area Reporter *newspaper. Ostensibly, the narrative extracted from the Mendenhall interview became Milk's first fulsome statement of goals, philosophy, ideology, and literal steps to be taken for reform during his time as City Supervisor. What follows is Milk's vision for change and unity as the City of San Francisco moved into 1978 with a new Board of Supervisors, which would be comprised of a Chinese American, an African American woman, a Jewish woman, and, of course, Milk, the city's first GLBTQ official. This new Board was, in Milk's estimation, the quintessence of San Francisco's "city of neighborhoods"—a palpable demonstration of its diversity.*

Milk reminded Mendenhall of his motivation to run for office in the first place—the notion that "hope" was vital to inspire in all people. Of course, "hope" was specifically centered on gay rights first and foremost for Milk. In another Bay Area Reporter *piece a few weeks later, Milk wrote about this very inspiration: "We can look to 1978 with the sparks of hope as we see the potential leap of Gay power taking place. Gay political power will move forward on many levels . . . the impact will be felt." In the Mendenhall interview, Milk discussed how he remembered what it was like to be a teenager discovering his sexuality. Milk's election, he averred, could potentially sound a clarion call to those in doubt and in hiding that there were possibilities for political power but, perhaps most vitally, for personal safety, empowerment, and happiness. He reiterated this memory and its connection to "kids" earlier that month when writing about his legacy, noting "I think I've already achieved something. I think that it's been worth it. I got that phone call from Altoona, Pennsylvania [from a gay teenager who expressed to Milk that his election helped him come out], and there's at least one person out there who has hope . . . and after all, that's what it's all about." Milk's role in the process of voice and liberation was to prove to others that change could and will happen.*

Milk understood his role as the central GLBTQ leader in San Francisco and, perhaps, his stature as one of the most famous GLBTQ leaders in the nation. As with the "You've Got to Have Hope" speech, he wove his own ethos and personal experiences into a narrative with which others could connect. In a heteronormative society—then in Milk's time, as is the case now—where marginalization and (worse) invisibility are the central travails of GLBTQ peoples, Milk seemed to come to grips with his place in the movement. Oftentimes aligning himself with Martin Luther King, Jr., and analogizing the GLBTQ cause to the mainstream civil rights movement, he charged ahead with both credibility as the movement's primary leader and the stresses that came with the assumption of that very role.

The text below describes Milk's plans for improvement as he would take office the following month (January 1978). Those plans included the need for a gay caucus to suggest modes and policies for change, the importance of educating the GLBTQ community on issues of rights and privileges, the demand for motivating the GLBTQ community to exercise its duties in the enfranchisement process and in organizing in unified ways, and the need to work with officials like Mayor George Moscone to enact negotiated tactics in the service of social change.

. . .

B.A.R. is pleased to present excerpts from a taped speech by Supervisor-elect Harvey Milk. He spoke before the November meeting of the San Francisco Gay Democratic Club. . . .

VICTORY

I will never forget it. I cannot. I know where it comes from. I don't have any power or influence yet. It really doesn't take place until January 9.

I am just a figurehead, the one who happened to step out of the back room. I am the one who happens to have done it. It is your victory, and I do not mean just the ones who worked and voted for me . . .

The opponents threw everything against us—innuendos, phony endorsements, and all—and we still won.

WALKING FROM THE CASTRO

The swearing in will be at noon on Monday, Jan. 9. We will be walking from Castro Street.

I was elected to represent the City of San Francisco and the 5th District. I also have a responsibility of being a Gay leader. I hope the walk will include everyone.

In the 98 precincts in the district, we were first in 60 and second in 33. We worked all over the district and our victory was broad-based. I knew that it would be.

WHAT THIS VICTORY MEANS

I ran three times before succeeding. Traditionally it is three strikes and you're "out," but I play by different rules.

When the mayor asked me a year ago what my motivation was, I told him that I remember what it was like to be 14 and Gay. I know that somewhere today there is a 14 year old child who discovers that he or she is Gay and learns that the family may throw that child out of the house. The police will harass that child. The state will say that the child is a criminal and that the intelligence of the Anita Bryants will be screaming at that child. Maybe that child read in the newspaper, "Homosexual Elected in San Francisco," and that child has two options: move to San Francisco or stay in San Antonio or Des Moines and fight. The child has hope.

THE OBLIGATION OF GAY PEOPLE

Picture a country of hundreds of Gay clubs and organizations. National conventions with 8,000 people who are electing to national office friends of the Gay community. Maybe we never had it so good, compared with what went before, but the future can be greater.

We are now split: Republicans, Democrats, Socialists, Independents. Many people say, "I cannot get involved in politics and why should I? Who is going to bother us here?"

We must begin now to be involved so statespersons will go out and change the laws. It can still happen here as it did in Germany. The Briggs' are the Hitlers. If the Briggs' win, they will not stop. They will taste victory . . .

It is vital that people join Gay groups even if they cannot attend the meetings. We must have members. The politicians want to know how many people are involved. Our protection is strength.

If we don't have the money, we must have numbers. We must register people to vote. Gay people have registered 5,000 voters in front of my camera store on Castro. . . . When I first started the Castro Street Fair the city would not close the street for me. The next year I took them photos of the crowds that had been there and they closed the street.

LEARNING & BUILDING GAY POWER

There were an incredible number of speeches made at the Democratic National Convention about rights, rights, rights—but we could not get a Gay plank into the platform. This is so even though we make up 5–7% in a voting bloc. They walked away from us. My answer to that is that we shall never again go back. We must start to build toward the national convention so that we cannot be ignored. . . . The Jewish vote is estimated at a 4% bloc vote. The Democratic convention was geared to get that Jewish vote.

We have to start to learn what to do and what not to do. We must educate ourselves as the Black movement and the Jewish movements have done. Why have they been so successful and why have we been such a failure? We may not find the answers immediately, but we will learn and we will make our presence felt.

When "push comes to shove," there are more of them than there are of us. We are going to need their support, and we had better start playing their games now. We must get into battles such as the International Hotel or whatever. We should work openly as Gay people so they know who is supporting them; so they will be there when we need their support.

Get involved in someone's campaign for the June primary elections. Let them know that you are Gay. If they don't want you, we will be finding out who is who.

A STRATEGY FOR GAY POWER

We must have a statewide caucus of Gay people, not just Gay Democrats, but also Gay Republicans, Socialists, Communists, Fascists and Independents. Then we must invite all of the candidates for state office to speak to us—not about the aerospace industry, but about their positions on Gay rights.

The time has come to embarrass our friends. We must ask ourselves some questions now that will have to be asked sooner or later. We can sit in the back of the bus where we may get shoved out when it is unpopular to have us around. We might as well find out now who our real friends are. If it embarrasses certain candidates, so be it. I am embarrassed by some of them.

NATIONAL STRENGTH

We must begin now to put together a statewide movement and learn from our mistakes in doing that. Maybe in three years we can have our own nationwide convention and invite the national candidates to find out where they are. If neither presidential candidate shows up, there may be a third candidate. There is no reason why we should vote Democratic or Republican just because we are ourselves Republican or Democratic.

What good is a nation which is economically healthy, that is beautifully run, if you are in jail because you are Gay. We must learn from history that the time for riding in the back of the bus is over; that we must ride up front or ride by ourselves. We must make that decision—not just for ourselves but for that young person in Altoona, Pennsylvania . . .

THE BOARD PRESIDENCY

Five of the ten on the coming Board want to be President, and they are very nice to me. Eventually, I will vote for one of them. Then I will have the other four to worry about.

The freshmen on the new Board may get together and share their thoughts. I have had two meetings with Supervisor-elect Dan White, who is thought of as all for Mother, God, and Apple Pie. He seemed comfortable at the Oyster House on Castro [where the two met and dined].

There are many issues: speculation, rent control, etc. I believe that we will have the votes on the new Board on Upper Market Street. I would like to see the new Gay ordinance (expanding Gay employment rights citywide) considered by the new Board so we can see how they vote. . . .

RELATIONSHIP WITH THE MAYOR

I went in to see the mayor when I was elected this time. I told him, "When I criticize you, you will hear it first in this office. It is only if there is no satisfaction that they will start to hear it outside. There are certain things that the Gay community wants and needs. I will be lobbying and watching. . . . As soon as I decide who I personally think should be the next mayor, I will come and tell you. You will be the first to hear it."

THE MAYOR'S RACE

If Mayor Moscone, who made promises to us a couple weeks ago (in a published transcript in B.A.R.), does not live up to them, look for the next candidate. He knows that he made some promises and we can no longer just sit back and let promises be enough. We must have our share—no more, but no less. He has two years.

We must get involved in the mayor's race. If the mayor does not live up to his promises, then we will be involved in finding another candidate. He knows that. You are going to make the difference. Not me.

Last time I said early, "With five major candidates for mayor and two possible in the run-off, we can wait until close to the election and then say, 'We offer you enough votes to put you in the run-off and this is what we want. . . .'" Many "leaders" in the Gay community who were desirous to retain their token positions let this slip out of our hands. They stopped the Gay community from making a major move at that point. Let us never let that happen again.

WORKING TOGETHER

We must stop fighting among ourselves because someone is not liberal enough or someone is not conservative enough or someone doesn't have the right personality. We must stop fighting and work together. Even if we can't stand each other, we have to work together. . . . There are also lots of people still "coming out" and you know what they are going through. Some are petrified about their careers. They need us to help them in their coming out.

FOCUS ON THE GAY ISSUE

It is not that the Gay issue is more important or that the other issues do not count, but we must focus on the Gay issue. There is no reason why other groups cannot discuss Gay issues. We cannot allow them off the hook.

I understand the problems of Women, Blacks, Chicanos and others, but I don't want to give them a way out. We are the only group discriminated against by the law. I would like to see support for us on this one issue.

I don't think that we should fall into the trap of trying to accomplish too much and allow others to say, "We are for human rights and thank you very much." I have heard that too often. . . . I don't see other movements speaking out against Briggs.

I want to say to the governor, "We know where you stand on employing women. We read it in the papers. How many Gay people do you employ?" I don't see Governor Brown dumping some orange juice and announcing, "Enough of Anita Bryant."

MY COMMITMENT

I have already scheduled meetings in the Haight area. There are about 15 District 5 neighborhood and association meetings a month. Either one of my two aides or myself will be at those meetings. I will also be available and accessible to the broader community and the Gay community.

We have to keep pushing. The mayor was right when he said, "The supervisors would have closed Polk Street for Halloween if there had been 70,000 head of cattle down there." How far do we push?

We must be strong and be heard. We must push as hard as they push and then push a little stronger.

Since I speak as a Gay person, I am very much aware of the responsibility that I have. I will make mistakes, and when I do, my aides will remind me of them. I hope that the mistakes will not be too serious.

27

"A City of Neighborhoods: First Major Address I and II"

Reprinted speech, *Bay Area Reporter*,
January 10, 1978, and February 2, 1978

*The day following his inauguration, Milk attended a fundraising din-
ner for the California State Democratic Committee. Though Lieutenant
Governor Mervyn Dymally, who was running for re-election, was the
official keynote speaker, all anecdotal accounts (most notably journalist
Randy Shilts's impressions in his book* The Mayor of Castro Street*) indicate that Milk stole the show. Speaking of Dymally, Milk noted in a letter to his movement that the politician was "more than a good 'friend'"
because he had taken a stand alongside the gay liberation movement. In
fact, part of the fundraising dinner was dedicated to helping Dymally win
the election, as he had "been singled out by the conservative Republicans
for defeat" due, in part, to this very support. This message carried over
to Milk's "City of Neighborhoods" address presented here. Seen in this
public limelight was his charming and theatrical delivery that had so at-
tracted people in San Francisco to his causes, leadership, and personality.
During this first "official" speech as Supervisor, Milk relished the media
attention he received and set the lively tone for his future public addresses
as one of the city's most popular politicians. In the speech that follows, as
one might expect from a populist, his message spotlighted the importance
of San Francisco's diversity and the class idea that people matter more
than "big business." To remedy the influence of those big businesses pur-
porting to "transform the city," Milk's discourse here took as its core
issue the importance of people in San Francisco lifting themselves out the
problems befalling the city—crime, overpopulation, gentrification, and*

discrimination against Latina/os, African Americans, and the GLBTQ community. He was always concerned about those people living outside the city who commuted in to work. These folks, Milk was fond of noting, did not care much for San Francisco's neighborhoods. They only felt "condemned to live in them"; these were heteronormative white-flighters who could barely wait to move away from the city's centers.

In the end, Milk's message in this document is another example of his populist rhetoric. San Francisco was about people, about communities blending together in powerful ways to improve communal and public life. His victory was for all in the city; as he wrote in the Noe Valley Voice *a month after the speech that follows, "[The election] must be taken as a victory for the entire districts and not any one part. I accept this widely-based, broad support with warmth." To Milk, only "the people" could save San Francisco, a municipal mecca that could potentially be the city of the future. San Francisco, according to Milk, could mean "new directions, new alliances, new solutions for ancient problems."*

.   .   .

In 1977, a large seaport city on the East Coast voted to take away the rights of some people. Later that year, a large seaport town on the West Coast voted into office one of those same people. That same West Coast city once had a frightening nightmare of the future—and the next morning promptly voted against Richard Nixon. That same city voted to decriminalize marijuana and now sees states like Mississippi follow its lead.

That city, *our* city—San Francisco—has now broken the last major dam of prejudice in this country and in so doing has done what no other city has done before.

How does one thank a city? I hope, with all my heart, that I can do the job that I have been charged to do and do it so well that the questions raised by my election will be buried once and forever—and that other cities once again will follow San Francisco's lead.

I understand very well that my election was not alone a question of my gayness but a question of what I represent. In a very real sense, Harvey Milk represents the spirit of the neighborhoods of San Francisco. For the past few years, my fight to make the voices of the neighborhoods of this city be heard was not unlike the fight to make the voice of the cities themselves be heard.

Let's make no mistake about this: The American Dream stands with the neighborhoods. If we wish to rebuild our cities, we must first rebuild our neighborhoods. And to do that, we must understand that *the quality of life is more important than the standard of living.* To sit on the front steps—whether it's a veranda in a small town or a concrete stoop in a big city—and talk to our neighbors is infinitely more important than to huddle on the living room lounger and watch a make-believe world in not-quite living color.

Progress is not America's only business—and certainly not its most important. Isn't it strange that as technology advances, the quality of life so frequently declines? Oh, washing the dishes is easier. Dinner itself is easier—just heat and serve, though it might be more nourishing if we ate the ads and threw the food away. And we no longer fear spots on our glassware when guests come over. But then, of course, our friends are too afraid to come to our house and [we] to go to theirs.

And I hardly need to tell you that in that 19- or 24-inch view of the world, cleanliness has long since eclipsed godliness. Soon we'll all smell, look and actually be laboratory clean, as sterile on the inside as on the out. The perfect consumer, surrounded by the latest appliances. The perfect audience, with a ringside seat to almost any event in the world, without smell, taste, and feel—alone and unhappy in the vast wasteland of our living rooms.

I think that what we actually need, of course, is a little more dirt on the seat of our pants as we sit on the front stoop and talk to our neighbors once again, enjoying the type of summer day where the smell of garlic travels slightly faster than the speed of sound.

There's something missing in the sanitized life we lead. Something that our leaders in Washington can never supply by simple edict, something that the commercials on television never advertise because nobody's yet found a way to bottle it or box it or can it. What's missing is the touch, the warmth, the meaning of life. A four-color spread in *Time* is no substitute for it. Neither is a 30-second commercial or a reassuring Washington press conference.

I spent many years on both Wall Street and Montgomery Street and I fully understand the debt and responsibility that major corporations owe their shareholders. I also fully understand the urban battlefields of New York and Cleveland and Detroit. I see the faces of the unemployed— and the unemployable—of *this* city. I've seen the faces in Chinatown, Hunters Point, the Mission and the Tenderloin and I don't like what I see.

Oddly, I'm also reminded of the most successful slogan a business ever coined: the customer is always right.

What's been forgotten is that those people of the Tenderloin and Hunters Point, those people in the streets *are* the customers, certainly potential ones, and they must be treated as such. Government cannot ignore them. Businesses ignore them. What sense is there in making products if the would-be customer can't afford to buy them? It's not alone a question of price, it's a question of ability to pay. For a man with no money, 99¢ reduced from $1.29 is still a fortune.

American business must realize that while the shareholders always come first, the care and feeding of their customer is a close second. They have a debt and a responsibility to that customer and the city in which he or she lives, the cities in which *they* the businesses themselves live or in which it grew up in. To throw away a senior citizen after they've nursed you through childhood is wrong. To treat a city as disposable once your business has prospered is equally wrong and even more short-sighted.

Unfortunately for those who would like to flee them, the problems of the cities don't stop at the city limits. There are no moats around our cities that keep the problems in. What happens in New York or San Francisco will eventually happen in San Jose. It's just a matter of time. And like the flu, it usually gets worse the further it travels.

Our cities MUST NOT be abandoned. They're worth fighting for not just by those who live in them but by industry, commerce, unions, everyone. Not alone because they represent the past, but because they also represent the future. Your children will live there and hopefully so will your grandchildren. For all practical purposes, the eastern corridor from Boston to Newark will be one vast strip city. So will the areas from Milwaukee, Wisconsin to Gary, Indiana. In California, it will be that fertile crescent of asphalt and neon that stretches from Santa Barbara to San Diego. Will urban blight travel to the arteries of the freeways? Of course it will—unless we stop it.

So the challenge of the '80's will be to awaken the consciousness of industry and commerce to the part they must play in saving the cities which nourished them. Every company realizes it must constantly invest in its own physical plant to remain healthy and grow. Well, the cities are a part of that plant and the people who live in them are part of the cities. They're all connected; what effects one affects the others.

In short, the cheapest place to manufacture a product may not be the cheapest place at all, if it results in throwing your customers out of work. There's no sense in making television sets in Japan if the customers in the United States haven't the money to buy them. Industry must actively seek to employ those without work, to train those who have no skills. "Labor intensive" is not a dirty word, not every job is done better by machine. It has become the job of industry not only to create the product, but also to create the customer.

Costly? I don't think so. It's far less expensive than the problem of fully loaded docks and no customers. And there are additional returns: lower rates of crime, smaller welfare loads. And in having your friends and neighbors sitting on that well-polished front stoop.

Industry and business has made our country the greatest military and economic power in the world. Now I think it's time to look at our future with a realistic eye. I don't think the American Dream necessarily includes two cars in every garage and a dispose-all in every kitchen. What it does need is an educational system with incentives. To spend 12 years at school—almost a fifth of your life—without a job at the other end is meaningless. Every ghetto child has the *right* to ask: Education for *what?*

It's time for our system to mature, to face the problem it's created, to take responsibility for the problems it's ignored. Criminals aren't born, they're made—made by a socio/economic system that has turned crime into a production line phenomena. "In 1977 there were so many burglaries per second, so many murders per hour. . ."

It sounds simplistic to constantly say that jobs are part of the answer. But there are things to consider. As huge as they are, corporations and companies frequently have more flexibility than the people who work for them. A headquarters company can leave town, a factory can literally pull up stakes and move someplace else. But the workers they leave behind frequently can't. The scare that's left isn't just the empty office building or the now vacant lot; it's the worker who can no longer provide for his family, the teenager who suddenly awakens from the American Dream to find that all the jobs have gone south for the duration.

It was an expensive move the company made. You see the empty buildings but you don't see the hopelessness, the loss of pride, the anger. You've done a lot more than just lost a customer. And when I say losing a customer, I don't mean just *your* customer. There are other businesses and when they move or shift, the people *they* leave behind are *also* your customers, just like you are theirs.

I think, perhaps, many companies feel that "city" is a form of charity. I think it more accurate to consider it a part of the cost of doing business, that it should be entered on the books as amortizing the future. I would like to see business and industry consider it as such because I think there's more creativity, more competence perhaps, in business than there is in government. I think that business could turn the South of Market area not only into an industrial park but a neighborhood as well. To coin a pun, too many of our cities have a complex, in fact, too many complexes. We don't need another concrete jungle that dies the moment you turn off the lights in the evening. What we need is a neighborhood where people can walk to work, raise their kids, enjoy life.

It's that simple.

And now, I suspect, some of the businesspeople in this room are figuring—perhaps rightly—that they've heard all this before. Why is it always business that's supposed to save the city? Why us? Why isn't somebody else doing something? How about *you,* for a change, Harvey? What the hell are the rest of the people in this room doing?

And you've got a point. But I merely suggested that business must help, that we must open up a dialog that involves all of us. Business decisions aren't his or hers alone for the simple reason that they effect far more people than just him or her. And we have to consider those other people. These are the ghosts that sit on your boards of directors and they must be respected.

And now I think it's time that everybody faced reality. *Real reality.* So for the next few minutes, it's going to be slightly down and dirty.

A small item in the newspaper the other day indicated what the future might be like. Mayor Koch of New York turned his back on the elegance of Gracie Mansion and opted for the comforts of his three-room apartment—and I'll refrain from any comparison to our good Governor.

Mr. Koch chose his three-room apartment because he likes it. Nothing more complicated than that. He likes it.

And believe it or not, that's the wave of the future. The cities *will* be saved. The cities *will* be governed. But they won't be run from three thousand miles away in Washington, they won't be run from the statehouse, and most of all they won't be run by the carpetbaggers who have fled to the suburbs. You can't run a city by people who don't live there, any more than you can have an effective police force made up of people who don't live there. In either case, what you've got is an occupying army.

The cities *will* be saved. The cities *will* be run. They'll be saved and they'll be run by the people who live in them, by the people who *like* to live in them. You can see it in parts of Manhattan . . . on the far north side of Chicago, and you can certainly see it in San Francisco.

Who's done the most for housing in our city? The Federal Government? The State? Who's actually renovating this city, who's buying the houses and using their own sweat and funds to restore them and make them liveable? And just how many homes do you think that includes by now? How many *thousands?* The people who are doing this are doing it out of love for the city. They're renovating not only the physical plant, they're renovating the spirit of the city as well.

The cities will *not* be saved by the people who feel condemned to live in them, who can hardly wait to move to Marin or San Jose—or Evanston or Westchester. The cities will be saved by the people who like it here. The people who prefer the neighborhood stores to the shopping mall, who go to the plays and eat in the restaurants and go to the discos and worry about the education the kids are getting even if they have no kids of their own. . . .

That's not just the city of the future, it's the city of today. It means new directions, new alliances, new solutions for ancient problems. The typical American family with two cars in the garage and 2.2 kids doesn't live here any more. It hasn't for years. The demographics are different now and we all know it. The city is a city of singles and young marrieds, a city of the retired and the poor, a city of many colors who speak in many tongues.

That city will run itself, it will create its own solutions. District elections was not the end, it was just the beginning. We'll solve our problems—with your help if we can, without it if we must. We need your help—I don't deny that—but you also need us. We're your customers. We're your future.

I'm riding into that future and frankly I don't know if I'm wearing the fabled helm of Mambrino on my head or if I'm wearing a barber's basin. I guess we wear what we want to wear, we fight what we want to fight. Maybe I see dragons where there are windmills. But, something tells me the dragons are for real and if I shatter a lance or two on a whirling blade, maybe I'll catch a dragon in the bargain.

So I'm asking you to take a chance and ride with me against the windmills—and against the dragons, too. To make the quality of life in San Francisco what it should be, to help our city set the example, to set the style, to show the rest of the country what a city can really be. To prove that Miami's vote was a step backwards and that San Francisco's was too forward.

Yesterday, my esteemed colleague on the Board said that we cannot live on hope alone. The important thing is not that we cannot live on hope alone, but that life is not worth living without it. If the story of Don Quixote means anything, it means that the spirit of life is just as important as the substance.

What others may see as a barber's basin, you and I know is that glittering, legendary helmet.

28

"The Word Is Out"

Public letter, February 1, 1978

On occasion, Milk used his new political office to take nonlegislative stands on issues related to gay rights. In October 1977, the Canadian province of Quebec passed a law banning discrimination against GLBTQ communities in the public franchise, workplace, and schools. The larger English-speaking Canadian nation refused to do so, and, in fact, key political leaders spoke out against protecting GLBTQ folks. Actually, some Canadian officials went so far as to suggest that GLBTQ individuals not receive workplace rights, in particular, at all. Milk called this discrimination "economic sanctions." Just as he had done with the Coors beer episode, Milk specifically insisted on a boycott as a tangible tactic. In a different memo a few days later than the document presented below, he wrote, "I strongly support a boycott of tourism in the English-speaking Canadian provinces in order to get those governments to recognize the rights of their gay citizens." He felt the need to issue a remonstration against the Canadian government; the press release below represents his larger protest. Note that Milk's discussion hints at a pan-GLBTQ community—the insistence that there was a GLBTQ diaspora that could come together in order to countermand Canada's willingness to support public homophobia. Moreover, it is clear that Milk worked through coalition building in connecting other minority groups to the GLBTQ community's causes. Essentially, the press release spoke to Milk's promise to use his office not just for gradualist strategies of negotiation when dealing with policy decisions but also for clear and ideologically potent immediatism regarding issues of gay rights. The release also demonstrated Milk's commitment to global causes in addition to those situated in the local San Francisco scene.

. . .

The word is out . . . The word is out that we are out . . . That just as the black community tossed aside the establishment's wanting blacks to "stay in their place" so too does the gay community toss aside the establishment's concept that we will "stay in our closets." . . .

The word is out that we will no longer go forth with hat in hand and be thankful for a crumb. . . . The word is out that we want our fair share . . . Not more, no less . . . And that we will *demand* our fair share.

The word is out that if the Canadian government wants to apply economic sanctions against the gay community, that the gay community of the United States will apply economic sanctions against the English speaking Canadian provinces whenever possible.

The word is out that discrimination against blacks or women or Spanish or gays or French-speaking peoples is discrimination against all people. The word is out that to attack one minority is to attack all minorities.

The word is out, and let the Canadian government and all bigots hear it loud and clear. Gay people are coming out, speaking out and we have no more intention of going back into our closets than black people have of going back into chains and slavery.

29

"Letter to 'Abe' on Domestic Politics"

Private letter, February 7, 1978

Milk wrote a number of personal letters involving political matters. In the one that follows, he addressed Abe Forten, a local businessperson and Chamber of Commerce leader, about the difficulties of people outside the city making their living in San Francisco. His words here echo his "City of Neighborhoods" speech, wherein he said, "the cities will not be saved by the people who feel condemned to live in them, who can hardly wait to move to Marin or San Jose—or Evanston or Westchester. The cities will be saved by the people who like it here. The people who prefer the neighborhood stores to the shopping mall, who go to the plays and eat in the restaurants and go to the discos and worry about the education the kids are getting even if they have no kids of their own." Milk was particularly upset about businesses setting up shop in town only to force their ideas for city planning while actual residents had to sit by idly as their neighborhoods changed around them. The letter below indicates a change of tenor for the city, at least as Milk perceived it. To him, San Francisco's old guard, business-centric ideologies were gone; instead, a people-oriented city had replaced big business. Milk argued that the city's big change was its dynamic and diverse people. "The old minorities have become the new majorities," he wrote. No longer primarily white and middle class, San Francisco was witnessing a change in ethnic makeup and class composition. The city was becoming a bastion of working class folks of myriad races, nationalities, and heritages. A November 1977 Bay Area Reporter article discussed these shifts as they related to the 1977 citywide elections, where "the white Richmond District elected an Asian, Gordon Lau, while the area that includes Chinatown elected an Italian, John Molinari." This mix of people sought to control their own destinies, and Milk stood as an advocate for his city's many diverse neighborhoods. Not much is known about Abe Forten, but he stands as a synecdochal business leader—one of the people whom Milk approached about adjusting to the city's economic changes and populace shifts.

. . .

Abe:

You have my "foreign policy" . . . here are some thoughts on one of my "domestic policies."

People who make their money in San Francisco, but don't live in San Francisco have at best an intellectual/financial commitment to the City. But they *don't* have an *emotional* commitment. They're not emotionally involved with the problems of the Police Department, the Fire Department, the conditions of the streets, the Muni, housing, etc. And it's that emotional commitment that makes all the difference.

As a Supervisor and as a resident, I think that I can truthfully be described as "patriotic" when it comes to San Francisco. The most I'm doing when I attack people who make their money here but don't live here is accusing them of a lack of local patriotism. Good God, the local boosters want the baseball team to stay in San Francisco, or the local football team, or whatever. What's wrong in asking the business leaders of the city to stay in the city as well? It's the same sort of boosterism.

How can the business leaders ask new industry and commerce to move to the city if they themselves don't? How can the business leaders ask people—families—to move back to the city if they themselves don't? The business leaders have a great opportunity to lead . . . to stop the exodus. To turn the tide. To start to move back to the city that they say they love.

Nobody has any intention of forcing people to live in San Francisco. In one sense, that would be denying them their right to live wherever they want. But then, aren't those who *have* to live here—the poor, the retired—also being denied their rights if these outsiders run the city?

This is going to be an unpopular statement, but I think it might be a true one. Those of us who are left behind, or who desire to stay in the cities, are compelled to deal with the city's problems. We *have* to. It's only natural that we resent those who copped out, those who fled to the sanctuaries of suburbia but who still make their money from the city and want to run it their way.

In considering the problems of the cities, one factor becomes of extreme importance: the old minorities have become the new majorities. The city is no longer primarily white, established, middle class, or even primarily married with children. It's yellow, brown, black, with a steady influx into the middle economic class of people who were formerly lower economic class. It's also increasingly young marrieds with no children, or young couples who aren't married, or extended families, or gays, or singles, and most certainly seniors. Some of the answers they see for the problems of the cities may differ drastically from some of the answers desired by those who used to live in the city but no longer do so. Above all else, we must consider the new demographics of the new city.

It should also be obvious, in considering the cities, that America is no longer in the position of tearing down and building anew. We no longer have those kind of resources. We no longer have that kind of wealth. And, increasingly we no longer have that desire. America is becoming Europeanized. In many cases, it's cheaper to renovate than to rebuild. And it may be more aesthetically pleasing. The new generation doesn't live in the future alone; it also lives in the past. We have an ancestry; we have roots. It's nice to be able to look at that ancestry as we walk down the street. With the past still part of the present, we won't suffer so much from future shock.

"Letter to Council Members re Judging People by Myths"

Public letter, March 13, 1978

One of the issues Milk was most passionate about that related to gay rights involved the popular and public misrepresentation of GLBTQ communities. He was specifically concerned about stereotypes and how a homophobic America accepted the "myths" passed around by a larger hegemonic system of oppression that painted GLBTQ folks into a corner of deviance. As he wrote in this letter to his fellow City Supervisors, his election as the city's first GLBTQ political leader held the promise to shake up these myths. Of course, such stereotypes often translated into public policy, as it did for California State Senator John Briggs and his campaign, later in 1978, to ban GLBTQ individuals from working in public education. The specter of such myths were raised during Anita Bryant's 1977 "Save Our Children" campaign that become the template for Briggs' initiative. Calling GLBTQ people "human garbage" and aligning them discursively with prostitutes, pimps, and drug dealers, Bryant—followed by Briggs—fashioned a popular rhetorical career by misrepresenting GLBTQ communities. Just under a year following "Orange Tuesday," Milk was back to stemming the tide of homophobic ideologies as he moved to curb yet another anti-GLBTQ campaign. This initiative, Proposition 6 (the Briggs Initiative), was ripe with stereotypes issued by Briggs. He often talked about GLBTQ teachers recruiting their students and in one pro-Proposition 6 pamphlet he reproduced pictures of men in drag with the caption, "Take a good look at this man in this photo wearing an earring and fingernail polish.

Ask yourself this question, 'Is this the kind of man I want teaching my children?'" Obviously playing to performative stereotypes, the underlying messages of Briggs' rhetoric was one of bigotry through essentialization. Also, a New Times article reports that Briggs' television spots often included "still photographs of young boys killed by homosexual Dean Allen Corll of Houston and of the victims of the trash bag murders in California, followed by film of their bodies being dug up or lifted out of garbage cans." In this example, Briggs equated every GLBTQ individual with one particular criminal—who just happened to be gay. By extension, Briggs attempted to convince Californians that GLBTQ folks were dangerous—in the classroom and elsewhere. As he was fond of saying, "What scares me is people going into the booth and voting for that last great taboo."

Milk's present letter likely came as a precursor to his internal Board campaign to urge for a gay rights ordnance for the City of San Francisco. The law would protect GLBTQ communities against discrimination in the workplace and in education. Moreover, safeguards against police brutality and economic discrimination (i.e., banking, loans) would later be considered as a part of the reform Milk urged. Milk was successful in getting committee support, and ultimately he persuaded the Board to vote in the affirmative. But he never had a chance to see the citywide law come to fruition, as he would be assassinated some eight months later by fellow Board Supervisor Dan White. Coincidentally and tellingly, White was the only Board Supervisor to vote against Milk's gay rights ordnance.

. . .

Dear Council Members:

As the only openly gay elected official in California, I would like to share with you a few comments on what my election to the San Francisco board of Supervisors means.

For too many years, gay people have generally not taken any active part in the government. For many years, many gay people, feeling disenfranchised, have given up hope for a better tomorrow. Hope that all will be right. Hope that the system does in fact work.

With that kind of background, many gay people and their energies are not put into use in the democratic society that we have.

We have learned from the past that once any group of people who are excluded from the system are brought into it, they not only dispel the fears and myths about them, but also add greatly to the general welfare of the society. So it was in the earlier days of this nation when the Irish were regarded as second class citizens, so it was with the Asians who worked on the railroads, so it was with the Blacks, the Jews, the Spanish-speaking persons. We no longer judge any of these people by their myths about them. We judge them by their elected officials and their leaders.

Now we have come to the test of our tolerance. We are judging gay people by the very few gay criminals and the myths about gay people. As more and more gay people move into positions of leadership, we are seeing all the myths being shattered. We are finding out as one of our presidents once stated, that "We have nothing to fear but fear itself."

I have found out since my election that gay people and other minorities across the nation see in my election a symbol of hope. That if I can achieve my position that [means that] the system is now open to all people, be they Black, Brown, Asians, the handicapped, seniors or gays. My election was a green light that the nation says we can all indeed move forward.

The future will follow the paths of prior history. Sooner or later, gay people will follow the roads of the Irish, Jews, Asians, Blacks, and Latins we have all accepted. And as that happens, more people will be given hope. While one cannot live on hope alone, I feel strongly that without hope, life is not worth living. Thus, the move toward acceptance of all people and their rights follows in the great tradition of this nation.

Gay Pride Week means just that. In San Francisco, we now not only recognize the importance of that Week, we now fund the Gay Pride Parade. We understand the need to give a nation of people hope. Nothing more, nothing less. Giving hope is, indeed, the greatest thing that any elected official can give.

Warmly,
Harvey Milk

"Resolution Requiring State Department to Close the South African Consulate" and "Closing the Consulate"

Press releases, March 22, 1978

A champion of human rights, Milk often took stands on international issues, for as he reasoned oppression knew no region, color, gender, religion, or sexuality. As a populist, he was committed to coalition building in San Francisco, to be sure. But he also viewed the joint oppression of people across geographical boundaries as vital to those in his own community. Milk was quoted in a 1978 Desert Sun *article issuing a charge to President Jimmy Carter: "I'm tired of all the silence from the White House. Jimmy Carter, you talk about human rights—in fact, you want to be the world's leader for human rights. Well, damn it, lead!" His suggested resolutions to close the South African Consulate and to withdraw investments in South Africa in the midst of the segregationist policy of apartheid spoke to his emphasis on human rights. His commitment in this milieu was similar to his challenge to the Canadian government to withdraw its proposed homophobic initiatives. As Milk told his supporters in two letters (also included) asking them to attend the Board of Supervisors meeting where the resolution would be debated, "I think this would be an emphatic statement that San Franciscans support human rights for all people and are outraged at the South African government's continuing policies of racial hatred." In the end, the resolutions garnered support from the Board of Supervisors but did not move beyond the governmental channels from there. Regardless, the four documents below exhibit just how passionate Milk was about joint oppression. Even in the crucible of San Francisco's and California's own struggles in 1978—not too mention the travails of Milk's own GLBTQ community—he took the time and energy to include a much larger public than his "city of neighborhoods" in his reform goals.*

. . .

Dear Friend,

I appreciate your interest in supporting the human rights of blacks in South Africa. As you may know, there are currently two resolutions in the Board of Supervisors which would be strong statements of San Francisco's outrage at the South African government's continuing policies of racial hatred.

I have introduced a resolution requesting the State Department to close the South African consulate here. And a resolution was introduced recently by Supervisors Hutch, Silver, Feinstein and myself urging withdrawal of investments from South Africa.

Both resolutions will be up for a public hearing in the State and National Affairs Committee on Friday, April 7 at 2:00 PM in Room 228, City Hall.

I urge you to attend the meeting to express your concerns. Hopefully, the Board will take these strong actions and your support would be very helpful.

Warmly,
Harvey Milk

Dear Friends:

On January 30th, I introduced a resolution in the Board of Supervisors requesting the State Department to close the South African consulate in San Francisco.

I think this would be an emphatic statement that San Franciscans support human rights for all people and are outraged at the South African government's continuing policies of racial hatred.

The matter will most likely come before the Board's State and National Affairs Committee on Friday, March 3 at 2:00 PM. The Committee is composed of Supervisors Gonzales, Pelosi and Silver.

I would be deeply grateful for your support of this resolution, both in testimony before the Committee in letters to the Committee members. If you are willing to testify, please call Dick Pabich at my office, so that we can organize the testimony. And please send me a copy of any correspondence you have with the Committee members.

Thank you for your interest.

Warmly,
Harvey Milk

THE STATE DEPARTMENT TO CLOSE THE SOUTH AFRICAN CONSULATE IN SAN FRANCISCO

WHEREAS, The City and County of San Francisco has long upheld equal rights and opportunities for anyone regardless of race; and

WHEREAS, The racial policies of the Republic of South Africa are a violation of the rights of many of its citizens; now therefore be it

RESOLVED, That the Board of Supervisors requests the State Department to close the South African consulate in San Francisco.

RESOLUTION URGING THE WITHDRAWAL OF INVESTMENT FROM AND DISAPPROVAL OF FUTURE INVESTMENT IN CORPORATIONS AND BANKS DOING BUSINESS IN OR WITH SOUTH AFRICA

WHEREAS, In many countries in South Africa, the racist apartheid government of four million whites totally dominates the lives of fifteen million Blacks and three million "Coloreds" (those of mixed blood and Asians); and

WHEREAS, Apartheid, the complete subjugation of Blacks and "Coloreds" to white supremacist rule, is the law of the land, denying the most elemental civil liberties—the right to move about freely, the right to a job with fair wages and working conditions, the right to live where one wants to live, and more—are officially denied to Black people; and

WHEREAS, The anti-apartheid freedom movement has been ruthlessly outlawed and subjected to fascist terror, its leaders have been imprisoned with maximum sentences, brutalized and slain, driven into exile; and

WHEREAS, United States corporations and banks which invest in and do business in these countries in South Africa perpetuate these undemocratic, political and economic practices against the majority of its citizens; and

WHEREAS, The City and County of San Francisco has substantial investments in corporations and banks which do business in countries like South Africa practicing apartheid; and

WHEREAS, The City and Country of San Francisco, on behalf of all its citizens, could make an impact on corporations and banks involved in such South African countries by withdrawing its investments in such corporations and banks; be it

RESOLVED, That the Board of Supervisors of the City and County of San Francisco urges the immediate withdrawal of all City funds invested in corporations and banks which do business in South African countries practicing apartheid; and be it

FURTHER RESOLVED, That the Board of Supervisors communicates directly to corporations and banks informing them of its action; and be it

FURTHER RESOLVED, That copies of this resolution be forwarded to the Mayor, the Retirement System Board and the City Treasurer.

32

"Letter to President Jimmy Carter"

Private letter, April 12, 1978

As 1978 moved ahead, Milk's leadership efforts garnered intensively more visibility and authority on local, state and national political scenes. He was interested in the establishment of party politics and the importance of organizing GLBTQ individuals within those political circles. One of the projects that Milk completed was successfully organizing the California Gay Caucus, a gathering across party, ideological, and social divides to create a politically united front that political candidates would (hopefully) have to address in both official rhetoric and in person at public events. This would be so if those mainstream politicians hoped to receive increasingly vocal and consequential GLBTQ votes. The caucus enacted Milk's political vision long sought in his voter registration efforts and calls for GLBTQ economic and political power and GLBTQ-centered leadership, embodying his belief that "Gay political clout must move forward in the face of the recent defeats in St. Paul and Wichita"—what he presciently called "the rise of the Right."

On April 12, 1978, Milk invited President Jimmy Carter to deliver the keynote address at the annual dinner of the San Francisco Gay Democratic Club. Though Carter declined the invitation, Milk nonetheless took the opportunity in his invitation to exhort the President about the importance of GLBTQ citizens and, of course, GLBTQ voters. In his letter, Milk wrote of a distant future in the Democratic Party where not only traditional minorities and labor unionists would be a party majority, but also GLBTQ groups. His immediate point seemed clear. That was, dominant politicians ought to consider expediency in listening to, and supporting, GLBTQ communities. As the minority caucus would grow, so went the argument, so too would its influences. Perhaps not rendered as a political threat, Milk's letter to Carter nevertheless resounded with the oncoming inevitability of GLBTQ power and the potential mistakes of ignoring its breadth on the local, state, and national landscapes.

Interestingly, Milk's letters to Carter did not stop with the rejected invitation to the San Francisco Gay Democratic Club. Rather, Milk pushed the President throughout the Briggs Initiative battle. In one June 1978 letter, Milk wrote with the niceties and pleasantries befitting a presidential appeal: "I called upon you to take a leadership role in defending the rights of gay people. As the President of a nation which includes 15–20 million lesbians and gay men, your leadership is vital and necessary." In a Desert Sun *article titled "Gays Hit Carter on Human Rights" that same month, though, Milk issued a bit more vehemence in his approach: "If Briggs wins he will not stop. They never do. There will be no safe closet for any gay person!" Whether he worked through normative tactics or firmer exhortations, Milk was unrelenting in getting Carter involved in the gay rights fight.*

Again, Milk wanted Carter to understand the impact of gay voters on the Democratic Party's success and on the President's re-election bid down the road. And over time, Milk intended to "make these gay people aware of their responsibility to vote as a major block in all elections, especially in those that can affect them greatly." The message was unequivocal in this letter to Carter.

. . .

Dear President Carter:

Like most people in this country, I am very concerned about human rights abroad and supportive of your efforts. I have worked in San Francisco towards affecting change in the South African government's racial policies and on other human rights concerns.

But I am also deeply concerned about the millions of fellow gay women and men in this nation who have been under attack from those who believe only in myths and fears about gay people and who lack an understanding of just who we are and why we are.

We are doing a strong educational campaign to dispel those myths and fears. We hope that soon the people of this nation and the world will judge gay people by our leaders and our elected officials rather than by our stereotypes, just as they do with Blacks, Asians, Italians, and other groups.

In San Francisco, we have a relatively strong political involvement. We—and particularly, myself—are putting together a strong political base within our own community and state and are forming alliances with the traditional minorities, feminists and union members. It is the goal of Lt. Governor Dymally that by 1990, the Democratic Minority Coalition, with the active support of gay people, will be the backbone of the Democratic Party in this state.

More to the point, the most active and politically aware group in San Francisco's large gay community is the San Francisco Gay Democratic Club. We will be holding our annual dinner this year on June 23rd. We have the long range goal to make that the most important political gathering in the gay community in the nation. Inviting guest speakers from all over to make their views known, we intend to let the millions of gay people who are looking for national leadership know where to look. We intend to make these gay people aware of their responsibility to vote as a major block in all elections, especially in those that can affect them greatly.

With this in mind, we would like to have you be the honored guest at this year's event. We are fully aware of your certainly crowded schedule and the political risks you might be taking by making such an appearance. But the other side of the coin is the role of leadership that you would be playing. Sooner or later, the massive gay population will indeed win their rights as other groups have already done. Sooner or later, the strife and anger and hatred and violence against gay people will be put aside. What we seek now is to leap over the many years and great turmoil that will take place by having the person who represents these many people speak out now. We seek a strong leadership role from someone and no one is better suited for that than a president who has taken a strong position on human rights across the world.

Naturally, we would appreciate a reply as early as possible. Or, if you see fit to discuss this with Vice President Mondale and decide that he might be the one to reach out to these millions of people, we would also be honored.

Thank you in advance for your consideration.

Warmly,
Harvey Milk

33

"Untitled (on Gay Caucus and Gay Power)"

Column, *Bay Area Reporter*," April 27, 1978

Part of Milk's successful City Supervisor campaign involved a robust call for a statewide gay caucus that would mobilize and gather community across political, social, and coalition-building lines. The goal in this effort was to establish a united front and to foster an influential voting block rendered to put political and electoral pressure on mainstream politicians to keep GLBTQ reform issues on their radar (see Document 32 and Document 34). And of course, politicians were invited to come; it's not that they were required, but Milk put some pressure on them. In a press release, for instance, he noted, "The caucus will . . . publicize who does and doesn't attend and the remarks of those who do attend." The threat to those wishing to skip the caucus meeting was clear enough—the GLBTQ community and larger public would be able to monitor which candidates thought little or nothing of gay rights.

In an April 25, 1978, public memorandum, Milk celebrated the promise of what a gay caucus could do. He wrote, "In no other state, and certainly not in California, has such an undertaking taken place. It marks another forward step for the gay movement. Maybe all the candidates will show up. Maybe none will. But now, for the first time, those who want the gay vote are being given the chance to seek it openly." Of course, there was a clear, utile motivation behind establishing the gay caucus—political power and a check and balance of mainstream politicians. However, Milk's insistence on a united front also emboldened the constitutive efforts of the GLBTQ community to gather strength from the caucus internally. The caucus, that is, could be a rallying point and a node of pride—pride that voice could be enacted and that a "good life" together was possible. As Milk reminded his readers in the editorial that follows, "We will see gay women and men from all over the state do what must be done and set the groundwork for the next four years and beyond. It is exciting." Milk's excitement punctuated this text; moreover, it translated into the eventual success of the California Gay Caucus. The caucus's success helped enact his political vision long sought in his voter registration efforts and calls for GLBTQ economic and political power. Moreover, the caucus would ultimately help the GLBTQ community challenge what Milk called "the rise of the Right." Part of this "Right" would eventually help launch the Briggs Initiative.

. . .

The Mayor tossed out the opening pitch for the beginning of the Community Softball League Season this weekend. The D.A. was there. The Fire Chief was there. To many of us in San Francisco, there is little new in that scene. Gay power, including power at the ballot box, has been growing to a point where no one running for a city office can ignore it. Even those who run by district, be they Supervisors or Assembly people, pay more and more attention to the gay vote.

The same thing is happening in Los Angeles, and Long Beach and San Diego are moving in that direction. And, now the full state? Why not?

The next logical extension of gay political power is to influence state-wide elections. As soon as more gay people all over California come to the realization that voting for their pocketbook is not as important as voting for our rights, then the gay vote will become solid and powerful. It could certainly become as important as any other minority vote bloc in the state. If Jerry Brown faces Ken Maddy in the general election this year, the gay vote might make the difference as to which becomes Governor. If not this year, most certainly in four years, the gay vote will be powerful enough to tip the primary race or even the general election.

The task for the gay community, statewide, is to start the organizing of a true non-partisan California Gay Caucus which will put all candidates for statewide office in the same position as those who run for office in San Francisco. Votes, money, workers—they are available. The candidates must seek them and earn them.

This year will be the start of the state Gay Caucus. The first attempt to bring the candidates and the gay community together is being tried in

Los Angeles on Saturday, May 6th. Some have questioned the wisdom of doing it this year when there is no race within the Democratic Party for Governor or Lt. Governor to provide interest. But I look at it as a training ground for putting together such a state caucus. The very fact that it is taking place makes it a success.

In no other state, and certainly not in California, has such an undertaking taken place. It marks another forward step for the gay movement. We will see gay women and men from all over the state do what must be done and set the groundwork for the next four years and beyond. It is exciting.

Every candidate for every statewide office was invited. Democrats and Republicans. It will be interesting to see who attends and what is said by those who do. The Gay Caucus will publish the results throughout the state. We will not endorse, but we will say who felt it was important enough to attend and what they said.

Maybe they will all show up. Maybe none will. But now, for the first time, those who want the gay vote are being given the chance to seek the gay vote. Up front. Not private meetings with a handful of gay people.

May 6th at the Bonaventure Hotel in Los Angeles. It will tell us a lot. Lt. Governor Dymally, Senator Cranston, Mayor Moscone and Los Angeles Mayor Bradley have all joined our side. Senator Briggs and Ex-Police Chief Davis are on the other side. On May 6th, we may see some more move to one side or the other. It must happen sometime.

For those who can make it, please join us in LA on May 6th.

34

"California Gay Caucus"

Article draft, *Alternate*, May 12, 1978

Milk's desire to establish a California Gay Caucus came to fruition as the first statewide convention took place in Los Angeles in mid-May of 1978. As noted previously (see Document 32 and Document 33), Milk had both promised to support such a caucus in his City Supervisor campaign and to take a firm leadership role in its efforts for social change related to GLBTQ communities. His excitement and pride came across clearly in an editorial published in The Alternative *newspaper in San Francisco. Therein, he informed readers, "The first statewide political caucus of this type happened and another step towards full gay power and gay rights was taken. It was a small bit of history and a training ground for all other states and for California to improve on. That it took place as a success in itself. That 'they' came was interesting. That 'they' spoke out and joined our fight was exciting." By "they" Milk referred to mainstream political leaders like Lieutenant Governor Mervyn Dymally, who was a speaker at the caucus's meeting. Dymally's presence was an outward sign that the "checks and balances" inherent in the motivation to organize a gay caucus were working.*

The California Gay Caucus meeting in Los Angeles came in the midst of two noteworthy strands of political and social context. First, several U.S. cities had suffered anti-GLBTQ legislation limiting where GLBTQ individuals could work and live—cities like Miami, Florida, where Anita Bryant's campaign was successful. Milk used these examples of homophobic policy making as flag events to push his community forward. Second and related, California State Senator John Briggs was in the process of stumping across the state for Proposition 6, his referendum project for putting similar blockades in front of gay rights efforts. The bottom line for Milk was that what happened in places like St. Paul and Wichita could potentially happen in California. In fact, as Briggs gained popularity, the so-called possibility was quickly becoming a legitimate reality. And at one point midway through Briggs' campaign, the possibility turned into a palpable reality for a great many Californians. This difficulty forced Milk to work even harder to organize a caucus and to use it as a launching point for his anti-Proposition 6 campaign during his first and only year in office.

The California Gay Caucus meeting could not have come at a better time. For one, the GLBTQ community needed to refocus its political efforts and concretize its commitment to each other. Also, though, Dymally's presence in particular spoke volumes to the general California public. When Milk mentioned that "they" came out to listen to GLBTQ leaders, he also meant that Dymally railed—of his own accord—against Briggs. Or as Milk put it, "Dymally shifted to a bitter, blistering attack on Senator Briggs and his anti-gay initiative. His emotion and anger against what Briggs is trying to do came out in statement after statement." Milk now had mainstream political support and the internal caucus that he needed to move forward against the eventual Briggs Initiative and for increased gay rights. As he had written in an earlier Bay Area Reporter *reporter issue, "The battle against Briggs will be hard and dirty on his part. We must reach out to every possible group of people everywhere in the state. I urge every Gay person to get involved in their local races . . . we need as much help as we can get, and there is no better way of getting help than to start to help others now." In the end, the caucus would serve as a catalyst for "help" both with Milk's in-groups and his external political audiences.*

. . .

It was another milestone in gay political history on Saturday, May 6th in Los Angeles. The first statewide gay political caucus took place at the new Bonaventure Hotel.

Gay people from all over the state and all political parties were invited. They came. Candidates from all parties running for state offices were invited. They came. The potentially powerful statewide gay vote finally emerged. No longer will candidates running for state office be able to avoid facing gay people. If they want our votes, they will have to seek them, out front and out of the closet.

The highlight of the day-long caucus was the remarks by Lt. Governor Merv Dymally. I use the word "remarks" because the Lt. Governor started his comments with a low-key statement, "I'm not going to give a speech, but I would like to talk about myself." He gave a little of his experience as a black person and talked about the oppression that he has faced and the attempts by the ultra-right wing to seek a candidate to run against him. Then Dymally shifted to a bitter, blistering attack on Senator Briggs and his anti-gay initiative. His emotion and anger against what Briggs is trying to do came out in statement after statement: "Briggs is trying to constitutionalize bigotry," "every ounce of tolerance is going to be attacked; every bit of bigotry will surface," "Incompetent teachers threaten the lives of our children more than any gay teacher could," "American politics survives on scapegoats," "If blacks want their equality, if women want their equality, then they must fight for the equality of gay people." Finally, the Lt. Governor made the pledge to make the anti-Briggs campaign part of his campaign and to take that message into the minority communities and throughout the state.

It was a powerful speech. Every gay person in the state would have joined those many gays in attendance with the rousing standing ovation that was given the Lt. Governor. He set the standards against which all other candidates seeking the gay vote should judged. It will be impossible to surpass that standard.

The first statewide political caucus of this type happened and another step towards full gay power and gay rights was taken. It was a small bit of history and a training ground for all other states and for California to improve on. That it took place is a success in itself. That "they" came was interesting. That "they" spoke out and joined our fight was exciting.

Gay political clout must move forward especially in the face of the recent defeats in St. Paul and Wichita. The counter balance must be the grassroots organization of the gay community. No longer can we vote one way for economic reasons or any other reasons. We must reach out to support only those who reach out and ask for our support . . . in public.

This was an experiment and it worked. Hats off to those in Los Angeles for putting it together, especially Don Amador, the gay liaison for LA Mayor Tom Bradley. . . And my thanks to all of "them" and "us" who came.

PART FOUR

Milk and the Politics of Gay Rights

35

"Keynote Speech at Gay Conference 5"

Tape cassette transcription of speech,
June 10, 1978

Moving beyond San Francisco and California politics, Milk gained more and more popularity on the national scene during his year in office as the District 5 City Supervisor. By the summer of 1978, he was entrenched in his epic battle with California State Senator John Briggs over Proposition 6. And this campaign had the national "eye" focused on the state and "ear" tuned into its larger implications for GLBTQ communities across the United States. But Milk's story—in and of itself—also became fodder for political pundits and extra motivation for GLBTQ communities facing similar oppressions and concomitantly celebrating small in-roads.

Milk was invited to Dallas, Texas, on June 10, 1978, to address a regional meeting, called the Gay Conference 5, which included GLBTQ leaders and caucuses from states in the western area of the United States. Undoubtedly, Milk entertained the same themes he had attended to in his 1977 campaign addresses and his 1978 stump speeches in favor of anti-Proposition 6 efforts. Overall, the summer of 1978 was a busy time for Milk, especially as he and his political ally and anti-Briggs debate partner, Sally Gearhart, inaugurated their Fund to Defeat the Briggs Initiative on June 6. Their press release from that day notes, "To defeat Briggs, campaigns have to be waged on many levels. Because different voters are motivated by different things and different people have misconceptions about gays, many approaches will be needed."

Certainly, the fund was one way of defeating Briggs. So, too, though, was bringing the anti-Briggs message to the Gay Conference 5. Much of what follows involves Milk's larger, nationwide appeals to support Californians in their fight against Proposition 6.

However, another spotlight of what has been deemed the "Dallas Speech" was Milk's insistence that regardless of the gay communities' coalition-building goals and his own populism, his sexuality was still core to his identity and public life. He told the Dallas audience, "I was always gay, and then something happened—I got elected and I was still gay." This self-identification was important because it exhibited a balance between Milk's mainstream political life and his sexuality—not to mention his sexual politics. At the same time, however, his sentiments below solidified that Milk centered his overall identity on being gay, an interesting move for a leader who had billed himself as a populist. Such a move, though perhaps unexpected (certainly during his walk to the inauguration wherein he held hands with Jack Lira, his boyfriend at the time), communicated both a pride and fearlessness. And if Milk was all about inspiring "hope," what better way then by showing how one could traipse the line between private and public, while ensuring that the private remained the focal point of one's subject position?

. . .

Thank you for being here. The you-s, wherever you are, make it possible for the us-es, in this case, to do our trip. Without you, without your support, the gay sisters and brothers all over the country some of us would never be able to do it. So, thank you for being here today.

In the six or seven years that I've been quite active, I've only given two written speeches—you know, wrote it out. I usually kind of like put some notes down and then don't even follow them. I gave one speech that night when the Lieutenant Governor was the guest, and I was told it was a very excellent speech, so I have one copy in case anyone wants to read it. [Laughter]

I was expecting the traditional Texas welcome when I got off the plane last night. I'd never been to that airport. And there was nobody there. [Laughter] And I said, Texas? And then it dawned on me. Very clever, you know, very smart. There's always that threat or fear that something's going to happen, that the extreme right wing, the paranoid people are going to get afraid and try to disrupt and maybe wait for me to come in and, you know, take me away someplace. And I figured if they didn't know what I looked like but they knew what Steve did, so they were watching him and waiting for him to go to the airport to get me. But he was smart. He stayed here, and figured I'd have to take the bus and nobody would interfere. So I got on a bus and it made about ten stops before it got out of the airport and thought I was in Disneyland. [Laughter] And had this magnificent ride from the airport to here, and I cruised the bus driver. [Laughter] And somebody with an aloha shirt kept saying, "My, it's cold tonight." You know, cause I'm dressed like this from San Francisco. And it was very clever. And I got here and there was no incident and I was safe and everything else. But very cheap. I had to pay the 4 dollars. [Laughter] Very tacky! [Laughter, applause] You know a New York Jew when you see one. [Laughter, applause]

Before I forget this, I was given one note by my administrative aide before I left. A gay woman by the name of Anne. And she wanted me to remind everybody that when you see the movie tonight, *Gay USA*, there's gonna be one scene where there's this lesbian in leather. And usually the audience responds pretty good, that's her lover Joyce. [Laughter] And you should see what City Hall is like . . . you know, Anne is probably one of the most together people I know, but when Joyce comes down to City Hall in leather. Picture that one. [Laughter]

Anyhow, I'm Harvey Milk and I'm here to recruit you. [Laughter, applause] I was reading the *Playboy* interview of that person from Florida [laughter], who wants to put all gay people in jail, and just stop and think about it, 20 million gay people in jail. [Laughter] We would have our own community center . . . hahaha, and instead of running for Supervisor, I'm going to run for Sheriff . . . haha. [Laughter]

Anita Bryant, last year, blamed the drought we had in San Francisco on the gay people in California. And, honest to God—this is true—honest to God, the day I got elected it started to rain. [Laughter, applause] And we had—we had a series of rainy days on and off. The day we were sworn in, some of us walked to City Hall from the Castro and—maybe I'll talk about that later—but we walked to City Hall, it was kind of clear, it was getting cloudy and—it's recorded, but I had my hand up and as I was getting [laughter] the—we do everything backwards. [Laughter] As I was getting ready to say "I do," it started to rain again! And then subsequent to that it started to rain and rain and rain! They want to recall me [Harvey laughing], to stop the rain! But it stopped and things are going pretty well.

I can't resist because you people are very political, I have one political joke. A real story joke. I only [get] to tell this about every six months or so and I told this in Chicago and they never heard it, but I couldn't believe that. So I'm going to tell it here and I don't know how many people know about Chicago politics. So this is an "in" joke if you don't know about it. It seems there was an ocean liner going across and it sank, and there was only one little, tiny piece of wood floating and 3 people were swimming towards it, but it could only hold 1. And the 3 people were the Pope, the President of the United States, and Mayor Daley. [Laughter] So, they had a discussion while treading water to see who should hold on to it and be saved. The Pope pontificated about being the spiritual leader of the world, and it was a good argument. The President, who was able to chew gum and swim [laughter, applause], said that he was the leader of the most powerful nation in the world, and he went on in his brilliant way, and there was a good argument. And Mayor Daley said that he recognized both positions but that Chicago was the hub of America, what took place in Chicago affected America. And the archdiocese of Chicago was the largest in the world, and you know it was a good argument. They all realized they all had real good arguments, so they did it the democratic way and voted . . . and Daley won 7–2. [Laughter, applause]

I've attended some of the workshops and—I look here, you know—I say that, you know, three, four, five years ago to think that this number of people would be gathered on a Saturday night in a major hotel that's used to conventions, and if anybody at that time would have said it was gay people, I would have said no. And it's so exciting to see it breaking out all over the country. That, the movement, the gay liberation movement is ready to explode. And you are part of it and you are helping it. And it's very exciting, and I watched the reactions in those seminars, workshops, and it was exciting to see the intensity. Ah, it's happening all over the country, and you realize where we've come and where we've got to go.

And my last whimsical part would be to remind you of Winston Churchill's famous statement, where he went to give a speech and the reception was the head of the temperance movement, and she said, "Sir Churchill, we've measured how much scotch you have drank in your life and in a room this size it would fill up this high." And he looked around, looked at her hand, looked at the ceiling, "So much to do, so little time left." [Laughter, applause]

And so much to do, and your being here is making that commitment. I jokingly said I'm here to recruit you, I don't have to because your being here is that commitment. And the message that anybody has to say is that without a commitment, you're just occupying space. We had better make that commitment, because we cannot afford not to. That the movement that we hear about, the Anita Bryants and the John Briggs in California and their counterparts throughout the country are trying to legalize bigotry. And we better be prepared for it, and we better make that commitment. And for those who don't understand, you better read the gay history, and I think Don Amador will let you know about that tomorrow. For those of you who have forgotten, read those history books because you've got to make that commitment, it is very dangerous. Based on what we've seen so far every ounce of tolerance is going to be attacked and every bit of bigotry will surface.

We just had a primary in California, and think about this, in San Francisco, we very seldom have races for judgeships—they usually are kind of fait accomplis. And when we do have a race it is probably the most dull race you can imagine, each telling which law school they went to. And this year we had a race, there were three people, and so in order to avoid a run-off you must get 50% of the vote. It just so happened that one of the people was a woman in which the gay community banded behind. She also was supported by other financial interests downtown, and it was probably the first time we've ever agreed on a candidate. And every wealthy name in the city was supporting her and so were every single gay person I knew, there were exceptions. And the weekend before, in liberal San Francisco, in a dull judge's race, a piece of literature went out—45,000 pieces went to homes in the most conservative area of San Francisco. And on the back it said who was supporting whom. And to this other judge, it mentioned the police officers group, this distinguished conservative, that distinguished conservative. And it said who was supporting [inaudible]. And it said "as she quoted herself in one of the gay publications she regards herself as an honorary homosexual and is supported by Harvey Milk and Carol Silver." And there was the fag hag smear. In liberal San Francisco, in a judge race. And I found out the names of the people who put that out and they were part of the progressive wing of the Democratic party. And you can be sure the bigots are smiling.

And so we better, better be prepared 'cause it's not going to be easy. 'Cause we've heard quite often today and yesterday and in the papers about this movement from the Right. I use a bad pun, I refer to it as the "third Right." And we know what they are doing, but what we don't there are two other aspects. And one is who is talking about it the most and you will find out it is the media that is controlled by the Right. Telling us about it over and again so that we are starting to believe that it is the package on the shelf that everybody's buying. And so that the legislators believe that indeed there's a movement to the Right and so the legislators are moving to the Right, and the media from the Right are saying the nation is moving to the Right to convince us it is happening, and we are buying it. We ourselves are buying it. We look at the defeats, but stop and think of what's really happening in the nation . . . in 1977, in Dade county, was an election that took away the rights of gay people, which in 1975 did not exist. And in the two weeks before and after Dade County, more was written about homosexuality than in the entire history of mankind. But in every household they talked about it; they may have said "you fucking queens," but they talked about it. And that was the opening of dialogue. And in every city of this country and in every town, the issue, the love that dare not speak its name, spoke its name. And dialogue is the beginning of understanding.

In 1977 a gay person was elected to public office in California. In 1977 the state of Mississippi lowered the penalties on marijuana. Mississippi! And in 1977 was the convention of conventions in Houston. And I say, yes, there's a movement to the Right, but there's a goddamn good movement to the Left too. [Applause]

And I'm not, and I'm not gonna buy, I'm not gonna buy their package here today. I'm concerned, I'm aware, I know what they are doing. I know the money they are putting together, I know the way they are chipping us away one by one. I know the way—their tactics. But I know ours. And I'll be on my defense but I'm gonna be on my offense too. I'm gonna put them on the defense, I'm gonna put then on real soon, real fast. And it is up to you to do the same thing. Let us fight, put them where they belong and let's turn the tide around. I think it's like 5 steps forward and a half a step back. And so they may win some victories, but it's easy to win victories. I told the editor of the *San Francisco Examiner,* the publisher, that if I were to put on the ballot in Atlanta, Georgia, should whites be allowed to teach, what would be the result? He said it would go down in defeat. It's easy! Those are easy victories, and based on those we think the world is caving in. Sure, ERA is getting beaten back, but 10 years ago it didn't exist.

And they are telling us the movement to the Right, it's their last ditch effort, and I think we are going to prevail based on history. And it's up to you to make sure.

So let me tell you a little of what's taking place in California, so you can relay it to Texas and maybe take the best of what we have learned from that. And take our mistakes and failures and learn from that so you can put together something that is even greater. So I would like to take a few moments to tell you about a few things that's taking place in California, to let you know that the Left is not remaining silent. You heard earlier about Lt. Governor Dymally who made some statements. You must understand that Lt. Governor Dymally is black, and as leader of the black community is speaking out for gay rights. And Lt. Governor Dymally is putting together the Democratic Minority Coalition. Forget for a moment whether you're Democrats or Republicans, just forget for a moment . . . if that's possible [Harvey laughs], but he's putting together the Democratic Minority Coalition, which is the traditional minorities, the feminist movement and the gay movement. And by 1990, by 1990 if we register the movement we will have control of the state. And so our goal is to register, not just our gay sisters and brothers, but the entire minority community in the state of California. And in the city of San Francisco we'll have a race for mayor next year, now I don't know who it's gonna be and I'm not that concerned at this moment. But I am concerned that in five years it is a member of a minority and that includes the gay and feminist movement as well. And that's our goal in California—to take over so that the Right is buried once and for all. [Applause]

And we are learning how to do it, because we are learning, and we're gonna make a lot of mistakes before it's over. But you can only make mistakes if you try. If you go back into the closet and hide you can't make any mistakes—you suffocate. And so we are gonna make mistakes.

But let me tell you what we've done as examples of where we're coming from. Governor Brown was up for re-election, Governor Brown was unchallenged in the primary, oh there were some minor characters running, people like Harvey Milk. But there was no competition. And the big, liberal meeting was the CDC convention—the California Democratic Club convention in San Diego, where the progressive wing of the Democratic party meets. And the gay caucus represented almost 15% of that membership. And we submitted to the Governor some questions, quite a few questions. And he didn't quite answer them and we didn't endorse him. And my statement was "the Governor almost answered our questions and we almost endorsed him." Subsequent to that, all of the sudden now he's meeting with the gay community. We tried to arrange meetings prior to that; we couldn't. But now he does because he's in a tough race for governor in the run-off and he needs us, and many of us will not go easy or cheap. We have questions and we want answers. Both candidates in the Democratic party for attorney general fought bitterly for the gay vote—bitterly and openly for it. And the mayor of San Francisco would not be mayor if it were not for the gay vote.

We've made the vote the end result. The ballot box, because that's where their answer is. You can have all the demonstrations you want, you can have all the rallies you want and all the meetings you want. But unless you go out there and push that button or punch the peg hole or whatever it may be, unless you cast a vote, it's meaningless. And the right understands that. And that's where their strength comes from.

And it's up to us to form our natural allies, whether we like them or not, whether they like us or not. But to form those allies, to once and for all, to get our way, to get our share—no more, no less.

And so we are using the vote as a way to get the rights. We are not ignoring the other tactics, everything's needed. But the end result is in that box. And if you can't get your gay sisters and brothers to understand that, then read them the pages of history. And those who say what difference does my one vote make? Let me give you an example, one district in our city, a candidate won, forgetting whether that candidate is good or bad, he won by twenty-one votes. Which meant that if one more person in every fourth precinct went out and voted against that person, he would have lost. One more vote in every fourth precinct. And so those people who say my vote doesn't count—you're crazy. It's vital, 'cause it's those one votes that make the difference.

And so we are learning, because of that we have many things happening. In Los Angeles the mayor appointed a gay as his advisor. In San Francisco, I don't think I could sit down and figure out how many gays are on important commissions. And because of my position I was able to appoint somebody to a state commission, the coastal commission. And we are putting gays in every spot we can. But not just gays, 'cause we are fighting with our natural allies.

Earlier this morning you heard a great speech that talked about the problems of the east. Where women were not being put in the right positions, they were being put into the traditional, stereotypical positions of health and so forth. San Francisco's a little different, we have five fire commissioners, three are women. We have five police commissioners, two are women. They are on the Board of Permit Appeals, the planning commission. And that goes for the Blacks, and the Asians, and the Latinos. We are making sure that we support each other, because that's the only way. We needed each other and we must stick together—whether we like each other or not or they hate us or not. The point is we have a common enemy. And so we are joining together our votes and I urge you people to do the same thing in Texas, and every other state.

You see, to me, I call us the us-es. If you look who's fighting against gays, if you look who's fighting against ERA, if you look who's for the Bakke decision, if you look who's holding back the Hispanic community, if you look who's trying to cut off funds for abortion, if you look who doesn't want childcare centers, if you look who doesn't want to put money into senior citizens—you come to the same person—the people who have control now.

And for us to vote our pocket book on an issue and not realize you are giving support to the same people who want to put us in jail—maybe not today—but tomorrow, you're crazy.

And all these groups are the us-es. Of course the thems say they have the right to control the destiny because it is their money. They have the big corporations and pay the huge taxes. But how do they get the money for the taxes? It's the bars of soap that you buy, it's the records you buy, it's the hamburgers you buy, it's the TV sets you buy, it's the automobiles you buy. The thems wouldn't have the money if it wasn't for the us-es. It's our money but they won't return it . . . while they throw a crumb and let us fight among it. And so that has to end. We must realize that there is a battle between the us-es and the thems. And when you forget that you're just giving more strength to the thems.

Of course right now there's someone in the audience who's one of them who's whispering into his lapel—did you ever see the secret service. I wonder what they talk about? [Laughter]. But they might as well know that some of us, and I'm sure there's somebody here, there always is, that if you're gonna take one of us, there will be ten more following up, because there are many of us. And we'll stick together.

So what is the advantage of getting involved? The advantage is many ways besides just getting your piece of the pie.

It seems very interesting, as an elected official, I'm an insider now. For those who don't know San Francisco is unique in many ways, it's both a city and a county—the only one in California. So the Board of Supervisors is both a city council and a county board of supervisors. And there are eleven of us, the city has a population of 675,000. During the day there's about a million people there with the commuters. And in the Bay Area there are some three million people that watch that city. [Question from someone]. I had to explain this 'cause a lot of people don't know. There are about a million people there whose lives are governed, and the budget is spent by 11 people. And one of them happens to be gay. And like it or not, the Chamber of Commerce, the Downtown Association, the unions, the environmentalists, the neighborhood people, the poor people—everybody has to deal with the Board of Supervisors. And in San Francisco, we are a very, very strong Board. We delineate the executive and the legislative [inaudible]. And so they must deal with me like it or not. And it's very interesting in how they do that.

The Chamber of Commerce assigns two members to each Board of Supervisors as their lobbyists, to have lunch with you. And guess who they picked to have lunch with me? Their president. Because I have been probably their greatest foe on the issues of San Francisco, forget about whether they're right or wrong because that's our little problem. But the chamber in trying to influence me, has picked their top person. Think of the education, when in the middle of lunch I talk about my lover. [Laughter, applause] Think of the education when I . . . we get, you know, tons of invitations to this dinner or that dinner, this opening, this council . . . well one came addressed to Mr. and Mrs. Harvey Milk. [Laughter]. And I call up and say "in case you didn't know . . . A., I'm gay and B., I don't think my lover would like to attend." And they get an education. And we send them a letter to follow up to explain that there are a lot of single people in the city who are not married, who are not gay, and their letters are an insult not just to gay people, but to single people. And think of the education they're all getting. Including the unions and so forth.

It's very interesting being an insider, in helping to educate people on the one-on-one. But how does it help the whole city? We kind of have a theme song, I was expecting it to be played when we came in, but I failed. It's Doris Day singing "what a difference a gay makes." [Laughter, applause]. You see I've been on the Board of Supervisors for all of five months, five months, it seems like an eternity, but five months. And a few things have happened, surprisingly, since my election, that for some reason or another would have happened eventually, but they have happened. I brought one along, it's a little document. And I say, "amending part 2, chapter 8, San Francisco municipal code, police code, by adding article 33 there to prohibiting discrimination based on sexual orientation in employment, housing, public accommodations and providing remedies therefore." And that's it. [Applause]

And they have to take me with them if they try to take this one away and I don't go easy. I go kicking and screaming and fighting. And I think San Francisco will back me up on that one.

It's gonna be a tough fight but this is it! [Applause]

And little things have happened, since I've been elected. For example, every year our city funds all the major parades, the Chinese parade, the Saint Patrick's Day parade. For some reason they would never fund the Gay Day parade. And the budget for this year was already locked up and there was no way to reopen the budget. But somehow or another it got reopened and somehow or another we got the money for a Gay Day parade. And it wasn't the money I was after . . . as soon as they gave us the money, some of them realized it was official sanction of the major gay event of the year. [Applause] And somehow or another we have a lot of gay people being appointed to positions. And somehow or another we are getting money for CEDA [California Enterprise Development Authority] jobs. And somehow or another we are getting money for a community center. And somehow or another . . . the list goes on and on, gay mental health workers. And somehow or another all these things are happening. And somehow or another, the police . . . there's less harassment, there's still some, but less and less. Somehow or another it does make a difference just being there.

And that's the nuts and bolts of the day to day problems that we can solve and help. So it does make a difference, and it's a very vital difference. But, it's very interesting, in the debate that went on in the gay rights, one of the more conservative supervisors, when the vote was obvious and she couldn't stop it, she got up and she said that, the gay people must set standards. And I arose, oh and then she talked about the S&M scene in the gay community. And I arose, and I said, "Supervisor Feinstein, of course you know the Marquis de Sade was heterosexual. And that the standards you want us to set are the standards of Richard Nixon and the people who made the Atom bomb and dropped it. The standards you want us to set, are the people who 50% of husbands beat their wives? The standards you want us to set are they the standards of the parents who abuse their children? The standards that you want us to set are the people who bring heroin into this nation and put people on drugs? What standards do you want us to set? Or do you want to set the standards in today's paper?" . . . 'cause I anticipated her question and I have written down, I've saved these, these were the headlines in one day's paper. "Trade deficit rose 20th month in a row," "U.S. rebukes Soviets," "U.S. said to weigh move against Chile," "capital punishment responds to crime," this is in New Jersey. "Nine Pennsylvania legislators are being investigated." There's articles: Vietnam, Panama, South Africa, the middle east, Ireland. I said "Those

are the standards? Because I don't think you'll find any gay people involved in any of those issues. So tell me about the standards you want
us to set." [Applause]

And so, and so, it's vital that there's gay people down there to raise
the dialogue that would go silent without it. And very interesting in San
Francisco, it's a gay person who has done a few things on the Board
that are non-gay. It was a gay person who introduced a resolution, that
asked the State Department to close the South African embassy in San
Francisco. The reason why, in case you don't know, South Africa has
quite a nice policy to non-whites. It's the only nation I know, if you are
born there and you are not white you are considered a foreigner and
must have a passport. And I could go on and spell out the horrors. Well,
half of San Francisco is non-white. And if half of San Francisco went to
South Africa they would be treated as third class citizens, and that's an
insult to me and to them.

And it's very interesting I'm the one who's fighting for the drug re-
habilitation centers for the Latino community in San Francisco. That
I'm the one fighting for the Asian community, in fact I've tried to get
an Asian elected president of the Board of Supervisors. And that it was
a gay person who, when Jimmy Carter announced that he wanted to
close down the Presidio, the army base there, which is a country club,
I said I don't sleep better at night knowing the Presidio is there. Close
it down. Turn it open to senior citizens, the handicapped, and to the
childcare centers. Let's make it a place that once trained people to kill,
to a place to train people to heal. And it was a gay person who introduced that and fought for that. And the list is very long of the dialogue
that the sensitivities that gay people bring to issues that are non-gay,
that surprises them, then they have to deal with it. And the whole city
is listening and watching and that can happen wherever we go, and it's
important that we do.

Then there's another aspect, that's very important, because for years
we were regarded as gay people but, see, Harvey Milk is known as a
gay person from San Francisco, and I was supported by teamsters and
firefighters, and construction trade workers and environmentalists and
senior citizens and the Chicano community. But I was always gay,
and then something happened—I got elected and I was still gay. The day
we got sworn in, I mentioned we walked, and there was a reason why we
walked. And for those people who were in the media conference, think
about this, the eleven supervisors were gonna be sworn in the same day.
And I thought it was vital that we were on the front page—so how do

you pick one out of eleven? So we walked, everybody else rode. So naturally the media said "hey that's interesting, we'll catch them walking." But what they didn't know until we got there was that I was walking arm and arm with my lover. And the front page of the *Examiner* was the photograph of Supervisor Milk walking to City Hall with his lover.

And for the first time, sex entered into it. I was not just gay—he's doing it to him! [Laughter, applause] Or maybe he's doing it to him! Well, they're both right. [Laughter] And when we were sworn in, we have a custom that each supervisor gets up and introduces their family [laughter] and so I said that—you know the cameras are there—and I said, "Of course you know I'm gay, and in this state it's illegal for two gay people to be married. But there's no law on earth that says that two people cannot love each other and I'd like to introduce my lover."

And I was amazed at the reaction of some of my progressive friends. Because sex had entered the picture. We were no longer just gay people, and they had to think about that humanistic part of us, for the first time. And an education was happening and it was great. And it's still going on and it's not gonna stop. And I get involved in these fights, everything from the budget on down. And sometimes we win the votes, and when I say win, I mean the progressive forces, and sometimes we lose. But the dialogue exists.

And on a few occasions, on the one vote, on environmental issues sometimes, on fiscal issues where I think they're irresponsive or they're just doing because of the power of the downtown association. And I don't know for sure whether I'm wearing a wash basin or that famed helmet of [Don Quixote] and tilting windmills, I don't know, and fighting dragons. And I may be fighting windmills or so, but, I think I may catch a dragon or two in the works. And if the story of Don Quixote means anything at all to me, it means that the spirit of life is more important than the substance. That the quality of life is more important than the standard of living. And I think I've brought that to the Board. And so the others may think I'm wearing just that wash basin, but I know I'm wearing that famed helmet.

And I bring another message, and that is about another gay movie that you're not going to see tonight, but that you might have seen or will see someday. It's called *The Word is Out* and I recommend it. 'Cause I think that we must put the word out. Let's put the word out—to come out. We must destroy the myths, the stereotypes and no offense to the stereotypes, we must let them know who we are. In San Francisco on Gay Day, some of us are showing up with one sign only. And that is the sign of the town and state that you were born in, to let them know, we are your children. That we are not all products of Hollywood, and San Francisco and New York; that we come from all over. We must come out so that they know we are doctors, lawyers, ditch diggers, cashiers. In fact I'm working with a group of some 90 some odd doctors and psychiatrists in the Bay Area to come out as a group—and if 90 psychiatrists and doctors come out as a group straight America would have a nervous breakdown. [Laughter, applause] We must let them know that we are not child molesters, that they are. [Applause] 95% of molesters are [heterosexuals; inaudible; lost in applause]. We must let them know if teachers affect the future of a child there would be a lot of nuns running around the streets. [Laughter, applause] We must dispel the myths of gay people who choose to be that . . . stop and think how ludicrous that is. And a child of heterosexual parents in the most fiercely heterosexual society, the child who wants to be equal with their peers, in which homosexuality is something to be sat on and spit on and killed, that child chooses homosexuality. Think how ludicrous that is. We must talk about that, we must talk about those issues on a one-on-one basis. And it's very important we do that. It's very important we come out. Not to stand on a street corner and say "hey, I'm gay." But to tell our parents. And people say "I can't tell my parents, it's going to hurt them." Think about what the hurt is gonna be when your parents go into a voting booth and vote against you without knowing. Who gets hurt? Not just you but that 13 year old who is coming out.

And so it's important that you come out to everybody that you know—to your relatives, to your friends, to your next door neighbor, to the person you work with, to the people in the restaurants you eat in, and to the people in the store where you shop. So that they know it's not the rights of some gay people, but it's your personal rights that they're discussing.

And I was very pleased in the time that I've been here, to know that there are some gay people contemplating running for political office in this state. We heard of some people running in New York, we know of some other cases. And I think it's important that I address the need for some of you to do that. And not just Dallas and Houston. It serves two purposes, one—it gives you a platform, so you don't win. It took me four times, you all thought that three strikes and you're out—in gay softball it's four strikes. [Laughter, applause] I think there is a tremendous and vital difference between a friend of the gay community and an avowed gay in public office.

36

"Gay Rights"

Article draft, *Coast to Coast*, June 16, 1978

Milk's editorial in the June 16, 1978, Coast to Coast *newspaper was a strong statement about his position on the Briggs Initiative, also known as Proposition 6. With the November referendum looming, Milk was intent on stymieing the anti-GLBTQ measure.*

Milk's attention during the summer of 1978 (and leading into the fall, just prior to his assassination) was turned toward the fight with John Briggs. The debate over gay rights between Milk and Briggs catapulted Milk into the media spotlight. At the same time, it punctuated his ethos as a local activist with a burgeoning national reputation. In the process, Briggs was cast as a brashly opportunistic and adamantly homophobic demagogue. Briggs's effort to rid the California schools of GLBTQ teachers became certified as Proposition 6 in May. Given Briggs' disrepute, even within his own party, he undoubtedly surprised most by taking up the moral inheritance of Anita Bryant's "Save the Children" campaign, which had the previous year led to "Orange Tuesday"—the day when Dade County, Florida residents voted to retract their gay rights ordnance.

Though other places like St. Paul, Minnesota; Wichita, Kansas; and Eugene, Oregon, were facing similar measures, Briggs ensured that California would be the ultimate battleground for homophobia. That California was the focus helped draw Milk into the debate, thereby ensuring his participation and, in the end, his reputation. By the time

November 1978 rolled around, the Proposition 6 battle would be Milk's crowning achievement. Ironically, even as Milk won the battle over Proposition 6, he would lose the war against homophobia—as he predicted, by the bullet of an assassin.

The editorial below preceded Milk's debates with Briggs. In this document, Milk outlined the first step of battling Proposition 6: dispelling the myths of the GLBTQ community espoused by Briggs and other Proposition 6 supporters who pitched the senator's bigotry to the public. Milk argued, "Thus, I feel that now—before they start in—we must talk about the false issues. They will be raised by Briggs, and if they wait to near the end, there will not be enough to time to speak out and explode the myths." Expediency was Milk's watchword. Always the strategist, he was looking ahead to what he assumed would be the core of Briggs' contentions. That is, Milk guessed correctly that Briggs, like Bryant before him, would angle toward so-called GLBTQ abuses of children and the deviancy of "choosing" to be salaciously GLBTQ. Here, Milk wrote about these myths, but he also established the baseline issue of "choice" in the context of sexuality.

He also challenged Briggs' reliance on the Bible as an argument from authority. In a Bay Area Reporter *retrospective decades later, Milk is quoted as saying, "I'm tired of listening to Anita Bryant and John Briggs twist the language and meaning of the Bible to fit their own distorted outlook. But I'm even more tired of [people] who know that they are playing fast and loose with the true meaning of the Bible. I'm tired of their silence more than their biblical gymnastics!" In that same article, Milk took Briggs to task for looking past society's larger, starker problems and focusing instead on so-called homosexual "ills" as described through stereotypes. He wrote, "What standards do you want us to clean up? Clean up your own act! Clean up your violence before you criticize Lesbians and Gay men because of their sexuality." In essence, Milk turned the mirror around on Briggs and his zealotry.*

Paired with the documents that follow, Milk's words below represent well his sentiments concerning the Briggs Initiative.

. . .

People are tired of talking about taxes and Jarvis-Gann. People will also get tired of talking about Briggs and gay rights. To these people, I say that the day we stop talking about gay rights is the day we no longer have them.

But the fact is that many people will get tired of the gay rights talks. Each day more and more people will make up their minds about the issue. WE and I stress the WE, must talk about some of the issues *now* while people are still listening and before they get fixed on a position that might be against us.

Many campaigns have already started. We have no control over the campaign against us—the Briggs side. Based on what took place from Dade County to Eugene, we know what to expect, especially at the end of the campaign. We must undermine their emotional campaign, geared to fears based on myths, now—before they start them up. And, they will.

The bigots waged campaigns of lies and hysteria in every city and there is no reason to believe that they won't here in California. To hope for something else is to be like Jews in Nazi Germany as they were being loaded into the box cars and hoping that they will be treated nicely and not put into the ovens.

I believe that we can win in November . . . but only if we mount a full-fledged campaign. One that covers all bases, both positive and defensive. Yes, defensive, too. For not to answer the false charges is, to some, an admission that the charges are not false. Otherwise, we would repudiate them.

There is no time like the present to start to repudiate them. For the sooner we start, the sooner we can lay them to rest. So, we need to have every gay person talk to as many non-gay people as possible about the issues—both real and false. It will be a monumental effort and, because many gays will remain in their closet, it makes it that much more important for those of us who are out.

Thus, I feel that now—before they start in—we must talk about the false issues. They will be raised by Briggs and, if they wait to near the end, there will not be enough to time to speak out and explode the myths.

We must talk about child molestation.

We must talk about role models.

We must talk about the Bible.

We must talk about "Chosen" lifestyles.

I would like to explode one of those myths right now. To me, the most pernicious is that gay people have deliberately "chosen" their homosexuality. I've known many more gay people than Anita Bryant and John Briggs have, and I have to tell you that they, and the churches that support them, deliberately lie.

Imagine a young girl or boy brought up by heterosexual parents in a fiercely heterosexual society, a society in which all "the role models" are strongly heterosexual, a society which considers a homosexual the low-est form of life, suitable fodder for queer-baiting, rape, murder. Now try to imagine this impressionable adolescent, who wants nothing more than to be a part of her or his own peer group, somehow deciding that homosexuality is the best of all possible worlds. As Anita Bryant would have us believe, on their 18th birthday, they suddenly say, "Gee, ma! I wanna be gay!" It's all a matter of "choice."

There is a perversity in that accusation of "choice" that chills my blood. It reeks of madness.

Where choice does play a part, of course, is in coming out. The choice is whether you should lead a secret life, subject to great personal agony, the threat of blackmail and the corrosion of self-respect or whether you choose pride. Pride in what you are, in the life you lead, in the emotions you feel.

A famous American coined the phrase that covers it all, "Give me liberty or give me death." Patrick Henry was talking about political lib-erty. But there is a more personal type, a more important type. If you are not personally free to be yourself in that most important of all human activities—the expression of love—than life itself loses its meaning.

To come out for a gay person requires a degree of courage that is rarely asked of a straight person. It involves the possible loss of one's job, the possible breaking of ties to one's families, the possible loss of one's friends and the realization that in the minds of most people you meet, you will not be seen as a stereotype.

And, once you've come out, there is no going back. Your gayness is now public, as much a part of you as the color of skin is to a black person. That's the only "choice" we have.

Our non-gay neighbors must be told that and they must understand that. The myths must be exploded. You as an individual can do that. And you must start to do it now. The last week of October will be too late.

37

"Gay Freedom Day Speech"

Reprinted speech, *Bay Area Reporter*,
June 25, 1978

One of the highlights of Castro life was the annual Gay Freedom Day celebration that included parades, performances, and community activities. Milk used the 1978 event as an opportunity to speak out on the Briggs Initiative.

As the summer of 1978 commenced, it was clear that the national wave of homophobia Briggs was both generating and floating atop was cresting. This was problematic as the November referendum deadline approached. As with Bryant's campaign, Proposition 6 inflamed the electorate because it concerned children, the specters of molestation and murder of the innocents, and the classroom as a recruitment space of so-called GLBTQ propaganda. These concerns seemed to resonate briefly with dominant California communities. In fact, the first poll in September 1978 indicated that 61 percent of the voters favored Proposition 6. The witch hunts, which would continue as teachers and public employees were "exposed," were too much to bear for GLBTQ activists. Even so, GLBTQ journalists and leaders like Milk asked for calm and tried to keep solidarity at the fore as the GLBTQ community faced a certain defeat in November.

Milk's response, as we might expect, was to fight. By his battle plan, one must ceaselessly talk, speaking out to explode the homophobic myths and hysteria that the Religious Right and opportunists such as John Briggs exploited to their ideological and political advantage. And talk he did, refuting the lies and distortions that asserted that homosexuality is a choice, that GLBTQ individuals are the primary perpetrators of child molestation and abuse, that GLBTQ people recruit by becoming "role models" for the "lifestyle," and simultaneously promoting the idea that homosexuality is natural, given, omnipresent, good, and undeserving of discrimination, harassment, and violence.

In mobilizing the GLBTQ community to rise up against Briggs, Milk employed a patriotic collective memory, quoting Patrick Henry, the Declaration of Independence, the Statue of Liberty's pedestal welcome, and "The Star Spangled Banner." In the address that follows, one gets a sense for the flavor of Milk's use of such memory. The analogies employed speak to Milk's insistence on linking gay rights with American liberation. Harkening back to a distinctly American past, in this vein, allowed Milk to connect GLBTQ communities to other oppressed groups who had both faced and fought the "long train of abuses" first articulated by the nation's forebears—from African Americans and Native Americans to women, laborers, and religious minorities.

Moreover, Milk began characterizing Briggs and his supporters as fascists and Nazis. This would become a common trope employed to expose the viciousness of Proposition 6. Raised in a Jewish home, it might not be a surprise that Milk favored the Holocaust trope, likening Briggs to Hitler and GLBTQ folks to Jews oppressed by the genocidal Nazi regime. This invective pivoted the debate in terms of good and evil. And such a Judeo-Christian theme of innocents and sinners was a necessary tactic, as Milk and his allies faced fighting what he continually called the Religious Right. Dismantling the proverbial master's house with the master's tools would eventually prove effective for Milk. And of course, the analogizing of anyone or anything considered "evil" with the ultimate enemy in Western history underscored Milk's savvy as a rhetor. Simultaneously, Milk made it clear that he was not afraid of these homophobic "Nazis." In a later Bay Area Reporter *article, Milk wrote, "Do you think gay people are going with their heads bowed to the gas chambers? I mean, I'll go kicking and screaming before I go with my head bowed. Three hundred thousand gays went into the gas chambers in Germany [sic] and then six million Jews. I don't think the Jews are going to go quietly next time, so why should gay people?" The fight against Briggs oftentimes boiled down to self-empowerment for Milk.*

One other noteworthy element of Milk's 1978 Gay Freedom Day Speech is what became his signature opening line during the months of

*the Briggs debate: "I'm Harvey Milk and I'm here to recruit you." This
announcement was a play on Briggs' insistence that GLBTQ teachers
"recruited" their students into an elusive and mysterious "gayness."
Milk's humor often set his discourse apart from other activists as lively,
comfortable, and witty.*

*Ultimately, 1978's version of San Francisco's Gay Freedom Day pa-
rade became incredibly political. As the* San Diego Union *noted in the
parade's wake, "The focus of the event [this year] was a voter initiative
on the November ballot that has been widely labeled anti-gay." The* Las
Vegas Review Journal *described the event for its readers in this way:
"Singing slightly altered songs like, 'When the Dykes Go Marching
In,' an estimated 240,000 gays and their supporters marched through
downtown streets Sunday. . . . A group of gay teachers marched along
chanting, 'Two, four, six, eight—our Miss Brooks wasn't straight.'" All
in all, the typical street theater bacchanalia became a fun and festive,
yet politically centered, event to both raise awareness about the Briggs
Initiative and to raise money to defeat it.*

. . .

My name is Harvey Milk—and I want to recruit you for the fight to
preserve your democracy from the John Briggs' and the Anita Bryants
who are trying to constitutionalize bigotry. We are not going to allow
that to happen. We are not going to sit back in silence as 300,000 of
our Gay sisters and brothers did in Nazi Germany. We are not going to
allow our rights to be taken away and then march with bowed heads
to the gas chambers. On this anniversary of Stonewall, I ask my Gay
sisters and brothers to make their commitment to fight. For themselves,
for their freedom, for their country.

Here in San Francisco we recently held an election for a judgeship.
An anti-Gay smear campaign was waged against a presiding judge because she was supported by Lesbians and Gay men. Here, in so-called
liberal San Francisco, an anti-Gay smear campaign was waged by so-
called liberals. And here in so-called liberal San Francisco, we have a
columnist for the *San Francisco Examiner,* Kevin Starr, who has printed
a number of columns containing distortions and lies about Gays. He's
getting away with it.

These anti-Gay smear campaigns, these anti-Gay columns, are laying
the groundwork for the Briggs Initiative. We had better be prepared for it.

In the *Examiner,* Kevin Starr defames and libels Gays. In the
Chronicle, Charles McCabe warns us to be quiet, that talking about

Gay rights is counter-productive. To Mr. McCabe, I say that the day he stops talking about freedom of the press is the day he no longer has it. The Blacks did not win their rights by sitting quietly in the back of the bus! They got off! We will not win our rights by staying quietly in our closets. . . We are coming out! We are coming out to fight the lies, the myths, the distortions! We are coming out to tell the truth about Gays! For I am tired of the conspiracy of silence.

I'm tired of listening to the Anita Bryants twist the language and the meaning of the Bible to fit their own distorted outlook. But I'm even more tired of the silence from the religious leaders of this nation who know that she is playing fast and loose with the true meaning of the Bible. I'm tired of their silence more than of her biblical gymnastics!

And I'm tired of John Briggs talking about false role models. He's lying through his teeth and he knows it. But I'm even more tired of the silence from educators and psychologists who know that Briggs is lying and yet say nothing. I'm tired of their silence more than of Briggs' lies.

Gay people are painted as child molesters. I want to talk about that. I want to talk about the myth of child molestations by Gays. I want to talk about the fact that in this state some 95% of child molestations are heterosexual and usually committed by a parent. That all child abandonments are heterosexual. That all abuse of children is by their heterosexual parents. That some 98% of the six million rapes committed annually in this country are heterosexual. That one out of every three women who will be murdered in this state this year will be murdered by their husbands. That some 30% of all heterosexual marriages contain domestic violence.

And finally, I want to tell the John Briggs' and the Anita Bryants that they talk about the myths of Gays, but today I'm talking about the facts of heterosexual violence and what the hell are you going to do about that?

Clean up your own house before you start telling lies about Gays. Don't distort the Bible to hide your own sins; don't change facts to lies; don't look for cheap political advantage in playing upon people's fears. Judging by the polls, even the youth of this state can tell you're lying Anita Bryant, John Briggs—your deliberate lies and distortions, your unwillingness to face the truth, chills my blood—it reeks of madness!

And like the rest of you, I'm tired of our so-called "friends" who tell us that we must set standards. What standards? The standards of the rapists? The wife beaters? The child abusers? The people who ordered the bomb to be built? The people who ordered it to be dropped? The people who pulled the trigger? The people who gave us Vietnam? The people who built the concentration camps—right here in California—and then herded all the Japanese Americans into them during World War II . . . The Jew baiters? The nigger knockers? The corporate thieves? The Nixons? The Hitlers?

What standards do you want us to set? Clean up your own act. Clean up your violence before you criticize Lesbians and Gay men because of their sexuality. . . . It is madness to glorify killing and violence on one hand and to be ashamed of the sexual act that conceived you on the other hand. There is a difference between morality and murder. The fact is that more people have been slaughtered in the name of religion than for any other single reason. That, my friends, is the true perversion!

Gay brothers and sisters, what are *you* going to do about it? You must come out. Come out to your parents, your relatives. I know that it is hard and that it will hurt them, but think of how they will hurt you in the voting booth! Come out to your friends, if indeed they are your friends. Come out to your neighbors, to your co-workers, to the people who work where you eat and shop. Come out only to the people you know and who know you. Not to anyone else. But once and for all, break down the myths; destroy the lies and distortions for your own sake, for their sake, for the sake of the youngsters who are being terrified by the votes coming from Dade County to Eugene. If Briggs wins he will not stop. They never do. Like all mad people, they are forced to go on, to prove they were right. There will be no safe closet for any Gay person. So break out of yours today; tear the damn thing down once and for all!

And finally, most of all, I'm tired of the silence from the White House. Jimmy Carter, you talk about human rights a lot; in fact, you want to be the world's leader for human rights. Well, damn it, lead! There are some 15–20 million Lesbians and Gay men in this nation listening very carefully. Jimmy Carter, when are you going to talk about THEIR rights? You talk a lot about the Bible, but when are you going to talk about the most important part: "Love Thy Neighbor"? After all, she may be Gay.

Jimmy Carter, you have the choice. How many more years? How much more violence? How much more damage? How many more lives? History says that, like all groups seeking their rights, sooner or later we will win. The question is: When?

Jimmy Carter, you have to make the choice. Either years of violence, or you can help turn the pages of history that much faster. And now, before it becomes too late, come to California and speak out against Briggs.

If you don't—then we will come to you! If you do not speak out, if you remain silent, if you do not lift your voice against Briggs, then I call upon Lesbians and Gay men from all over the nation, your nation, to gather in Washington one year from now on that national day of freedom, the Fourth of July. To gather on the same spot where over a decade ago Dr. Martin Luther King spoke to a nation of his dreams . . . dreams that are fast fading, dreams that to many millions in this country have become nightmares. I call upon all minorities and especially the millions of Lesbians and Gay men to wake up from their dreams . . . to gather in Washington and tell Jimmy carter and their nation: "Wake up . . . Wake up, America. No more racism; no more sexism; no more ageism; no more hatred. No more!"

Jimmy Carter, listen to us today. Or you will have to listen to all of us from all over the nation as we gather in Washington next year. For we WILL gather there and we will tell you about America and what it really stands for.

. . . And to the bigots . . . To the John Briggs' . . . To the Anita Bryants . . . To the Kevin Starrs and all their ilk: Let me remind you what America is. Listen carefully. On the Statue of Liberty it says, "Give me your tired, your poor, your huddled masses yearning to be free. . . ." In the Declaration of Independence it is written, "All men are created equal and they are endowed with certain inalienable rights. . . ." And in our national anthem it says: "Oh say does that star spangled banner yet wave o'er the land of the free. . ."

For Mr. Briggs and Mrs. Green and Mr. Starr and all the bigots out there: That's what America is. No matter how hard you try, you cannot erase those words from the Declaration of Independence. No matter how hard you try, you cannot chip those words off the base of the Statue of Liberty. And no matter how hard you try, you cannot sing the STAR SPANGLED BANNER without those words. THAT'S what America is, LOVE IT OR LEAVE IT!

38

"To Beat Briggs"

Column, *Bay Area Reporter*, August 3, 1978

As the "Summer of Briggs" continued, Milk's frustration with middle-of-the-road GLBTQ community members reluctant to join the fight increased. Ostensibly, complacency and apathy incensed his spirit of vigilant reform. His August 3, 1978, forum editorial in the Bay Area Reporter *presented his frustrations. In effect, he directly charged his readers with getting involved—monetarily as well as in spirit. Milk articulated this claim laden with guilt alongside a sense of fear. The latter pathos appeal spoke to the importance of self-safety (physical and public). Milk wrote, "Unless the Gay community, in total, starts to act now, it will be too late." Here, Milk reminded GLBTQ readers that Briggs's focus on exposing and occluding teachers was just the beginning of what such a homophobic law could propagate in terms of other, farther stretching anti-GLBTQ legislation. Just as Bryant's campaign had given way to Briggs's proposal, so to was the worry that the successful passage of Proposition 6 would give rise to other homophobic demagogues determined to restrict further the public liberties and personal freedoms of GLBTQ communities. Milk was recorded in a later retrospective as writing, "If Briggs wins, he will not stop. They never do. Like all mad people, they are forced to go on, to prove they are right; there will be no safe closet for any gay person. So break out of yours today; tear the damn thing down once and for all!" Again, this sentiment evinced the palpable fear that Milk held close; the essay below seethes with his anger for apathetic community members and teems with his insistence that they support the anti-Briggs campaign.*

. . .

In just about 90 days there will be an election in this state over the Briggs Initiative, Prop. 6. That could turn the mood of the nation more to the Right or more to the Left. It is more than just the rights of Gay teachers. Every Gay professional person—every Gay person who has any kind of license—has to realize that they may be next. The list will not end. *Every* effort by *every* Gay person must be made to defeat this initiative.

"I don't have to worry . . . it can never happen here in San Francisco!" That is a comment that I have heard too often these past few weeks. Sounds like some of the unaware Jews talking during the early days of Hitler. That attitude itself could very well bring about disaster. Letting others do the work . . . do the financing . . . etc., because it does not affect you personally—right now—is exactly why the Briggs Initiative could pass. No one is going to win the battle for Gay rights if the Gay community does not put its full effort into the battle. Yet, a vast number of Gays seem to think that by *talking* about how bad Briggs is will in itself do the battle. By the time the anti-Gay ads hit the media and mails it will be too late. The battle must be fought now, before the hate campaign starts. And sitting home, or in your friendly bar, won't help one bit. It will also take money.

NO MORE BAR MITZVAHS

Gays don't spend a lot of money on their children's education or birthdays. On their children's bar mitzvahs, weddings, confirmations. Gays don't put funds aside in large insurance policies or trusts for their mates and family. Thus the potential is there for Gays to contribute more towards a political campaign to protect themselves than non-Gays can. If every Gay person gave a small amount, there would be enough funds to mount a strong fight against Briggs. And if every Gay person contributed an amount equal to what they would have put into a child's education, clothing, food, gifts, etc., if they had one, then there would be enough money to mount a winning campaign. Yet, for some reason, Gay people don't seem to understand the need to fund this battle. For some reason Gay people feel someone else will put up the funds and volunteer their time.

THE HATE CAMPAIGN

Unless there is a rapid change in attitudes, unless there is a fast awakening of consciousness, there will be a rude awakening come November. I have a copy of the first volley against Gays put out by the Concerned Christians. It is not just against Gays teaching. It includes the ministry, police and fire fighters. It, in effect, links Gays and pornography as one and the same thing. And that is just the beginning.

Unless the Gay community, in total, starts to act now, it will be too late. It will not be a campaign that will be won on the last days as many "candidate" campaigns are. This will take a long time to win . . . people have to be talked to, on a one-to-one basis. And more than once. It cannot be done after the hate starts to pour out.

Already here in San Francisco the signs are for a rotten campaign to be waged against us. It ain't pleasant. Please get involved. Please give of your time and funds. *Both* are badly needed.

SNOW WHITE & SAFETY

Snow White made famous the concept of "Whistle While You Work." For the past several years, the Richard Harkness Butterfly Brigade has been making famous the concept of "Carry A Whistle For Your Protection." Several thousand are out there. More are needed. The concept has spread to Chicago and other cities. The "carry a whistle" works!

With the long hot summer still here and the Briggs hate campaign starting, there could well be an increase to the violence against Gays that already exists. The best protection is to carry a police whistle. Use it *only* when either under attack or when you see another person under attack. When you hear one being blown you, and you, and you, and you, respond. With yours and on the run. A lot of violence has already been abated by the use of whistles. A lot of violence may well have been abated by the simple knowledge that the whistle force exists. The cost: $1.00! It could very well make the difference between a safe neighborhood—no matter where you live—and a violent one. Many stores in the Castro Village area carry them. A good investment!

39

"I Have High Hopes Address"

Stump speech, 1978

Even in the midst of the Briggs fight, Milk never left his populist roots. Lest history look back at the final months of Milk's life as dedicated solely to the anti-Proposition 6 campaign, the stump address he delivered around San Francisco in the summer of 1978 concerning "the people" proved otherwise. As with his early discourse from 1978 (see Document 27), Milk kept his attention focused on his notion of a "city of neighborhoods." Below, he reminded his constituencies that "Perhaps the most valuable resource of any city—and the one that's ignored the most—is the people who live in it."

One of Milk's favorite citizen groups was the senior population. He was a constant advocate for senior rights, and had he lived longer, he indeed would have initiated plans for employing seniors and ensuring that their golden years were both fulfilling and comfortable. As fond as Milk was of children (one of his hobbies was dressing as a clown for community events), he also had a genuine affinity for seniors. As he saw it, both groups represented the bookends of life in San Francisco. Milk even considered putting the two groups together in his populist vision for the "city of neighborhoods": "And we might consider employing some of our seniors as PSAs—'Practical Student Aides'—to help out as tutors. We could even include them in the school's hot-lunch program." As always, Milk elevated people above business.

. . .

I have high hopes for the future of our cities. I have high hopes for the future of San Francisco. Granted its present problems, I have high hopes that the city of the future—*our* City of the future—will be one that will enrich the lives of all the people who live in it.

Most plans for the city of the future involve money—lots of it, more than any city could afford. But there are improvements that can be made in the city that don't necessarily involve lots of money. That require, instead, generous amounts of imagination—and heart.

Perhaps the most valuable resource of any city—and the one that's ignored the most—is the people who live in it, particularly the elderly. At present, we treat our senior citizens like so many beer cans, to be discarded after use. But the seniors are the very same people who made this city. They're you and I, twenty or thirty or forty years from now.

Senior citizens don't suddenly lose their expertise, their knowledge of what makes things work, and how, at the magic age of 65. Instead of scrapping them, why not use them? Why limit their contributions to civic life to service on the Commission for Aging, or related agencies? Why not appoint them to other boards and commissions? Their feeling for the human dimensions of a city would make them invaluable.

And there are other ways in which we could use our "Senior Power." I would like to see a complex that we might call a "people-center"—a complex that contains schools, hospitals, child-care centers and senior centers. It might even have a center for minor criminal offenders.

In such a center, our Seniors could be employed in the hospital section to read to patients or as aides to the staff. They might help staff our childcare center. Those who commit minor crimes might also be employed to work in various portions of the center. Perhaps the senior citizen would meet the "inmate" and discover that he's good at math. "Then why aren't you an accountant?" "Because I never went to school." And the next day the "inmate" might enroll in the center school, with the senior citizen as a tutor.

Someday, the "inmate" would leave the center for a decent job. And the senior citizen—and society—will have discovered that his own talents are still worthwhile, that he qualifies for something more than "no deposit, no return."

And perhaps the child enrolled in the people-center school will learn more than the Three R's. He will have discovered that prisoners, too, have hopes and aspirations, that being old need not be a period of uselessness, and that life is really about people helping people.

The great thing about imagination is that a little of it can go a long way. With not too much effort, we could turn small areas of our older hotels, or empty store fronts, into much-needed child-care centers. We might even pay some of our senior citizens to help staff them.

And we might consider employing some of our seniors as PSA's—"Practical Student Aides"—to help out as tutors. We could even include them in the school's hot-lunch program.

There are other problems that might yield to imagination. Why must an industrial "complex" be an area of brick buildings, railroad tracks and shanties that dies every evening at five when the workers go home? Why not intermix home and factory, make factories light and airy so people would enjoy working in them—and then ban the automobile!

40

"Harvey Milk vs. John Briggs"

Televised debate transcription, August 6, 1978

As the referendum vote on Proposition 6 inched closer and closer, Milk and Briggs engaged in numerous public debates. Many were not recorded; of those that were many are nearly inaudible and, at their best, difficult to translate. One of the extant (and clear) exchanges between the two adversaries was aired on August 6, 1978, on San Francisco's KPIX-TV. The heated chat was later rebroadcast around California. In this televised "discussion"—over a restaurant table with an unnamed moderator—the talk was anything but cordial. In the transcript that follows, Briggs attempted to reframe Proposition 6 as attending solely to GLBTQ teachers rather than denying "anybody the right to a job." Milk, of course, refuted this idea, suggesting that the Briggs Initiative would be the first of many dominoes to fall should GLBTQ teachers be banned in the state of California (see Document 38, Document 40, and Document 42). Interestingly, the discussion turned to the issue of "choice" as it related to sexualities—still a hotly contested and robust issue to this day. Milk chided Briggs for assuming that people simply stake out their sexualities "like you would choose your candidates." In the process, Milk addressed the myths that Briggs and his supporters espoused.

Throughout the series of debates over the summer (and into early fall) of 1978, Milk was calm and methodical in his approach. Working alongside debate partner and San Francisco State University professor Sally Gearhart, he stuck to verifiable statistics when talking about exploding homosexual myths (i.e., "90 to 95 percent of all known child molesters are heterosexual men") and reasoned narrative evidence when it came to the topic of choice (i.e., "I was born of heterosexual parents. I was taught by heterosexual teachers. In a society that's so fiercely heterosexual, who was there to tell me, 'Gee, Harvey, you ought to be homosexual!'").

On the other hand, Briggs remained true to form, demonstrating his constant and blatant heterosexism during the discussions. Oftentimes snapping and issuing non sequiturs, he once told a moderator who mentioned how Governor Ronald Reagan disagreed with the Briggs Initiative, "I really don't care what Gov. Reagan says. [He] comes from the same Hollywood crowd [that financed a great deal of the anti-Prop 6 campaign]. About 90 percent of the films that come out of Hollywood that are pornographic are homosexual films." Other times, Briggs became visibly and physically hostile. A San Francisco Examiner article from October 1978 reported that KSFO radio reporter Tony Russomanno was attacked by Briggs after one debate. Russomanno stopped Briggs to ask how the senator thought the debate went. Briggs called him "a first class liar . . . then seized Russomanno's microphone, pushed it against his chest and neck and shoved him out of the way." To many, Briggs's feigned statistics, outlandish comments, and—eventually—his physical responses smacked of desperation.

Indeed, as the documents preceding and following the present debate transcript indicate, Briggs's motivations were severely in question. Perhaps voters brought those very doubts to the polls with them in November of 1978.

. . .

Briggs: I'll tell you what [Proposition] 6 does not do. It does not deny you the right to be a supervisor. It does not deny anybody in this room a right to have a job.

Milk: Yes, it does, it denies people the right to teach.

Briggs: But there are no teachers in this room.

Milk: But we don't know; there are some other people in this room.

Briggs: It does not deny anybody the right to a job. It does not deny anybody the right to rent or buy a house. All it does is say that parents—parents have the ultimate right as to who is going to teach their children.

Milk: Wait, wait, wait. Based on that—on that "ultimate right," at one time parents didn't want blacks to teach. At one time they didn't want women to teach. You know, the old Bible says women shouldn't be teachers, in the Old Testament. At one time. Because parents are locked in—they're afraid of something different. They're afraid of change. Because of fears and myths put into their heads. . . . One of those myths in this new ordnance is that you choose your sexuality. You don't choose your homosexuality. Like you don't choose blue eyes. Like you would choose your candidates . . .

Briggs: I care about this country. And I care about the family. And I really, sincerely, honestly, and truly believe from the bottom of my heart that homosexuality is a real threat to the survival of this country, if we continue to tolerate it and approve it and let it be raised to an equal level and standard of heterosexuality. That's what I truly believe.

Milk: That's the oldest game in the world! That's why I keep saying to you, study! I would be surprised what your next step is! . . . [Homosexuality] is not ever done because of an experience. It is determined before school age. And as every scientific study done says, it is not a choice. It is not a choice. That's the most fundamental mistake conservatives like Briggs bring up.

Briggs: But children learn by example. Children emulate. People need heroes. I said at the opening of the show that the reason you wanted to be elected to high office is so you can recruit and convert every young, adolescent homosexual. Those were your own words!

Milk: No, no, no. I said that one of the reasons of being elected is I'm a role model to young gay people. To young gay people. You see? You mis—turn things around like you turn everything else around.

Briggs: What about a teacher who's a role model?

Milk: A teacher to a [particular] sexual orientation? You see, Senator, you're turning things around. My statement was, I'm a role model to the young gay people. To people who have already established themselves as gay. Period. I didn't say—you're the one who keeps bringing up this phony recruitment. You know you're lying. You know you're changing the statements around. And you're doing that all the way around, just like you shifted the money around in your campaigns. And you talk about morality! And I question, what is your real motive behind it? What is your real ambition behind this? What are you really using this for? And stop this phony issue!

41

"The Positive or the Negative"

Column, *Bay Area Reporter*, August 31, 1978

Toward the summer's end, Milk continued to worry about the divisions of ideological and spiritual commitments within the GLBTQ community regarding the Briggs Initiative fight. The editorial below outlined the three categories of community members that Milk saw implicated in the struggle to defeat the Briggs Initiative. He asked his readers to "Take your choice!" and, of course, recommended that they fall into the category of "The Positive Beat"—"those who feel that we can win against Briggs." As the campaign amped up and reached its climax, Milk's movement had lesbians and gay men pass around the following palm card as a means of educating heterosexual voters, but also firming-up the movement's members: "The purpose of this card is to make you aware of the fact that you ride with, talk to, eat with, and see gay people every day. I hope that the time you sent with me has helped you to realize that we are people just like you. Please think carefully about the Briggs Initiative before you vote in November, because it directly affects human rights, particularly mine as a gay person." The movement also inspired rallies in the days leading up to that fateful November election day, such as those in San Francisco, Los Angeles, and San Diego, not to mention solidarity parades in New York, Houston, and New Orleans. Milk even published an editorial during the summer, telling people, "If each person puts into the fight 2 hours per week, that is about 30 hours. A little more than one day in your life to win freedom—not just for Gays, but for all. It is a small amount of time . . . less than the amount of time each person

would spend in a bar one night a week or at a movie one day a week."
He and his allies were pulling out all the stops leading into the election.

In effect, Milk called to his community one last time—with just over
two months until the Proposition 6 referendum—for a last push. This
Milk Forum piece showed the pressure that was mounting, and that
Milk was experiencing, as the battle over the Briggs Initiative hit its
crescendo. In a sense, Milk's editorial struck fear in his audience; it ap-
peared to him that there was no safe haven or quarter for anyone out of
the closet. His last push for others' involvement in the anti–Proposition
6 campaign was serious business—expediency, worry, and frustration
framed Milk's tone in the following editorial.

. . .

Take your choice. Strong positive or strong negative. That seems to be
what's happening in the Gay community with the Briggs/Bryant forces
coming down on us. From input that I'm getting, Gays are falling into
one or the other category. Take your choice!

THE NEGATIVE BEAT

There are those in the Gay community who have given up the battle
against Briggs even before it gets under full steam. They take the position
that no matter what we, do we cannot win. So they start to crawl back
into their closets and try to shut out all light . . . all hope. They want to
have every Gay "be nice." They want Gay to become invisible. They are
willing to allow all the young people who are "coming out" to go through
the hell that so many people have gone through in the past—feeling alone
and frightened with no help, no hope. They have even taken the position
that since they are not teachers, the Briggs initiative doesn't affect them.
They won't register to vote! "What difference does it make?" is their line.

THE POSITIVE BEAT

Then there is the positive beat. Those who feel that we can win against
Briggs and will do everything possible to see that it can happen. And
that spirit runs across the lines out of the field of politics and into all
aspects. That spirit can be summed up by calling attention to the Gay
physicians and psychiatrists who in the face of a possible witch hunt
have broken down their closet doors and "come out," destroying myths
in doing so . . . giving hope in doing so. That spirit can be summed up

by the San Francisco Gay Freedom Day Marching Band and Twirling Corps and the powerful sense of excitement they bring at each of their performances. That spirit can be summed up by the Gay-Police charity softball game which, once again, on many levels, showed what co-existence means. The Bryants/Briggs would never be able to understand the spirit of that game and the long-range ramifications. Bigots don't understand. Finally, that spirit can be summed up by those who are taking an active part in the anti-Briggs campaign. The task set out to them is huge, and they are tackling it—now.

THE SIDELINERS

The rest of the Gay community, those who are on the sidelines, are those who are watching it all take place and just talk about it without getting up and joining one side or the other. If that multitude sitting on the sidelines were to get up and join the positive side en masse then Briggs/Bryant would be stopped. If they continue to sit on the sideline and just talk, then we are in serious trouble. And, if they get up and move to the negative side, then repression will become a reality. The sad thing is that right now that multitude is just sitting there and not making its positive move. It is a sad fact that when it does understand it has to move, it may be too late. The positive work takes longer and more effort than the negative approach. Maybe that is why such a relative few have made that positive move. They are not willing to fight for their rights. The hate campaign has yet to begin in full force. Once it does, it might be too late to beat it back. The fight has to begin right now . . . yesterday. It must be fired up now. Volunteers and funds are the only way to beat Briggs . . . good vibrations won't do it!

This is as deep and as urgent an appeal as I can make. Please! If everyone in the Gay community would just commit a few hours and/ or a few dollars per week, we can win. If everyone waits for the other person to move first, we lose. If you feel that your effort won't make the difference, you are wrong! If you think that tomorrow will do, you are wrong! The army needs to start its movement now. San Franciscans Against Briggs, BACABI [the Bay Area Committee Against the Briggs Initiative], No on 6, and A United Fund to Defeat the Briggs Initiative are making their moves, but they need you . . . badly! For they are you. Without you they really don't exist. If Briggs wins, he will continue his Gay-hunt. He must be stopped now, and only YOU can do it.

42

"Statement on Briggs/Bigotry"

Public letter, September 22, 1978

In September 1978, Milk and other leaders of the movement to defeat Proposition 6 organized a legal symposium at the Hastings College of Law regarding gay rights under the current law and what the contours of these rights—and other minorities' rights—would be reduced to in the event of a Briggs Initiative victory. The document below is an invitation to GLBTQ community members to attend this symposium. In the process of bringing people together to explore legal ramifications of Proposition 6, Milk laid bare some of the overt—and not so overt—"facts" about the current climate in California concerning gay rights and the larger issue of human rights. Namely, as he noted in a June campaign letter related to this topic, "We are a group of citizens who understands the Briggs Initiative to be an alarming and increasingly strong reactionary attitude in the U.S., and we further understand that gay people are linked with women, ethnic minorities, old people, disabled people and the bulk of the nation's labor force as immediate or eventual targets of the witch hunts that would be the result of any victory for this reactionary mindset." As always, Milk linked the GLBTQ community with other disenfranchised groups in the service of accomplishing larger goals.

Interestingly, his message in this invitation at once provoked terror while also indicating some collective strength. There is a sense of dread as the November election day drew near and Briggs seemed to be gaining momentum. At the same time, however, the power to stymie this oppressive initiative was in the peoples' hands. As with his earlier appeals for community involvement (see Document 39), Milk argued that defeating Proposition 6 could only be done if more GLBTQ folks, in particular, contributed their energies to the cause.

. . .

Recently, I faced Republican State Senator John Briggs in a two-hour debate. Every "argument" that Briggs used was based upon myths, fears, lies, innuendos and ignorance. He obviously knows little about the subject he is discussing and cares little for the truth.

I feel the Senator is using the gay community as scapegoats, much as Hitler used the Jews as scapegoats and Nixon used the communists in his drive for power.

Senator Briggs is trying to constitutionalize bigotry. He will not be successful. His stands fly in the face of why America was formed, why the Constitution was written and why it has been amended since to guarantee the rights of Blacks, women and others.

But the horrors of the Briggs Initiative are not the only problems faced by lesbians and gay men in this state and in this country.

One would like to think that most Americans are opposed to discrimination. But history tells us that is not so. For over 100 years, we were content to treat Blacks as property. For over 100 years we were content to deprive women of the simple right to vote.

And, of course, for well over 200 years, this country has been content to treat homosexuals as something less than human. The fact is that in 1978 it is perfectly acceptable to fire a gay person from his or her job, not for any reason related to the job, but simply because that person is gay.

The fact is that in 1978, it is perfectly acceptable for police in almost any city in this country to harass a gay person, not because that person has broken a law, but simply because he or she is gay.

The fact is that in 1978 it's perfectly acceptable to watch a gay person in jail be sexually assaulted because our sadistic morality tells us that he or she deserves it, simply because he or she is gay.

And in 1978 it's perfectly acceptable for courts to take a child from a gay parent and place that child in a foster home because people won't believe that a gay parent can love and take care of a child as well as any non-gay parent.

The concept of gay rights frightens people. And maybe it should. Not because it threatens their children; it does not.

Gay rights frightens people because it shatters the myths that have been perpetrated by this society ever since the days when homosexuals were set afire at the stakes in Salem with bundles of stacks called "faggots."

What is even more regretful is that many gay people have also been brainwashed with these myths and are struggling to find peace with themselves. They are not aware of what rights they *do* have, what rights they *should* have and what rights they *can* have.

Tomorrow and Sunday, Hasting College of the Law will host a Gay Rights Under the Law Symposium.

We have brought together leading attorneys and activists from across the United States to discuss the status and future of gay rights. The conference will provide the first opportunity for an exchange of litigation and lobbying strategies in the area of gay rights.

Representatives of the United Farmworkers and the NAACP will discuss how they have confronted the similar problems their groups have faced.

Hopefully someday soon, conferences like this will not be necessary and society will accept its gay citizens with the same respect and tolerance it affords everyone else.

43

"Overall Needs of the City"

Speech, September 25, 1978

Only six months into their terms, the newly elected San Francisco City Supervisors were accused of self-serving politics by powerful community leaders wishing to go back to citywide elections. Recall that district elections allowed individual neighborhoods to vote for their respective representatives. The overt concern of these critics was that San Francisco's overall needs would be pushed aside in the maelstrom of the Supervisors fighting for their particular districts' well-being. Covertly, there was speculation that these more oppressive forces did not like that one neighborhood could elect a Chinese American, one could elect an African American woman, and—of course—that one could elect an openly (and proudly) GLBTQ individual. Such a plurality of voices and diversity of backgrounds potentially threatened traditional power bases and monied interests in San Francisco.

There were a number of issues that raised doubts about the genuine care of these critics and the veracity of their claims. First, the Supervisors had barely begun their terms before a Grand Jury was called to review evidence provided by the anti-district election proponents. Clearly, there was not enough time to be able to ascertain a fair conclusion about the alleged corruption of district-elected Supervisors. Second, the critics failed to understand that any elected official represents, first and foremost, her or his district. Even in the case of citywide elections, localized neighborhoods were to be centered as key constituencies. Third, the Grand Jury focused—at least in terms of Milk—on his support of the gay rights ordnance as evidence that he only cared about District 5 (as if there were no GLBTQ individuals living in other districts). As a populist, stretching back to his foray into San Francisco politics in 1973, Milk had always been interested in overall reform. And indeed, in the press release that follows he reminded his constituents that he worked hard for every facet of the city's people and their myriad problems. For instance, his campaign materials from the 1977 election note that his platform involved building housing developments, reducing public transportation costs for citizens, cleaning up public green spaces, fundraising for community centers, and working with police to ensure more safety in the districts. Yes, of course, he also sought a gay rights ordinance and labored to fight Proposition 6. But in the end, Milk's populist sensibilities never gave way, even when a majority of his time and energy was focused on the Briggs Initiative.

The entire issue of the Grand Jury investigation exposed some of the fear of the power interests in San Francisco who were worried about what near-true representation of the city's people (i.e., through district elections) would do for monied interests. If power brokers could not control cross-city elections, as they had in the past, then seemingly people in the "city of neighborhoods" would have more say. As for Milk, he questioned what antagonists thought were San Francisco's true needs. Milk, often backed by supervisory assistant Anne Kronenberg, was fond of sending press releases from his desk in City Hall. He viewed this as a part of his daily responsibilities as a populist leader. Sometimes offering advice or a summary of doings in his office and other times seeking public support or making a scathing argument against monied interests, Milk's press releases pepper the archive. Most of the documents are mundane, but some stand out—examples of Milk's fiery political stances and forthrightness. Even the mundane releases are worth examining, to get a sense for Milk's daily work as a city and GLBTQ leader. The press release that follows, however, is not to be classified under the "mundane" category.

. . .

The Civil Grand Jury, in its report last week, chastised the current Board of Supervisors, the first one elected by district. It charged the Supervisors with being more concerned with their personal constituencies than with the "overall needs of the City." And it attempted to link this with its major concern, that of middle class flight from San Francisco. . . .

The new Board has been in office less than a year and hadn't been more than 6 months by the time the report was completed. This was hardly enough time for the Grand Jury to study the long-range, permanent effects of district elections.

I also question what the Grand Jury considers the City's "overall needs."

Many, many people have commented to me about how much more responsive the current Supervisors are to public opinion and participation. That's an important "need" for city residents.

I know that the dirty streets of District 5 receive much more attention now than they did before—as do the dirty streets of every District where the Supervisor cares. The same is true of the many small issues that concern people. That, too, is an important "need."

True, I spend much of my time dealing with issues of particular concern to neighborhoods and people of District 5. But I also work hard on the many city-wide issues like budgets, dog litter, Yerba Buena, housing costs, sewers and zoning and I also work on state issues, like Proposition 13 and now, Proposition 6. The same is true of the other members of the Board. This is a "need" that is being met.

But most puzzling about the Grand Jury report is how it tried to tie district elections to "middle class flight" from San Francisco. There has been no census since district elections went into effect and the current Board has been in office. I don't know on what basis the Grand Jury could have measured "middle class flight" in the last few months.

The problem of families leaving San Francisco has been in existence for over ten years, hardly the result of something we have done only recently. It is an important problem, to be sure, but it is not one that will be solved by spending millions of tax dollars from other San Franciscans, as the report suggests.

The plight of seniors and minorities in our City is also a major problem, though the Grand Jury overlooked them. The current Board has certainly paid a great deal more attention to these people than did the old, at-large Board.

Maybe the Grand Jury should have talked to the District Supervisors before they wrote their report. I know of at least one who they didn't bother to talk to.

Maybe that was because its members figured they knew what I'd say, just like they "knew" what the long-range effects of district elections were and they "knew" why the middle class was leaving San Francisco.

44

"Ballot Argument Against Proposition 6"

Public letter (with Frank Robinson),
November 7, 1978

By the time the Briggs Initiative referendum came and went, Milk and Briggs had engaged in countless debates across the state of California. In effect, the public debates involved mostly boilerplate arguments— those that were recycled time and time again. Both Milk and Briggs could anticipate each other's questions and answers. In strange ways, the two political gladiators fighting for the lives of their constituents had become friendly on the road and in the wings of their public verbal battles. Regardless of the repetition involved in the debates, Milk always shined. And the familiarity of Briggs' performance, in particular, allowed Milk to continually push Briggs into a corner as a vociferous homophobe. Briggs' energy seemed to wane and he became hyperbolic in his exhaustion. Meanwhile, a life on the road emboldened Milk, spurring on his biting critiques of myth making on the part of Proposition 6 supporters. Milk also began to link the Briggs Initiative to a slippery slope that would eventually harm free expression and free speech of everyone in San Francisco—regardless of their sexualities. When the votes were in, Milk had held sway. On November 7, Proposition 6 was defeated by more than a million votes, 3.9 to 2.8 million, 58–42 percent.

There is a sense in this document of the domino effect that Milk often talked about regarding the initiative. On one of the many "debate cards" that he carried to public meetings with Briggs, he wrote, "If this [Prop 6] is allowed to pass it could become part of an epidemic which will spread—as it did in Nazi Germany—to other individuals who are minorities by virtue of their race, religion, sex, political beliefs or national origins." Indeed, the Bay Area Reporter *and other California news outlets speculated that Briggs's witch hunts could potentially carry on if the voters moved in the direction of limiting individual freedoms.*

The press release below was crafted by Milk and his speechwriter and friend, Frank Robinson. The release rearticulated the anti-Briggs arguments one last time on the morning of the referendum. This would be Milk's last public, discursive push *for the defeat of Proposition 6.*

. . .

The initiative plays upon fears that homosexual teachers will automatically molest their students or will serve as "Role Models" with the result that their students will somehow become homosexual.

These assumptions are false.

Statistics available from the California Highway Patrol, the Los Angeles Police Department and the San Francisco Police Department show that more than 90 percent of child molestations are committed by heterosexuals, often members of the child's family.

The belief that homosexual teachers by their mere existence will serve as "Role Models" and thus alter the sexual orientation of their students is also unjustified. According to psychologists, a child's sexual orientation is determined during its pre-school years and the significant "Role Models" are the mother and father.

Every child is born of heterosexual parents and raised in a strongly heterosexual environment. The natural inclination of children to become heterosexual is further supported by their peer group. Nevertheless, 7–10% of children become homosexual, strong heterosexual "Role Models" having no effect. Likewise, the occasional exposure of a heterosexual child to a homosexual teacher will have no effect.

The initiative ignores the fact that California and its various municipalities already have laws concerning the molesting of children and these laws are rigidly enforced. The initiative also ignores the fact that classroom behavior which violates good taste and judgment is subject to censure by school authorities.

Besides the above, the initiative is pernicious and dangerous for the following reasons:

—It attempts to regulate a profession on moral grounds which have nothing to do with the profession itself. If passed, it would establish a dangerous precedent.

—It denies the rights of free speech to a substantial number of the State's citizens, forbidding them the right to even discuss homosexuality *outside the classroom* as well as in.

—It subjects every teacher in the state, heterosexual as well as homosexual, to blackmail. An accusation by a student that he or she overheard a teacher discussing homosexuality could lead to an automatic 30-day suspension.

—It raises the specter of a McCarthy-style witch-hunt in determining who may or may not be a homosexual.

—It allows further government intrusion into people's private lives and will cost every taxpayer money in administrative costs.

The initiative is politically inspired, designed to correct a situation that doesn't exist. It libels the entire teaching profession and limits the rights of free speech for teachers, effectively making third-class citizens of those members of a highly respected profession. For these and other reasons, the initiative has been opposed by both Governor Brown and Attorney General Younger, both Lt. Governor Dymally and Mike Curb, major newspapers such as the *Los Angeles Times,* the *Sacramento Bee* and the *San Francisco Examiner,* most public officials and school officials and labor leaders from all over the state.

They found this initiative repressive and against the basic principles of our democracy.

We urge you to vote *NO* on this initiative and reject the concept of legislation-by-myth with the intent of depriving *any* minority of the same rights enjoyed by the majority.

PART FIVE

Harvey's Last Words

45

"Political Will"

Tape Cassette Transcription,
18 November 1977

The final weeks between the defeat of Proposition 6 and the assassinations of Milk and Mayor George Moscone were exhilarating—there was, after all, so much promise in the wake of the Briggs Initiative going down in flames and in the sweet strains of Milk's swan song that folks could be heard singing across the Castro neighborhood. Liberation seemed possible. The "hope" that Milk talked about so very much had at long last come to bear. However, a number of events also occurred that put a damper, and a near cessation, on the GLBTQ community's elation. For instance: the emotional unraveling of Board Supervisor Dan White; his resignation from the Board of Supervisors; his strong-armed rescinding of that resignation and appeal for reinstatement; the political jockeying and lobbying that ensued during the interim; his learning from a reporter that Moscone would not reappoint him; his armed entry of City Hall through a basement window; his execution of George Moscone; his execution of Harvey Milk; Board President Dianne Feinstein's devastating revelation to City Hall employees and reporters, "Mayor Moscone and Supervisor Harvey Milk have been shot . . . and killed. Police have a suspect. Supervisor Dan White." Much too has been said about Milk's farsighted fatalism, his longstanding prediction that he'd die early, his preoccupation with the possibility of his assassination, and existential trembling no doubt exacerbated by proliferating death threats. Milk was, in fact, obsessed with his assassination.

So much so that he wrote a political will one year before the prophecy of his demise proved true.

The document below is a partial excerpt from his political will, recorded the year before his assassination. Readers will note a prophetic rhetoric and a palpable soberness as Milk realized he would never make it to the "promised land" with his GLBTQ brothers and sisters despite the successes that he would achieve. Ultimately, he wanted his legacy to live on not in political success, but in the spirit of hope: "And that's all I ask. That's all. I ask for the movement to continue."

Milk's political will was recorded on tape in the law offices of his attorney, Walter Caplan. The opening scene in Gus Van Sant's feature film Milk *depicts Milk recording the will at his kitchenette—a Hollywood embellishment.*

. . .

This is Harvey Milk speaking on Friday, November 18. This is tape two. This is to be played only in the event of my death by assassination. I've given long and considerable thought to this, not just since the election. I've been thinking about this for some time prior to election and certainly over the years. I fully realize that a person who stands for what I stand for—a gay activist—becomes the target of potential target for a person who is insecure, terrified, afraid, or very disturbed themselves. Knowing that I could be assassinated at any moment or any time, I feel it's important that some people should understand my thoughts. So the following are my thoughts, my wishes, my desires, whatever. I'd like to pass them on and played for the appropriate people. The first and most obvious concern is that if I was to be shot and killed, the mayor has the power, George Moscone's, of appointing my successor to the Board of Supervisors. I know there will be great pressures on him from various factions, so I'd like to let him know what my thoughts are.

I stood for more than just a candidate. I think there was a strong differential between somebody like Rick Stokes and myself. I have never considered myself a candidate. I have always considered myself part of a movement, part of a candidacy. I've considered the movement the candidate. I think there's a delineation between those who use the movement and those who are part of the movement. I think I was always part of the movement. And I think that. I wish I had time to explain almost everything I did. Almost everything that was done with an eye on the gay movement.

I would suggest and urge and hope that the mayor would understand that distinction and that he would appoint somebody to my position who also came from the movement rather than used the movement or never understood the movement. I think those people who actively opposed me—the Jim Fosters, Rick Stokeses, Jo Dalys, Doug de Youngs—those people never understood the movement. I'm not saying they're against it. They just never understood it. They used it. Maybe willingly, maybe unwillingly, but they never understood what it was about. I think those who remained in silence—the Frank Fitches, not wishing to play sides—never understood the movement. That silence is sometimes worse than speaking out. I would hope that the mayor would understand that appointing somebody who actively opposed me or subtly opposed me or kept quiet, stuck their head in the sand, would be an insult to everything I stood for, would be an affront to the campaigns and the people who worked.

I would hope he would give consideration, strong consideration, only to people who came from the movement. I've talked to several people and they know my thoughts, so I put them on tape so there's no doubt in anybody's mind about my thoughts. There are some people I definitely have in mind who I would like the mayor to consider.

The first person I would have is a gentleman by the name of Frank Robinson, who is quite an author in his own right. Frank even more so knows my thought processes. Not only has he read everything I've written and helped rewrite major pieces, but Frank is the one who almost daily we had conversations on various points of thinking and philosophies. So he knows my thoughts as well. He understands how I arrived at the decisions and he played devil's advocate time and time again. So if there's anyone who knows me from the depth of the intellect and emotions, it's Frank Robinson. And I think being who he is, he has that incredible ability to express himself clearly and concisely and if there were any problems, he would be able to carry on the philosophy and idea of what I stood for.

If there's some reason Frank is not the choice, the next consideration I would hope the mayor would give would be to Bob Ross. Bob has read everything I've written in the past four years and also has carried on extensive dealings with me and also has the ability to get along with a lot more people than I can, which is also going to be needed. And Bob is a strong person that will not bend and that's vital. You cannot have a weak person—the Rick Stokes types, the professional lawyers. The first few gay people must be strong. That doesn't mean obstinate or uncompromising, but they must be strong.

The third choice would be Harry Britt, who most people don't know. But I've watched Harry and Harry's been involved with three campaigns.

He knows where I am. I've watched Harry grow and grow and grow and become more articulate. Some people may find him wrong because he is somewhat emotional, but by God, what fabulous emotions! And he's a very, very dedicated and strong person and will not be pushed around. One that understands what the movement is and where it must go. Some day it will be there anyhow.

A fourth possibility is a person who is younger, newer, and learning every day. It's the woman who put my campaign together. Anne Kronenberg, who is strong. Who understands and learns fast and thinks fast. And would add a spirit, being a gay woman, that the others cannot add. And I think that would be an outstanding choice.

And I hope the mayor would understand that in cases like this, the tradition has been to replace a person who has been assassinated with someone who is close to the candidate in thought, rather than somebody who actively or quietly opposed the candidate. And it's important that it happens. I cannot urge the mayor strongly enough to hear what I'm saying. I think that if he did that, he would be gaining a tremendous amount of support.

The other aspect of the tapes is the obvious of what would happen should there be an assassination. I cannot prevent some people from feeling angry and frustrated and mad, but I hope they will take that frustration and that madness instead of demonstrating or anything of that type, I would hope that they would take the power and I would hope that five, ten, one hundred, a thousand would rise. I would like to see every gay lawyer, every gay architect come out, stand up and let the world know. That would do more to end prejudice overnight than anybody could imagine. I urge them to do that, urge them to come out. Only that way will we start to achieve our rights.

I hope there are no religious services. I would hope there are no services of any type, but I know some people are into that and you can't prevent it from happening, but, God, nothing religious. Until the churches speak out against the Anita Bryants who have been playing gymnastics with the Bible, the churches which remain so quiet have the guts to speak out in the name of Judaism or Christianity or whatever they profess to be for in words but not actions and deeds. God—and that's the irony. God—churches don't even know what it's about. I would turn over in my grave if there was any kind of religious ceremony. And it's not a disbelief in God—it's a disbelief and disgust of what most churches are about. How many leaders got up in their pulpits and went to Miami and said, "Anita, you're playing gymnastics with the Bible—you're desecrating the Bible." How many of them said it? How many of them hid and walked away? Ducked their heads in the name of Christianity and talked about love and brotherhood.

No services whatsoever. If anything, play that tape of Briggs and I, which is somewhere in the cabinet in the back—the file cabinet. Just play that tape of Briggs and I over and over again so people can know what an evil man he is. So people know what our Hitler is like. So people know that where the ideas of hate come from. So they know what the future will bring if they're not careful.

And that's all I ask. That's all. I ask for the movement to continue, for the movement to grow because last week, I got a phone call from Altoona, Pennsylvania, and my election gave somebody else, one more person, hope. And after all it's what this is all about. It's not about personal gain, not about ego, not about power—it's about giving those young people out there in the Altoona, Pennsylvania's hope. You gotta give them hope.

Document List

As editors, our goal has been to reproduce Harvey Milk's words in their "original" form, transcribed directly from his typed, hand-written papers, or published speeches, letters, editorials, columns, and interviews. We have erred on the side of leaving Milk's inscriptions largely alone when it came to our copyediting, which means that in some instances the reader will encounter his idiosyncratic sentence constructions and typographical peculiarities. In doing so, we believe we faithfully have preserved his rhetorical signature and style, which of course had so much to do with his politics. Any "translation" errors are our own.

1. "Interview with Harvey Milk," interview, Davidlee Rinker, *Kalendar* (San Francisco), August 17, 1973, pp. 1, 19, James C. Hormel Gay & Lesbian Center of the San Francisco Public Library, GLC35, Milk-Smith Collection, Box 3, Series 2a.

2. Harvey Milk, "Address to the San Francisco Chapter of the National Women's Political Caucus," speech, September 5, 1973, James C. Hormel Gay & Lesbian Center of the San Francisco Public Library, GLC35, Milk-Smith Collection, Box 26, 73–78, clippings.

3. Harvey Milk, "Address to the Joint International Longshoremen & Warehousemen's Union of San Francisco and to the Lafayette Club," speech, September 30, 1973, James C. Hormel Gay & Lesbian Center of the San Francisco Public Library, GLC35, Milk-Smith Collection, Box 9, Series 2d.

4. Harvey Milk, "An Open Letter to the Mayor of San Francisco," public letter, September 22, 1973, James C. Hormel Gay & Lesbian Center of the San Francisco Public Library, GLC35, Milk-Smith Collection, Box 26, 73–78, clippings.

5. Harvey Milk, "MUNI/Parking Garage," press release, September 27, 1973, James C. Hormel Gay & Lesbian Center of the San Francisco Public Library, GLC35, Milk-Smith Collection, Box 26, 73–78, clippings.

6. Harvey Milk, "Alfred Seniora," press release, September 28, 1973, James C. Hormel Gay & Lesbian Center of the San Francisco Public Library, GLC35, Milk-Smith Collection, Box 26, 73–78, clippings.

7. Harvey Milk, "Who Really Represents You," campaign flyer, September 1973, James C. Hormel Gay & Lesbian Center of the San Francisco Public Library, GLC35, Milk-Smith Collection, Box 26, 73–78, clippings.

8. Harvey Milk, "Milk Note," column, 1 February 1974, "Insider" (section), *Vector* (Newsletter of Society for Individual Rights, San Francisco), reprinted in *San Francisco Crusader*, December 5, 1978, James C. Hormel Gay & Lesbian Center of the San Francisco Public Library, GLC35, Milk-Smith Collection, Box 9, Series 2d.

9. Harvey Milk, "Anyone Can Be a Movie Critic: How Not to Find Leadership," editorial, *San Francisco Crusader*, February 1974, reprinted in *San Francisco Crusader*, December 5, 1978.

10. Harvey Milk, "Open Letter to the City of San Francisco Hall of Justice on Police Brutality," public letter, February 14, 1974, James C. Hormel Gay & Lesbian Center of the San Francisco Public Library, GLC35, Milk-Smith Collection, Box 9, Series 2d.

11. Harvey Milk, "Where I Stand," article draft, "Waves from the Left" (section), *Sentinel* (San Francisco) March 28, 1974, James C. Hormel Gay & Lesbian Center of the San Francisco Public Library, GLC35, Milk-Smith Collection, Box 9, Series 2d. Published in the *Sentinel*, March 28, 1974, p. 5.

12. Harvey Milk, "Where There is No Victim, There is No Crime," press release, April 1, 1974, James C. Hormel Gay & Lesbian Center of the San Francisco Public Library, GLC35, Milk-Smith Collection, Box 9, Series 2d.

13. Harvey Milk, "Political Power" article draft, "Waves from the Left" (section), *Sentinel* (San Francisco), May 23, 1974, James C. Hormel Gay & Lesbian Center of the San Francisco Public Library, GLC35, Milk-Smith Collection, Box 9, Series 2d. Published in the *Sentinel*, May 23, 1974, p. 5.

14. Harvey Milk, "Letter to the *San Francisco Chronicle* Concerning Anti-Gay Editorials," letter draft, July 1, 1974, James C. Hormel Gay & Lesbian Center of the San Francisco Public Library, GLC35, Milk-Smith Collection, Box 9, Series 2d.

15. Harvey Milk, "Library or Performing Arts Center?" press release, 4 December 1974, James C. Hormel Gay & Lesbian Center of the San Francisco Public Library, GLC35, Milk-Smith Collection, Box 9, Series 2d.

16. Harvey Milk, "Au Contraire . . . PCR Needed," column, "Milk Forum" (section), *Bay Area Reporter*, February 6, 1975, pp. 11–12, James C. Hormel Gay & Lesbian Center of the San Francisco Public Library, GLC35, Milk-Smith Collection, Box 3, Series 2a.

17. Harvey Milk, "Harvey Milk for Supervisor," campaign letter, February 26, 1975, James C. Hormel Gay & Lesbian Center of the San Francisco Public Library, GLC35, Milk-Smith Collection, Box 3, Series 2a.

18. Harvey Milk, "Statement of Harvey Milk, Candidate for the 16th Assembly District," campaign material, March 9, 1976, James C. Hormel Gay & Lesbian Center of the San Francisco Public Library, GLC35, Milk-Smith Collection, Box 3, Series 2a.

19. Harvey Milk, "Reactionary Beer," column, "Milk Forum" (section), *Bay Area Reporter*, March 18, 1976, p. 12, James C. Hormel Gay & Lesbian Center of the San Francisco Public Library, GLC35, Milk-Smith Collection, Box 26, 73–78, clippings.

20. Harvey Milk, "Nixon's Revenge—The Republicans and Their Supreme Court," column, "Milk Forum" (section), *Bay Area Reporter*, April 15, 1976, p. 12, James C. Hormel Gay & Lesbian Center of the San Francisco Public Library, GLC35, Milk-Smith Collection, Box 4, Series 2a.

21. Harvey Milk, "My Concept as a Legislator," column, "Milk Forum" (section), *Bay Area Reporter*, May 27, 1976, p. 22, James C. Hormel Gay & Lesbian Center of the San Francisco Public Library, GLC43, Randy Shilts Papers, *Mayor of Castro Street*, Box 1.

22. Harvey Milk, "'Uncertainty' of Carter or the 'Certainty' of Ford," column, "Milk Forum" (section),September 2, 1976, p. 8, James C. Hormel Gay & Lesbian Center of the San Francisco Public Library, GLC35, Milk-Smith Collection, Box 26, 73–78 Clippings.

23. Harvey Milk, "A Nation Finally Talks About . . . 'It,'" column, "Milk Forum" (section), *Bay Area Reporter*, June 9, 1977, p. 17, James C. Hormel Gay & Lesbian Center of the San Francisco Public Library, GLC35, Milk-Smith Collection, Box 26, 73–78, clippings.

24. Harvey Milk, "Gay Economic Power," column, "Milk Forum" (section), *Bay Area Reporter*, September 15, 1977, p. 12, James C. Hormel Gay & Lesbian Center of the San Francisco Public Library, GLC35, Milk-Smith Collection, Box 26, 73–78, clippings.

25. Harvey Milk, "You've Got to Have Hope," speech, June 24, 1977, James C. Hormel Gay & Lesbian Center of the San Francisco Public Library, GLC35, Milk-Smith Collection, Box 9, Series 2d.

26. "Harvey Speaks Out," interview, George Mendenhall, *Bay Area Reporter*, December 8, 1977, pp. 2, 4, James C. Hormel Gay & Lesbian Center of the San Francisco Public Library, GLC35, Milk-Smith Collection, Box 26, 73–78, clippings.

27. Harvey Milk, "A City of Neighborhoods: First Major Address", Parts I and II, reprinted speech, "Milk Forum" (section), *Bay Area Reporter*, January 10, 1978, pp. 13–14 and February 2, 1978, p. 9, James C. Hormel Gay & Lesbian Center of the San Francisco Public Library, GLC35, Milk-Smith Collection, Box 26, 73–78, clippings.

28. Harvey Milk, "The Word is Out," public letter, February 1, 1978, James C. Hormel Gay & Lesbian Center of the San Francisco Public Library, GLC35, Milk-Smith Collection, Box 9, Series 2d.

29. Harvey Milk, "Letter to 'Abe' on Domestic Politics," private letter, February 7, 1978, James C. Hormel Gay & Lesbian Center of the San Francisco Public Library, GLC35, Milk-Smith Collection, Box 9, Series 2d.

30. Harvey Milk, "Letter to Council Members concerning Judging People by Myths," public letter, March 13, 1978, James C. Hormel Gay & Lesbian Center of the San Francisco Public Library, GLC35, Milk-Smith Collection, Box 9, Series 2d.

31. Harvey Milk, "Resolution Requiring State Department to Close the South African Consulate" and "Closing the Consulate," press releases, March 22, 1978, James C. Hormel Gay & Lesbian Center of the San Francisco Public Library, GLC35, Milk-Smith Collection, Box 9, Series 2a.

32. Harvey Milk, "Letter to President Jimmy Carter," private letter, April 12, 1978, James C. Hormel Gay & Lesbian Center of the San Francisco Public Library, GLC35, Milk-Smith Collection, Box 7, Series 2c.

33. Harvey Milk, Untitled (on Gay Caucus and Gay Power), column, "Milk Forum" (section), *Bay Area Reporter*, April 27, 1978, p. 16, James C. Hormel Gay & Lesbian Center of the San Francisco Public Library, GLC35, Milk-Smith Collection, Box 26, 73–78, clippings.

34. Harvey Milk, "California Gay Caucus," article draft, *Alternate*, May 12, 1978, James C. Hormel Gay & Lesbian Center of the San Francisco Public Library, GLC35, Milk-Smith Collection, Box 9, Series 2d.

35. Harvey Milk, "Keynote Speech at Gay Conference 5," tape cassette transcription of speech, June 10, 1978, San Francisco Gay, Lesbian, Bisexual, Transgender Historical Society, Harvey Milk, Box 13. Courtesy of David Lamble.

36. Harvey Milk, "Gay Rights," article draft, *Coast to Coast* (San Francisco), June 16, 1978, James C. Hormel Gay & Lesbian Center of the San Francisco Public Library, GLC35, Milk-Smith Collection, Box 9, Series 2d.

37. Harvey Milk, "Gay Freedom Day Speech," reprinted speech, "Milk Forum" (section), *Bay Area Reporter*, June 25, 1978, pp. 11–12, James C. Hormel Gay & Lesbian Center of the San Francisco Public Library, GLC35, Milk-Smith Collection, Box 26, 73–78, clippings.

38. Harvey Milk, "To Beat Briggs," column, "Milk Forum" (section), *Bay Area Reporter*, August 3, 1978, p. 12, James C. Hormel Gay & Lesbian Center of the San Francisco Public Library, GLC35, Milk-Smith Collection, Box 26, 73–78, clippings.

39. Harvey Milk, "I Have High Hopes," stump speech, 1978, James C. Hormel Gay & Lesbian Center of the San Francisco Public Library, GLC35, Milk-Smith Collection, Box 9, Series 2d.

40. "Harvey Milk vs. John Briggs," televised debate transcription, August 6, 1978, Bay Area Television Archive at San Francisco State University, used with permission from Tom Spitz (KPIX/KBCW)

41. Harvey Milk, "The Positive or the Negative," column, "Milk Forum" (section), *Bay Area Reporter*, August 31, 1978, p. 14, James C. Hormel Gay & Lesbian Center of the San Francisco Public Library, GLC35, Milk-Smith Collection, Box 26, 73–78, clippings.

42. Harvey Milk, "Statement on Briggs/Bigotry," public letter, September 22, 1978, James C. Hormel Gay & Lesbian Center of the San Francisco Public Library, GLC35, Milk- Smith Collection, Box 9, Series 2d.

43. Harvey Milk, "Overall Needs of the City," speech, September 25, 1978, James C. Hormel Gay & Lesbian Center of the San Francisco Public Library, GLC35, Milk- Smith Collection, Box 9, Series 2d.

44. Harvey Milk and Frank Robinson, "Ballot Argument Against Proposition 6," public letter, November 7, 1978, James C. Hormel Gay & Lesbian Center of the San Francisco Public Library, GLC35, Milk-Smith Collection, Box 9, Series 2d.

45. Harvey Milk, "Political Will," November 18, 1977, tape cassette transcription, San Francisco Gay, Lesbian, Bisexual, Transgender Historical Society, Harvey Milk, Box 13. Courtesy of Walter Caplan.

Editor Biographies

JASON EDWARD BLACK is Associate Professor of Rhetorical Studies and an affiliate professor in Gender & Race Studies at The University of Alabama in Tuscaloosa. His research program is located at the juncture of rhetoric and social change, with an emphasis on American Indian resistance, GLBTQ community discourses, and Black liberation. His work in these areas has appeared in the *Quarterly Journal of Speech, Rhetoric & Public Affairs, Southern Communication Journal, American Indian Quarterly, American Indian Culture and Research Journal, Communication Quarterly,* and elsewhere. Professor Black is the coeditor of *Arguments about Animal Ethics* (Lexington Books, 2010). He has received the Wrage-Baskerville Award from the National Communication Association and the Rushing Early Career Award and the Owen Peterson Award in Rhetoric and Public Address from the Southern States Communication Association.

CHARLES E. MORRIS III is Professor of Communication & Rhetorical Studies and LGBT Studies at Syracuse University. He is the cofounding editor of *QED: A Journal in GLBTQ Worldmaking* (Michigan State University Press). His books include *Remembering the AIDS Quilt* (Michigan State University Press, 2011), *Queering Public Address: Sexualities in American Historical Discourse* (University of South Carolina Press, 2007), and *Readings on the Rhetoric of Social Protest* (Strata Publishing, 2001, 2006, 2013), and his essays have appeared in the *Quarterly Journal of Speech, Communication and Critical/Cultural Studies, Rhetoric & Public Affairs,* and elsewhere. For his work as an archival queer, Professor Morris has received two Golden Monograph Awards, the Karl Wallace Memorial Award, and the Randy Majors Memorial Award from the National Communication Association.

www.ingramcontent.com/pod-product-compliance
Lightning Source LLC
Chambersburg PA
CBHW030347270326
41926CB00009B/996